Cholesterol & Children

Also by Robert E. Kowalski

The 8-Week Cholesterol Cure

Robert E. Kowalski

CHOLESTEROL & CHILDREN

A Parent's Guide to Giving Children a Future Free of Heart Disease

Foreword by Dennis M. Davidson, M.D.
Preface by Paul Y. Qaqundah, M.D.

1817

Harper & Row, Publishers, New York
Grand Rapids, Philadelphia, St. Louis, San Francisco
London, Singapore, Sydney, Tokyo

Library of Congress Cataloging-in-Publication Data

Kowalski, Robert E.
    Cholesterol and children.
    1. Atherosclerosis in children—Prevention.
2. Low-cholesterol diet.   3. Low-cholesterol diet—
Recipes.   I. Title.
RJ426.A82K69   1989   613.2′8   87-46151
ISBN 0-06-091589-7

89 90 91 92 93 FG 10 9 8 7 6 5 4 3 2

This book is dedicated with love and devotion to Ross and Jenny, my son and daughter, who inspired me to research and write these pages. For them I wish long years of health and happiness.

Contents

Tables

Acknowledgments

No book, especially this one, is the result of the work of only the person whose name appears as author. Simply stated, the book could not have been a reality if not for the enthusiastic support of my agent, Clyde Taylor, who has believed in me from the beginning. I also greatly appreciate the courage of my publisher, and of my editor, Larry Ashmead, to publish a book that will do a lot of kids a lot of good even if such books are not typically commercial successes. My thanks to Bill Siarny for guiding me through the mountains of literature with his trusty computer. And finally, a journalist's appreciation to all those sources whose brains I've picked over the phone, by mail, and in person. I thank you all, and my children thank you all for your expertise, knowledge, and wisdom.

Foreword

by *Dennis M. Davidson, M.D.*
Director, Preventive Cardiology
Associate Professor of Medicine
University of California College of Medicine
Irvine, California

A great man is he who does not lose his child's heart

—Mencius

Among the many countries and cultures I have been privileged to visit, one observation is paramount: every society loves its children. Specific concerns range from basic survival in war-torn developing countries to enrollment in the "best school" in economically advanced nations, but all people express their hopes for the future as goals for their children.

Parents traditionally mention "good nutrition" as an important goal for their girls and boys. However, adults in all countries often depend more on custom and folklore than on sound scientific principles in deciding what to feed their children.

Fortunately, advances in nutrition knowledge in the past few decades have significantly improved the prospects of children throughout the world, most dramatically in developing countries faced with famine and disease. International agencies have vigorously pursued the application of this new knowledge in many Third World nations with a remarkable improvement in infant and child mortality rates.

More subtle—and often overlooked—are the nutrition prospects for children in economically advanced countries. For such children, the major threats to a long and healthy life are the "diseases of civilization," such as cancer and heart disease due to atherosclerosis.

It is now quite clear that atherosclerosis is a problem that begins in childhood. Focusing on those risk factors most important in the adult population (cholesterol, blood pressure, and smoking) that are preventable, several long-term studies of children have been done in the United States and elsewhere. Their findings are quite consistent: as children grow from infancy to school age and on into early adulthood, their blood cholesterol level and blood pressure tend to remain in the same relative position as their classmates. For example, these studies indicate that approximately 10 percent of 10-year-old children already have blood cholesterol levels of 200 milligrams per deciliter or more; this is the value currently recommended as the upper limit for adults. Without nutrition changes by the family and by the school, these "high risk" children are likely to stay at the upper levels of cholesterol throughout their life, making them more prone to accelerated atherosclerosis and an early heart attack. And many more children show values that would indicate future levels in their adult years far above ideal. Perhaps 50 percent or even more of the children in the United States would profit by cholesterol reduction now. And all children would benefit from a low-fat diet in terms of total health for today and the future.

How can we detect which of our children are at risk? A family history of heart attack or bypass surgery in parents or grandparents before the age of 50 may indicate genetically linked high levels of blood cholesterol in their offspring. However, our studies show that less than half of 10-year-olds with blood cholesterol levels above 200 have such a family history. This indicates to me the importance of screening all children to detect those who appear to be at highest risk.

Fortunately, technological advances have allowed manufacturers to produce analytic equipment to reliably measure blood cholesterol from a drop or two of blood in only three to five minutes. In mass screenings of fourth-graders at school sites, our costs for materials and reports to parents and physicians have been less than $2 per child. Those children found to have high cholesterol levels are being followed closely by their physicians.

Given a reliable and inexpensive screening program, can we actually hope to change children's cholesterol values? In large part, this will depend on the dietary and exercise patterns established by the family and reinforced by the school curricula. We have been gratified by the parental response to our school screening, and early follow-up indicates that many parents are significantly altering the family diet.

As a physician, I find it most helpful to offer practical advice to all families regarding alternatives to the "typical American diet" and to refer the "high risk" families to our registered dietitian for in-depth counseling on heart-healthy eating. Such individual counseling goes slowly, however, and we have often wistfully hoped for a book on this topic which would be so informative and clearly written that it would become a bestseller and could then serve as a home reference guide for our patients.

Our wishes came true with the appearance and overwhelming success of Robert Kowalski's *The 8-Week Cholesterol Cure.* Shortly after its publication, I had the pleasure of meeting Bob to thank him for his valuable contribution to parents and children everywhere. I was even more delighted to learn that he was completing a book specifically on children and cholesterol.

His success in this endeavor will become quite apparent as you read further in this volume. The book is perfectly up to date and accurate regarding the application of research to personal nutrition for both children and adults. Even more important, Bob has faithfully transferred his scientific knowledge into practical advice (including marvelous recipes) for the concerned family. It covers (with much greater eloquence) all the important points we mention to our patients during individual counseling. Finally, he has "spoken from the heart" about his topic, making the book a joy to read.

Rabindranath Tagore wrote: "Every child comes with the message that God is not yet discouraged of man." With a greater concern for global peace and well-being of all people, and our rapidly expanding knowledge of nutrition, I am confident that we will someday be able to offer the legacy of life to every child on this earth. Let's begin here and now, and follow Robert Kowalski's lead in giving our kids a healthy and happy heart.

Preface

by Paul Y. Qaqundah, M.D.
Clinical Professor of Pediatrics,
University of California, Irvine

Charter Chairman,
American Academy of Pediatrics
California Chapter IV

Coronary heart disease is the major public health problem in our country. Arteriosclerosis (hardening of the arteries) is responsible for more than one-third of the deaths in the United States. It claims more than half a million lives each year and cripples over five million Americans with symptomatic coronary heart disease and many more having asymptomatic covert illness. Many studies show that cardiovascular disease starts in the young. It begins with fatty streaks lining the arteries, graduates into fibrous plaques in the young adult, and grows to full calcification by early middle age, which makes the individual prone to myocardial infarction (heart attack).

Factors that help speed this process are numerous. Some of them we cannot change, such as being a male or carrying a gene of familial hypercholesterolemia, for which very high cholesterol levels and arteriosclerosis start very early in life. In this case, one should be under medical supervision in addition to using the information in this book. Children with familial hypercholesterolemia constitute only a small number, but the majority of children with that hypercholesterolemia have their problem related to a diet high in fat and cholesterol. Dietary intervention now may very well reduce their chance of coronary incidence in the future. Overweight, high blood pressure, smoking, and a sedentary lifestyle, if treated early, add to well-being and help prevent this disease.

We all agree that preventing the problem is better than treating it. Physicians, especially pediatricians, struggled to fight many epidemics such as infantile diarrhea, whooping cough, poliomyelitis, and measles. Organized preventive medicine started late in the nineteenth century by providing pure water and milk to combat the big killer of that time, infantile diarrhea. In the first half of the twentieth century, the development of immunizations gave future impetus to preventive health care. Today more than half the pediatrician's time is spent on preventive services. Screening tests for a variety of asymptomatic diseases have assumed increasing importance. In the early fall of 1987, the Department of Health Services in California successfully completed the newborn screening program in which they tested well over 2.7 million infants for phenylketonuria (PKU) and other asymptomatic infantile diseases. They found 111 cases of PKU, with an incidence of 1 in every 25,378 births. If this is a screening test done to detect and protect children from a very rare disease, it behooves us to screen routinely for high cholesterol levels in children and protect them from the number one killer, coronary heart disease.

The Orange County Health Education Department, in conjunction with the University of California at Irvine, the American Heart Association, the American Academy of Pediatrics, and others, recently screened about 450 schoolchildren ranging in age between 9 and 11, and found 14 percent of them with cholesterol levels of over 200 milligrams per deciliter, 11 of whom had levels considered to be very excessive and alarming for their age. They found many more of the children with levels that need to be lowered. In this study, a positive family history of coronary heart disease correlated with only one-third of the children with high cholesterol levels. This means that two-thirds of them would not have been recognized if routine screening had not been carried out.

In the pediatric age group, the basic intervention should be toward diet rather than drugs. If dietary intervention is to be effective, the eating habits of the entire family should be changed. Some of the guidelines from the National Institutes of Health's Consensus Conference on Lowering Blood Cholesterol to Prevent Heart Disease are: "It is desirable to begin prevention in childhood because patterns of lifestyle are developed in childhood. The moderate-fat, and moderate-cholesterol diet recommended for the population at large in this report should be suitable for all family members including healthy children older than 2 years. For children, the diet should provide all nutrients in quantities adequate to growth and development, and meet energy requirements. Excessive gain in weight should be avoided."

We now know that cholesterol buildup is slow, is certain, and goes unnoticed. When symptoms occur (angina or myocardial infarction), simple measures such as changing dietary habits, stopping smoking, and instituting exercise and relaxation are still necessary but might not be enough; more severe measures might be necessary to correct the disease. Pediatricians and parents alike start protecting children early in life by giving them the best medical services available, immunizing them against infectious diseases, educating them to avoid smoking and drugs, informing them about sexually transmitted diseases, and helping them survive their teenage years. By following Robert Kowalski's advice in this book, you can also help them sail through their middle age without the threat of the big monster—cardiovascular disease.

It has never worked to advise somebody to relax and take it easy, and it will never work to tell somebody to avoid fatty foods and cholesterol. Robert Kowalski helps you change your family's diet gradually, to meet the need of the "healthy heart." In showing you how and where to eat, this book distinguishes itself from others. It explains, in a language you can understand, what cholesterol, saturated fats, unsaturated fats, and poly- and monounsaturated fats are, where to find them, and how much of each of them to use. It helps you know where and how to shop, and gives you very practical recipes that are very acceptable to all family members (especially children)—recipes that follow the recommendation of a low-fat, low-cholesterol diet and at the same time give nutritional values that promote growth and development.

Robert Kowalski recognizes and discusses very intelligently in this book the other risk factors that contribute to cardiovascular disease. I have recommended his previous book, *The 8-Week Cholesterol Cure,* to many of my patients, and it has helped them lose weight and follow a healthful diet. I am waiting impatiently for this book because it will help children alter lifestyle factors that contribute to cardiovascular disease in their later years, while at the same time giving them a practical and easy way to develop good eating and other health habits that will last them all their lives.

Introduction

CHILDREN, CHOLESTEROL, AND HEART DISEASE

What genetic gifts did you receive from your parents? Blue eyes? Curly hair? Athletic ability? Like father, like son, the saying goes. But far too often children inherit a genetic endowment that predestines them to heart disease.

Like Sleeping Beauty, who was cursed by the wicked witch to prick her finger on a spinning-wheel spindle and fall into a death-like sleep, genetically predisposed children live happy normal lives, oblivious to problems that lie ahead. Do you remember the fairy tale? Sleeping Beauty's parents tried to eliminate all the spinning wheels so the prophecy couldn't come true.

The witch was not to be put off, however, and lured Sleeping Beauty to her fate. Luckily for her, a handsome prince broke the spell with a kiss and they lived happily ever after.

The ending of the story for today's children can be just as happy. The spindle in their story is cholesterol. But parents today can do a far more effective job than Sleeping Beauty's in eliminating the risks so that no handsome princes—in the form of coronary bypass surgery or other medical intervention—will be needed.

For my family, that cholesterol spindle has been wreaking havoc for generations. My grandmother died of a massive coronary attack, my father died prematurely of a heart attack at 57, his brother suffered a heart attack and had a subsequent coronary bypass, and his sister likewise died at an early age, also of heart disease.

Those were the genes I inherited. That endowment led to a heart attack at age 35. If I had not been under medical care, taking a heavy dose of medications, I probably would not have survived. But I was lucky, and lived to have coronary bypass surgery that same year. The problem was not resolved, however, and at 41 I needed a second operation.

The common denominator for those of us in our family with this disease is cholesterol. Our bodies are just not equipped to handle it properly. Our livers produce too much, our digestive tracts eliminate too little, and our diets add fuel to the fire. We're certainly not alone in this, as millions of Americans and others throughout the world are afflicted in the same way.

As I have described in my first book *The 8-Week Cholesterol Cure,* I found a way to effectively control the cholesterol problem to the point that my cholesterol level is well within the safety zone. The same can be said for the many men and women who have followed the program.

Because of my own condition and my immersion in writing a book on the subject, I am very aware of the health implications of an elevated cholesterol level. That's why I had my son's blood cholesterol level checked at the time of his annual exam before entering second grade. Ross was 7½ years old at the time, and the cholesterol blood test is definitive by that age. In fact, we can now test for cholesterol in children at any age, with confidence that the results will indicate both present and future tendencies toward normal or elevated levels. Authorities once questioned whether there was a minimum age for testing. Today they agree that the earlier the test, the better.

For a child before puberty, total cholesterol should be less than 140 milligrams per deciliter, and the LDL cholesterol should be less than 100. We'll explore the significance and meanings of those numbers later in this book. Suffice it to say that figures in excess of those levels pose a clear and certain danger of coronary heart disease. Ross's numbers were 181 and 123, respectively.

As we'll see, those levels don't mean that Ross was in immediate danger, or even that he would be a candidate for a heart attack in his teens, as some children are. But the numbers provided indisputable proof that my son had inherited the family's coronary curse. Sooner or later he would be pricked by the figurative spindle.

That's the bad news. The good news is that we are now aware of Ross's problem and that, unlike Sleeping Beauty's parents, we can entirely eliminate the risk posed by cholesterol. It will take a lot of extra effort, a degree of sacrifice, and more than a little understanding, but with Ross's cooperation we can vastly improve the odds against his ever developing coronary heart disease. Already, with the program I designed for him, Ross has lowered his cholesterol level significantly.

Ross is not alone. Millions and millions of boys and girls carry the genetic predisposition toward heart disease. Medical authorities estimate that as many as one-half of all Americans have elevated cholesterol levels that put them at risk of heart disease. That means that half of all children carry the same genetic burden. For them, too, the good news is that, with a simple blood test for detection and subsequent modification in diet and lifestyle, the risk of developing heart disease can be greatly reduced.

It has long been a truism that one of the best ways to assure a long and healthy life is to wisely choose one's parents. Of course that's impossible; our children are stuck with us and with our genes. But we can do our level best to turn the odds in their favor.

Before we go any further I want to emphasize as strongly as possible that a recognition that the household must make a few modifications to reduce cholesterol risk does not have to cast a black shadow over the family. In fact, the complete opposite is true. This recognition should be viewed as a positive opportunity for the entire family to improve its health status. There's no doubt that everyone will benefit—not only in terms of lower cholesterol, but also through lower blood pressure, decreased weight, and better physical fitness. The changes we've made in our family, for example, have not been drastic. There's no doom and gloom in our home. Sure, Ross misses a few foods that aren't good for him, but, as you'll read in his own words, everything is just fine.

Since we discovered Ross's elevated cholesterol level, we now know exactly what we're dealing with and can plan accordingly. We've worked out a complete list of foods and recipes that all of us can enjoy and that are low in fats and cholesterol. We know how to handle the situation when Ross is invited to birthday parties or other events at which the wrong kinds of foods will be served. Ross fully understands what is happening and takes it all in stride.

But most important, I believe to the roots of my being that if

Ross stays on his course of cholesterol control he can live a long and happy life free of heart disease. The genetic chain can be broken and the curse removed for the first time in our family's history. That's the feeling you can have about your children's future as well. What better gift can you give your youngsters? This book can help you every step of the way.

As a medical writer trained in both journalism and medical science I've had access to information from the world's leading medical authorities. I've visited their laboratories and read the voluminous and often complicated literature. This book is my opportunity to share all that knowledge with you in an understandable manner that I hope you'll also find enjoyable.

In these chapters you'll have all your questions about cholesterol answered. You'll also learn what you can do to offset the additional health threat of high blood pressure. You'll learn how to discuss the future with your children and how to deal with the present. And you'll see how easy it really can be to modify—not drastically alter—your family's eating habits so that everyone will benefit.

Let's face it: kids have certain favorites that just can't be replaced. Yet while slashing cholesterol and fat intake your children can continue to enjoy such goodies as sloppy joes, burgers, chili, pizza, pancakes, waffles, and even cakes and cookies. Other traditional family meals can be modified so that everyone in your home can continue to enjoy them.

Who hasn't at one time or another wanted to jump into a fairy tale to rescue the hero or heroine from the wicked witch? Who didn't cheer when Dorothy discovered that water melted the Wicked Witch of the West? The health threat of high cholesterol levels and heart disease is far more real to your children. You can be the hero to banish that villain forever!

1

One Family's Fight

To take one look at my son, Ross, is to see the picture of all-American health. He loves playing games and sports in the playground after school. Running, skateboarding, and bicycling are some of his favorite activities. His eyes are bright and his body strong and growing. And on top of it, he has a remarkable record of freedom from even common colds. The boy is just never sick.

To make sure that both my children are developing properly, my wife and I take Ross and my daughter, Jenny, for an annual examination by the pediatrician each year just before school starts. The pediatrician they saw in Chicago, before we moved to California, asked about family history and recommended that Ross have a blood test to determine his cholesterol level. At the time, there was some question as to whether tests on children were really predictive, and, if so, when the proper time was to do them. Ross was only 3 years old then. I had moved to Los Angeles a few months earlier, leaving my family in the Midwest until I could get established as a writer in California. Understandably, things were in a bit of turmoil domestically, with two households half a continent apart. And, to cloud the issue more, I planned to bring Ross out to the West Coast with me. There was just no time to get a cholesterol test or to worry about it.

Ross and I enjoyed a remarkable relationship when he flew out with me in January 1981. We learned a lot about each other, and the bonding that happened was a wonder. Every father should have an opportunity to get to know his son in such a one-on-one manner.

When it looked as if I could build a career as a writer specializing in medical assignments, my wife, Dawn, moved out with our daughter. Things started coming along nicely. Dawn got a teaching job in a local high school. My work was starting to pay off. And we were about to buy a house.

Then I got the news that changed my life forever.

I had had a triple coronary bypass operation in 1978, when I was only 35 years old, following a heart attack. While I appeared healthy and vigorous in all ways, it seemed that my arteries continued to clog. My cardiologist recommended a second bypass. We cancelled all plans.

Happily, however, the second surgery went very well. I recovered completely in record time, and was back to my typewriter after just two weeks. Within a month I was working full time.

After the second surgery I resolved that I would never need a third trip to the operating room. There was no question in my mind that cholesterol had been the culprit. My elevated cholesterol level just had to be brought down.

After an extensive review of the medical literature, I came up with a personal cholesterol-lowering program that included dietary modification, the inclusion of certain foods found to reduce cholesterol in the blood, and supplementation with the B vitamin niacin. The results were remarkable. My original cholesterol count was a dangerous 284 milligrams per deciliter. Diet modification alone had done very little in the past. But with this new program my cholesterol level plummeted to a safe, comfortable level of 169 in only a couple of months. My cardiologist was so impressed that he agreed to work with me on a clinical study at Santa Monica Hospital Medical Center to see if the program would work for others. It certainly did. Literally all the participants in that study dramatically reduced the level of the "bad" LDL cholesterol and increased their counts of the "good" HDL cholesterol. (I'll explain what all that means in more detail later.) The full story of that program designed for adults was told in the book *The 8-Week Cholesterol Cure*.

But while I stopped eating hot dogs, steaks, eggs, and butter, I didn't ask Ross and Jenny to do the same. Let's face it: certain kinds of foods just seem to go with childhood. I didn't want to take away the fun of munching on McDonald's cheeseburgers and fries. Then, too, there was a bit of ostrichlike thinking on my part. Ross and Jenny were just kids, after all. They weren't about to have a heart attack or need surgery; they were really healthy kids.

So for months I ignored the issue. I just didn't think about it—until September and time for the annual trip to the pediatrician. This time I didn't wait for him to suggest the cholesterol test; I asked for it.

Sure enough, Ross exhibited an elevated level of cholesterol in his young blood. The numbers weren't in the astronomical range, though some children at his age actually can have life-threatening levels. But they indicated that, left alone to progress through the years, his cholesterol level would increase during young adulthood. Not that, regardless of what Ross continued to eat or how he lived his life, we would have noticed it. The process of cholesterol buildup is a slow but certain truth. What we got was a yellow light indicating danger ahead. Now was the time to do something about the situation.

Ross did *not* have heart disease then or now, but I didn't want him to experience the pain and horrors of heart disease and surgery—*ever*. His elevated cholesterol level simply pointed to the likelihood of his developing heart disease later on.

Now you may be thinking, "Wow, the guy became a wild-eyed zealot and forced his whole family to eat nothing but fruits and vegetables." Nothing could be further from the truth.

Today Ross eats hot dogs, hamburgers, burritos, tacos, spaghetti, French toast, pancakes, waffles, pizza, and virtually every other goodie known to kids. And, yes, he still goes to birthday parties and eats cake and ice cream. He even goes to fast-food restaurants. We all do.

And when it's time for snacks and desserts, we enjoy cookies, cakes, granola bars, brownies, and cupcakes. Would you believe they're actually *good* for us all? Yes, it's true. My wife makes excellent desserts, and now she does so with little or no fat.

All this came as an evolution in our eating habits—and, I must say, as the result of more than a little effort to develop the recipes and approaches to make it all happen. Now my kids—and yours—can eat the foods they love without the threat of clogged arteries. In this book you'll read all about how to prepare foods fit for a kid. But there's much more than that to preventing future heart disease.

Another major risk factor in heart disease is smoking. There's no question in anyone's mind that this habit has a direct link to the development of atherosclerosis and heart attacks. Many adults would like to quit but haven't been able to do so. Yet in spite of all we know, tens of thousands of children are starting to smoke cigarettes.

The time to influence children is before they reach for that first smoke. It's my sincere belief that Ross and Jenny will never acquire the cigarette habit. They've been exposed to education in school, certainly, but in addition, in a very nonthreatening manner and without heavy-handed tactics, I've extended the antismoking message to the home. My kids have become avid antismokers—so much so that my wife quit at their urging! I'll tell you all about it in Chapter 8, dealing with other risk factors.

By now you've probably heard about the role of what's called Type A behavior in the development of heart disease. The Type A personality is marked by hostile, angry, time-driven behavior and has been correlated with heart disease. The Type B individual, on the other hand, is more relaxed and exhibits fewer traits of time-urgency. Most researchers and physicians agree that the way we deal with stress is an important risk factor. There's no doubt in my mind that stress was influential in my early disease onset. But the most frightening thing was to see much of my behavior pattern inherited by my son.

Ross is very much like me in many ways, and not all of them are positive. For example, at a very early age he was showing signs of anger and frustration when a toy wouldn't work right. At other times he'd burst into tears when an argument with his sister would frustrate him. If he was this way at age 8, what could we expect in the future?

Interestingly, most psychologists agree that this sort of negative behavior starts like a storm. First you see the clouds forming, and before you know it, the rain is pouring down. Similarly, anger and hostility grow from a small seed into a full-blown rage. And those of us with Type A traits don't know what to do about it. In fact, we don't even know we're beginning a tantrum; once we're there, we can't stop the flow of emotions.

Are you like that? Do you get outraged over a traffic jam or a missed appointment? Does an argument with a merchant over an unsatisfactory purchase lead to inordinate outbursts? If so, you too have the signs of a Type A personality. But what about your kids? Can you see some of those traits in them?

I'll get into lots more detail about this important issue in the chapter on today's stressful child. But for the moment let me share one approach to diminishing Type A behavior that has really worked well in our family.

One day I sat down with Ross and Jenny for a serious talk. We have these frequently, so this came as no surprise to them; in fact, they like the opportunity to clear the boards about various things. This time I brought up the topic of emotional outbursts.

I explained my own problem first. I told them that too often I yelled about things that didn't really matter that much. I'd get angry about something, and the anger would grow rather than dissipate. Here's just one example: Like most kids, mine leave things lying around the house. Sometimes I pick them up without comment. Sometimes I tell the kids to clean up the mess. But other times, especially when I'm tired at the end of the day, I yell. And every once in a while I lose my temper. Afterwards I feel guilty about my behavior, but once that beastly temper gets out of its cage, I can't put it back.

In the same way, Ross gets frustrated about a toy that won't work. Or about a homework problem that seems impossible to solve. Jenny starts to cry in response to a real or imagined injustice —little sisters always seem to feel deprived about one thing or another. And with both kids, once the emotions start to flow they grow and grow.

So I calmly told them I needed some help in controlling my temper. I asked them to do me a favor: when they heard me start to yell, I wanted them to say, "Daddy, please stop."

But how about the kids? When Ross would lose his temper, we decided that one of us would say, "Ross, please stop." The same for Jenny. None of us was beyond improvement, I explained, and they both quickly agreed that the happiest home was one in which there was no yelling, screaming, and crying.

Now that may sound like a simple, commonsense thing to propose. How can a comment like "Please stop" do any good? Well, let me tell you, it can and it does. It actively defuses that emotional outburst—for all of us. It's helped me, it's helped my kids, and it's made for a nicer way of life. But very important, this simple little trick has started my kids on the right track of controlling their tempers and coping with stressful situations.

Living a Type B way of life doesn't mean that a person must become docile and less goal-oriented, as some people believe. Rather, it's a way to actually make all of us far *more* productive by eliminating wasteful displays of emotion. There are so many things parents can do to start their kids toward Type B healthful living. In Chapter 7, I describe in detail a deep-breathing program I began with Ross and Jenny, which has helped all three of us tremendously to cope with stress; and they love doing it.

As with deep breathing, many if not most of the ways to prevent future heart disease in your children also provide direct benefits for you as parents. Take physical fitness. We know that a sedentary lifestyle is a risk factor in heart disease. One of the best ways to get children interested in physical fitness, in fact, is to make it a family affair. While Ross naturally enjoys the active life, Jenny seems to lean toward more sedentary behavior. She'd rather play in her room than ride her bike. Ross loves to run. Jenny walks. Slowly.

In the same vein, my wife had been putting off a return to regular exercise. Dawn worked out in a health club when we lived in Chicago, but never seemed to get around to joining one after moving to California. So I suggested that we join a health club here that the whole family could enjoy. The club offers family swim days, and even features a Sunday family exercise program. Now all four of us routinely include exercise in our lives. In addition to the club, we try to do some biking together and other activities as well.

Avoiding another risk factor also presents extra benefits. It's well recognized that overweight persons have shortened life expectancies. Obesity increases the risk of hypertension, high cholesterol levels, diabetes, and heart disease. Unfortunately, Dawn brings with her a family history of being overweight. Ross inherited my body structure and tends to be lean. But from the very start, Jenny showed the signs of being chubby. Dawn's mother and grandmother both were overweight, and she also has a tendency to put on pounds.

Each time Jenny went for her annual physical checkup, the pediatrician pointed out that her weight was well above average. Jenny didn't really seem to be eating that much more than her friends. Was her weight genetically predetermined? The thought disturbed me quite a bit.

Then, because of Ross's cholesterol level, the family diet began to change. Little by little, bit by bit, the fat level of the foods we ate started to fall. Actually, the evolution was almost imperceptible.

First it was the little things, such as switching to low-fat mayonnaise. Such products naturally have fewer calories. Then came improved methods of cooking; using a vegetable-oil cooking spray instead of butter or margarine for frying. Hamburgers on the grill looked and tasted the same as always, but they were made with a fraction of the fat, which slashed their calorie content. And on and on it went.

The happy news is that Jenny has thinned down considerably. Now there's not a trace of chubbiness. And we never even had to concentrate on the problem or remind her about it. She just ate the food served, and enjoyed every bite. In fact, she brags about how she eats more "good" food than Ross in some instances. For snacks, Jenny loves sliced fruit far more than Ross. But for both kids I've found delicious and nutritious ways to keep them healthy, happy, and growing.

As time goes on, there are more and more reports linking diet with this or that disease. And each report has one thing in common: the conclusion that we need to reduce the total and the saturated fats in the foods we eat. Doctors now link fat intake with a variety of cancers, including those of the colon, prostate, breast, and lung. There's no question that the symptoms of Type II, non-insulin dependent diabetes completely disappear when patients control their diet and attain optimal weight.

Another dietary link that most of us have heard a lot about is that between sodium intake and high blood pressure. Cut down on the salt, the authorities tell us. In our family, sodium intake has gone way down since we've gotten "heart smart," and it's all happened without even trying. The approaches I share with you just naturally have less sodium, so you don't miss it at all.

Some risk factors we just can't do anything about. I can't change Ross's sex. Nor can I re-engineer his genes, or take away his predisposition to high cholesterol levels. But many of the risk factors can be controlled.

Yet while it's easy to decide to cut down on fat and cholesterol, it's not so easy to figure out just how to do it—especially for children. Do heart-smart kids have to live entirely different lifestyles from others? Absolutely not!

What about birthday parties, you might ask. Doesn't a parent lose control? Well, yes and no. Certainly you don't want to tell a boy or girl not to attend such parties. And yet you don't want them to gobble up all the traditional goodies. I have a way of solving this problem that is painless, and I describe it in Chapter 4, "Fighting Killer Cholesterol." There are also tricks I've come up with for special occasions throughout the year, such as Easter and Halloween.

How about eating out—especially in fast-food places, which kids love? There are ways around this dilemma, too, explained also in Chapter 4. The list goes on and on, and I've done a lot of research for both your family and mine.

I am not a physician. And while it's true that I've written exclusively about health and medical matters for the past twenty years, I have never put myself forward as a doctor. But as a medical writer, I assigned myself the project of finding out all I possibly could about children, cholesterol, and heart disease. That research has been done in supermarkets, restaurants, doctors' offices, research laboratories, library files, medical journals, computer searches, and, very noteworthy, my kitchen. I've asked the questions and gotten the answers. What I do offer is my services as an expert guide through mountains of information written in medical jargon—advice of not one physician, but dozens of top authorities in the world. I did it all for the best of reasons: I dearly love my kids and want the best for them. And now your kids can benefit as well.

Let me take you step-by-logical-step through the entire issue. I've spelled out every bit of information I've gathered over the years, and all the ideas and tips I've come up with myself as well as those from others.

Some of the things you'll be reading about in the pages to come are pretty straightforward. There's no controversy about the cholesterol issue anymore, and there's no question that everyone benefits from a bit of weight control and ways to control destructive behavior patterns.

But what about approaches such as vegetarianism? Is this something you'll want to consider for your family? To help you make that decision I've outlined the advantages and disadvantages. Am I an expert in vegetarianism? Of course not. But I've had the advantage of learning from the best. I've worked closely with researchers at California's Loma Linda University in developing the First International Congress on Vegetarian Nutrition, which has become a major event, with authorities participating from around the world. I bring you all the information you need from these top people.

When shopping, which cooking oil should you choose? Can you continue to eat cheese? Which breakfast cereals should go into the shopping cart? How can you get your kids to eat the ones you want them to? It's all spelled out in the pages that follow. But let me preview with a particularly successful ploy in my family.

Like other kids, mine were drawn to two kinds of cereal: those with special prizes inside and those with specialty shapes and colors. Needless to say, those cereals are not the best kinds when considering nutrition. So what's a parent to do?

When my Jenny asked for the multicolored cartoon-character cereals she saw advertised on TV, she was surprised when I said yes during a trip to the supermarket. There was one catch, though: that cereal was to be eaten only as a snack, not for the breakfast meal. She agreed eagerly to the deal. Now think about it. Candy eaten as a snack is 100 percent sugar; the cereal is only half sugar. So while it's a terrible choice for breakfast, it's *quite OK* for a snack. And Jenny promised to rinse her teeth with water after munching.

Ross, on the other hand, loved the prizes at the bottom of the box. No matter that the cereal was sugary and contained only those vitamins sprayed on the flakes during processing. I spoke with him matter-of-factly about all this, and we too made a deal. Now I get him the cereal I want him to eat—especially oat bran, which helps lower cholesterol levels—and he's rewarded with a prize I purchase, such as a pack of collector's cards, stickers, or some such little trinket.

Oat bran is one of the many foods on the market today that can actively cause a drop in cholesterol levels. When reading the findings of researchers who have attempted to lower children's cholesterol, I noted that practically all achieved a drop of about 10 percent with dietary measures of cutting back on fat and cholesterol. Sometimes the drop is less. But when you add special foods like oat bran, the cholesterol levels plummet even more. This book discusses all the various foods you can incorporate into your family's meals to ensure the most complete cholesterol control, and to obtain the greatest cholesterol reduction possible without drugs.

What started as a lifesaving necessity for Ross and Jenny and myself has turned into a virtual hobby. I've really enjoyed coming up with ways to control my family's cholesterol and thus preventing future heart disease. My attitude about the whole process shows in the pages to come.

Good health should be a positive idea, not a "downer." The last thing you need to hear is a depressing litany of "Thou Shalt Nots." What I offer is an upbeat way to enjoy food, family, and health.

To help put things into perspective—to show the way kids might view healthful changes—I asked Ross and Jenny to share their thoughts with you in their own chapters. Ross wrote his own responses to a series of questions I posed to him—the kinds of questions your kids might want to ask him if they came to visit. Jenny and I talked while a tape recorder took down her thoughts. I think you'll agree that these are two happy kids who don't view themselves as at all deprived.

Finally, I invite you to turn the page and begin reading about just what cholesterol is and what you can do about it. I think you'll find it fascinating reading, and I'm confident it will convince you to start making the changes necessary to fight killer cholesterol in your home.

Why not start this evening by preparing one of the recipes in Chapter 18, "Food Fit for a Kid"? In the mood for Mexican food? Try the enchiladas; they're delicious. Or how about a pizza? You'll be amazed at how many mouth-watering and kid-pleasing menus you'll devise to share with your family tonight and every night.

From my family—Dawn, Ross, Jenny, and me—to yours, welcome to a generation of kids free from heart disease! Good eating and good health to you and yours from me and mine!

2

The Cholesterol Primer

Although "cholesterol" has become a household word, few of us have a complete understanding of the substance and its chemical cousins. Whenever one begins a study of a new area, be it art or wine or real estate, the first order of business is to learn the vocabulary. So let's begin with a straightforward yet thorough overview of the terms and concepts that will help you understand the principles of preventing heart disease in your children.

The term *cholesterol* refers to a waxy substance in the chemical family of alcohols. It is one of many related chemicals all referred to as sterols. A certain amount of cholesterol is required for your body to produce hormones and to form the sheath around nerves. However, your liver produces all you need. There is no need to take in any cholesterol in your food.

The only foods that contain cholesterol come from animal sources. Some foods, of course, contain more cholesterol than others: eggs, cheese, and liver contain large amounts, while skim milk and certain fishes contain little. Of course, many of our favorite foods come from animal sources, and it would be difficult if not impossible to eliminate those foods completely. The answer, as we will see, lies in the old adage of moderation.

While all animal foods contain some cholesterol, plant foods contain none at all. Thus those commercials on TV touting peanut butter or salad oil with no cholesterol mean absolutely nothing. Regardless of fat content or other attributes, no vegetable foods contain any cholesterol at all.

As mentioned, the liver produces cholesterol every day and releases it into the bloodstream. The amount produced is controlled by an enzyme called HMG Co-A reductase. Some of us have more or less of that enzyme, and that is one of the reasons why some people have elevated levels of cholesterol in their blood.

Another reason for elevated cholesterol levels is that in some people the body does not eliminate as much cholesterol as it might. Cholesterol leaves the body through the colon in the form of bile salts and acids. The more bile acids are eliminated, the more cholesterol must be drawn from the blood to make more. There are ways we can help our bodies eliminate bile acids and thus drop cholesterol levels. We'll talk more about that later.

The third reason for elevated cholesterol levels is, of course, the food we eat. Interestingly, it is not only the cholesterol we consume, but also the total amount of fats, and especially saturated fats, which drives those levels up. In fact, *saturated fats elevate cholesterol levels even faster than cholesterol itself.*

People living in countries where their diets contain little fat and cholesterol typically have lower levels of cholesterol in their blood. Many studies have shown that native men and women leaving countries such as Japan and Ireland find that their blood cholesterol levels rise significantly as they consume more fats and cholesterol in keeping with the American way of life.

There's no question that some people can consume much more fat and cholesterol than others and still keep their blood cholesterol levels down. Genetics play a strong role in such metabolic affairs. However, everyone's cholesterol will rise, regardless of genetic endowments, if his or her diet becomes laden with fats and cholesterol. It's a matter of both nature and nurture.

There are three types of fat in the diet. They are designated chemically by the number of hydrogen atoms in the fat molecule. If the molecule can accept no more hydrogen atoms, the fat is said to be saturated. Such fats tend to be solid or semisolid at room temperature, and they include butter, lard, and other animal fats, as well as certain vegetable oils. In addition, food manufacturers may add hydrogen atoms to vegetable oils to retard spoilage; you'll see them listed as "partially hydrogenated."

If one space on the fat molecule remains unfilled by a hydrogen atom, the fat is monounsaturated. Olive and peanut oils contain primarily monounsaturated fat, as do cashew nuts, avocados, and olives.

Finally, if many spaces on the molecule remain open, the fat is said to be polyunsaturated. Principal sources of polyunsaturated fats in the diet are vegetable oils other than olive and peanut oils.

As we will learn in more detail in Chapter 4, authorities recommend that no more than 30 percent of our total calories come from all fat. And of total calories, no more than 10 percent should come from saturated fat. Don't let that confuse you. There are much easier ways to determine the proper amounts of fat in your family's diet without calculating percentages. However, scientists always use percentages in their discussions, so for the moment we'll stay with that. Suffice it to say that the typical American diet derives much more than 30 percent of its calories from fat, and that it is not at all difficult to reduce fat intake to reach the desired levels. The American diet averages over 40 percent fat!

Now let's get back to cholesterol. The substance does not float in the blood by itself. Rather, cholesterol is carried in the blood by molecules made of protein and fat. Since *lipid* is another term for "fat," those molecules are called *lipoproteins.* Some are heavier than others, and thus are called high-density lipoproteins as compared to low-density lipoproteins.

Scientists have learned that cholesterol carried by high-density lipoproteins (HDL) remains in the blood, to be returned to the liver for metabolism to bile acids and salts, which are eliminated through the colon. Low-density lipoproteins (LDL), on the other hand, carry cholesterol to be deposited in tissues, specifically in the tissues lining our arteries. HDL cholesterol, often simply called HDLs, then, plays a protective role, while LDL cholesterol, or LDLs, is detrimental.

There is a third classification referred to as very-low-density lipoproteins (VLDL). Eventually these VLDLs become converted to the detrimental LDLs.

After having a blood test to determine your cholesterol level or that of your child, the results will be stated in terms of the amounts of total cholesterol, "good" HDL cholesterol, and "bad" LDL cholesterol. Currently they are measured as milligrams of cholesterol per deciliter of blood, abbreviated as mg/dl. In Europe and, some say, eventually in America, the metric equivalent will be stated in terms of millimoles.

Researchers have learned that the ratio between total cholesterol and HDL cholesterol can more effectively predict risk of heart disease than total cholesterol alone. For example, if someone's total cholesterol is 200, with an HDL of 50, the ratio is 4. The higher the ratio over 4, the greater the risk; the lower the ratio, the lower the risk. The average ratio for adult men is about 5. "Average risk" implies no added risk; you want to be at no higher than the average risk, and preferably lower. We still do not know the ideal ratio for children, although it is important to have a high HDL and a low LDL, combined with a low total cholesterol reading.

Your blood test results will contain one more bit of information in the blood lipid profile: a triglyceride level. Triglycerides are a storage form of fat composed of molecules called chylomicrons. Since chylomicrons are used by the liver to produce VLDL, and subsequently LDL, it's best to have a relatively low level of triglycerides in the blood.

Now, you might ask, how can I control those lipids? Both nature and nurture play roles in levels of blood concentration. Women and blacks tend to have higher levels of HDL, while men and whites have lower values. However, environmental factors also are involved. People engaged in vigorous exercise typically have higher HDLs than sedentary individuals. Obesity tends to reduce the protective HDLs. While alcohol in moderate amounts is known to raise HDL levels, there is some current controversy because the specific portion of the HDL cholesterol raised may not be the one involved in the protective role. Thus there should be no temptation to have a drink or two to raise your HDL levels. Conversely, smoking cigarettes absolutely decreases HDL concentration. Apart from these measures, there is little a person can do to affect HDLs per se; rather, a person can decrease the amount of LDLs so that the ratio improves.

Some individuals may be able to lower LDL and total cholesterol levels dramatically just by cutting back on fat and cholesterol in the diet. Others, because of their unique metabolic makeup, may not respond to dietary measures as well. Such persons may need drugs designed to lower cholesterol levels in the blood.

Triglyceride levels are greatly elevated in only a relatively small portion of the population. When levels go very high, drugs typically must be used to reduce them. But for moderate elevations, dietary modification does the job. Elevated triglycerides frequently are the result of excessive intake of simple carbohydrates, including sucrose and other sugars, and alcoholic beverages. Triglycerides will markedly decrease with weight reduction.

Physicians and other health professionals have terms to describe individuals with elevated cholesterol and fats in their blood. Hypercholesterolemia means elevated cholesterol levels. Hyperlipidemia means elevated levels of fats. And hyperlipoproteinemia refers to elevations in the level of molecules carrying cholesterol in the blood. Actually, the terms are used almost interchangeably in medical literature.

The effects of elevated levels of fats in the blood are now almost universally agreed to begin early in childhood. The process is insidious, progressing without any symptoms until well into adulthood. Later symptoms might include chest pains (angina pectoris), heart attack (myocardial infarction), and even sudden death. It's frightening to think that often the first sign of coronary heart disease is death.

As you will read in the next chapter, when young children and adolescents are autopsied after accidental death or death from other causes, signs of the beginnings of heart disease can already be seen.

Very early in life, fatty streaks can be found in the aorta, the large artery leading from the heart. In some children, fatty streaks also appear in the coronary arteries, those providing blood to the heart itself. As the child matures, those fatty streaks progress to fibrous plaques, which become raised. Plaques are composed of cholesterol, fibers, calcium, and cells known as macrophages.

Slowly but surely, the plaques begin to occlude the lumen, or opening of the arteries, to the point eventually where significant narrowing occurs. This process is called atherosclerosis, from the Greek words meaning "gruel" and "hardness."

Such hardening can develop in any of the body's arteries, most typically in the coronary arteries of the heart, the neck's carotid arteries supplying the brain, and the peripheral arteries in the legs. Hardening of the coronary arteries is referred to as coronary heart disease, coronary artery disease, or ischemic heart disease, the latter relating to the lack of oxygen supplied by the blood to the heart.

If the carotid arteries in the neck become occluded, the result can be a stroke, referred to as a cerebrovascular accident, or CVA in medical parlance. Clogged arteries in the legs can lead to severe cramping pain called intermittent claudication. Surgery can be performed to bypass the affected area to supply sufficient blood and oxygen to the leg muscles and prevent that pain.

Bypass surgery can also be performed on the arteries of the heart, shunting blood by way of transplanted bits of vein taken from the legs. That procedure has been with us since 1967, when it was developed at the Cleveland Clinic in Ohio. Today more than 150,000 coronary bypass surgeries are performed annually.

Cardiologists can detect the occlusion of arteries through a number of evaluations. The electrocardiogram (ECG) records by tracings on paper the electrical activity of the heart in a series of waves familiar to anyone who has ever seen a medical drama on TV. If one of those waves, the ST segment, becomes depressed in a measurable degree, it means insufficient blood and oxygen are reaching the heart's muscular tissues. Sometimes this can be seen in patients at rest. More typically, though, cardiologists have the patient exercise on a treadmill or stationary bicycle while wired to the electrocardiograph machine. As the demand for oxygen increases during exercise, the ECG may show increasing depression in that ST segment, indicating occlusion of the arteries.

To see where specific narrowing of the arteries, called stenosis, may have developed, patients may require angiography, whereby a catheter is threaded through arteries in either the legs or arms into the arteries of the heart itself. An injected dye, seen on a video screen, shows exactly where the narrowing has developed. By viewing the film and carefully measuring the degree of narrowing, physicians determine whether the patient can be treated medically or surgically.

Research efforts are now underway to develop new and improved methods of clearing out occluded arteries. Much has been written on the promise of lasers in this regard. Other doctors are working on methods of shaving the interior of the arteries in a manner similar to the Roto-Rooter for sewer drains.

Certainly I'm pleased that medical research developed the coronary bypass surgery which kept me alive to watch my children grow. And I'm confident that additional procedures will come along down the line. But I would much rather prevent the necessity for such drastic measures in my own children.

We now know the risk factors for developing coronary heart disease. They are elevated serum cholesterol levels, obesity, high blood pressure, lack of physical exercise, stress, cigarette smoking, sex, and family history. Happily, we can control all but the last two factors. You can guide your children toward a lifestyle that is not only healthful in a general way, but also drastically reduces their risk of ever having heart disease.

The statistics on heart disease are absolutely horrifying. Each year, 500,000 Americans suffer a heart attack. One million persons die of heart disease each year, making it the nation's number one killer. The odds that a child born today will have a catastrophic cardiac event before age 60 are one in three. Those are really lousy odds by anyone's standards.

One would think that with all we know about the disease, the future would look much brighter. But figures issued by the federal government provide a gloomy outlook, since coronary heart disease is predicted to remain the leading U.S. killer for decades. Despite lifestyle changes in the general population and improved medical therapies, researchers predict heart disease will still be the number one cause of death in the year 2010. In dollar figures, heart disease will cost about $44.7 billion that year.

Using a computer to simulate conditions expected in the next twenty years or so, a team from the Harvard School of Public Health, Brigham and Women's Hospital, and Harvard Medical School determined that the annual number of newly diagnosed heart disease cases will rise to about 900,000 by the year 2010. The total number of patients will be about 8.5 million Americans. More than 600,000 people will die each year from coronary heart disease alone, not counting other forms of heart disease such as valve failure and so on.

Reporting their results at a meeting of the American Federation of Clinical Research in 1986, the team said the next project would be to determine the impact of a medical breakthrough or a change in risk factors on coronary heart disease.

My family doesn't have to wait for the results of that computer simulation or the actuality of the year 2010. We know how to change our risk factors so that the children will not be among those statistics. With the information in the coming chapters, you too will have the capability of saving your children's lives and preventing needless pain and suffering.

3
The Kids' Cholesterol Connection

In 1961, a pediatrician first asked whether diet was somehow linked to cholesterol levels in children.[1] Today we have a mountain of evidence to answer that question with a resounding *yes*. The medical literature contains dozens if not hundreds of articles spelling out the connection among childrens' diets, their cholesterol levels, and their likelihood of developing coronary heart disease.

Writing in the *Journal of the American College of Nutrition,* Dr. William Kannel of Boston University said "the responsibility of the pediatrician for his young patients' health should not end at adolescence.... The average American child presently has one chance in three of a cardiovascular catastrophe before reaching age 60. The predisposing factors arise from habits conditioned in childhood. There is a compelling need to protect the young from an atherogenic way of life."[2]

As a parent, especially one with a history of heart disease, I feel particularly compelled to protect *my* children from that atherogenic way of life. With the assistance of a librarian friend of mine, I've reviewed the writings of experts from all over the world; this chapter summarizes those writings, and I feel confident that after having read it, you'll want to protect *your* children as well.

In research on coronary heart disease, it is only within the past ten years that attention has shifted to children; until then the focus was exclusively on the problem in adults. And not much earlier than that, there was still a scientific controversy regarding the link among diet, the amount of cholesterol in the blood, and coronary heart disease.

Seeing indisputable evidence mounting, physicians soon agreed that persons suffering heart attacks and showing the symptoms of coronary heart disease almost always had elevated levels of cholesterol in their blood. They knew that cholesterol was a component of the diet, but did that diet affect the blood cholesterol levels?

Early on, those who said there was a correlation between cholesterol in the diet and cholesterol in the blood pointed to comparisons between Western countries and other populations around the world. People consuming significant amounts of animal foods contributing saturated fats and cholesterol had high levels of cholesterol in the blood. Those eating little such food, relying instead on grains, vegetables, fruits, and low-fat fish and poultry, had low cholesterol levels.

But on the other hand, scientists pointed out, the Eskimos who ate practically nothing but high-fat animal foods such as whales, seals, and fish had unexplained low serum cholesterol levels, and virtually no heart disease. And what about studies with healthy young men fed extra eggs in their diets? Their cholesterol levels did not rise as a result. Therefore, those investigators said, there was no reason to change the American way of eating.

As time went on, those discrepancies and others were eliminated. It was realized that while the Eskimos ate a lot of high-fat meats, the fats in whales, seals, and other marine animals in cold waters are polyunsaturated rather than saturated. In addition, the particular oils in their diet have a protective effect.

The young men fed those extra eggs demonstrated a phenomenon now known as the "saturation effect." The human body can metabolize only so much fat and cholesterol. After a while, one hits a saturation level; it's like trying to put 10 ounces of fluid in an 8-ounce glass. But if a person who normally eats a low-fat, low-cholesterol diet is fed egg yolks, the level of cholesterol in the blood indeed rises.

Slowly the consensus in the medical community swung to accepting the idea that diet does affect cholesterol levels. But there remained a "So what?" attitude. There was no proof, the nay-sayers maintained, that lowering cholesterol levels in the blood would have any effect on heart disease.

That evidence was delivered in a report published in 1984 in the *Journal of the American Medical Association*.[3] A major study conducted through the National Heart, Lung, and Blood Institute showed that men who reduced their cholesterol levels by 25 percent achieved a 50 percent drop in the incidence of coronary heart disease. The authors stated without reservation that for every 1 percent fall in blood cholesterol level, there would be a 2 percent reduction in heart disease risk. The men in this study cut their risk in half!

That report became a historic medical landmark, a milestone in our progress against heart disease. Finally the nation's top authorities convened in December of 1984 to form a consensus on lowering blood cholesterol levels to prevent heart disease.[4] The panel consisted of experts in lipids, cardiologists, family practitioners, epidemiologists, biomedical scientists, statisticians, authorities in preventive medicine, and representatives from the lay community. They came together to answer five questions:

1. Can elevated blood cholesterol levels cause heart disease?
2. Can reducing blood cholesterol levels help prevent heart disease?
3. When and how should treatment be started?
4. Should the general population be concerned?
5. What further research is needed?

The panel concluded that "it has been established beyond a reasonable doubt that lowering definitely elevated blood cholesterol levels will reduce the risk of heart attacks caused by coronary heart disease." The greater the level of cholesterol elevation in the blood, they said, the greater effort should be expended in treatment to cut that level to normal.

And, the experts advised, "All Americans (except children younger than two years of age) should be advised to adopt a diet that reduces total dietary fat intake from the current level of about 40% of total calories to 30% of total calories, reduces saturated fat intake to less than 10% of total calories, increases polyunsaturated fat intake but to no more than 10% of total calories, and reduces daily cholesterol intake to 250 to 300 mg or less." We'll discuss the everyday implications of that advice throughout this book so you and your entire family can benefit from this expert counsel.

But before we do, let's dig further into the literature regarding cholesterol and children. You'll soon see why experts in preventive medicine believe that the children of today can be saved from the coronary heart disease of tomorrow. In the coming pages, you'll read the opinions of authorities across the country and around the world.

Physicians writing in the *Southern Medical Journal*[5] say that atherosclerosis begins in childhood and that the disease progresses through several stages before becoming clinically apparent in adults. They believe that "the serum cholesterol concentration has an almost linear relationship to the risk of developing coronary heart disease." The greater the cholesterol level, the greater the risk.

A leading authority on children and heart disease, Dr. Charles Glueck, has said that "we know that approximately one-third of all children of parents sustaining myocardial infarction before age 50 will be found, on sampling, to have primary dyslipoproteinemia [elevated blood lipids]."[6]

Reporting on studies done at the University of Michigan,[7] researchers said that 62 percent of all boys and girls studied had at least one risk factor for heart disease. Those children were only 7 to 12 years old.

Another study examined the coronary arteries of 1,500 infants, children, and adolescents.[8] They were abnormal more often than not by the age of 15, frequently by the age of 5, and not uncommonly in infancy. Looking at the incidence of coronary-heart-disease risk factors in boys aged 8 to 12, researchers at the University of California found that 46 percent had at least one such factor; only one-third had no risk factors at all.[9]

In a major investigation called the Muscatine Study, nearly 5,000 schoolchildren in Muscatine, Iowa, were evaluated.[10] The researchers reported that "perhaps the fifty percent of children in the Muscatine Study with serum cholesterol levels above 180 mg/dl can be considered at risk for the future development of coronary heart disease."

Cholesterol levels of children as well as of men and women are listed in Tables 1–9. These values are listed as percentiles; for example, only 5 percent of the population would have higher levels than those in the 95th percentile. The "mean" refers to the average level.

Dr. Kannel[2] has written that although values encountered in children may seem "normal" by the usual or adult standards, children with cholesterol levels in the upper end tend to become adult candidates for coronary heart disease. As we'll see in more detail

Table 1. PLASMA LIPIDS IN CHILDREN AND ADOLESCENTS*

Age in Years	Total Cholesterol (mg/dl)			Triglycerides (mg/dl)			HDL Cholesterol (mg/dl)			LDL Cholesterol (mg/dl)		
	5th	Mean	95th	5th	Mean	95th	5th	Mean	95th	5th	Mean	95th
0–4												
Males	114	155	203	29	56	99						
Females	112	156	200	34	64	112						
5–9												
Males	121	160	203	30	56	101	38	56	74	63	93	129
Females	126	164	205	32	60	105	36	53	73	68	100	140
10–14												
Males	119	158	202	32	66	125	37	55	74	64	97	132
Females	124	160	201	37	75	131	37	52	70	68	97	136
15–19												
Males	113	150	197	37	78	148	30	46	63	62	94	130
Females	120	158	203	39	75	132	35	52	74	59	96	137

* Data from the Lipid Research Clinic Data Book (1980). Figures reflect percentiles.

Table 2. PLASMA TOTAL CHOLESTEROL (mg/dl) IN ADULT MALES[11]

Age/Years	Average	5%	75%	90%	95%
0–19	155	115	170	185	200
20–24	165	125	185	205	220
25–29	180	135	200	225	245
30–34	190	140	215	240	255
35–39	200	145	225	250	270
40–44	205	150	230	250	270
45–69	215	160	235	260	275
70+	205	150	230	250	270

shortly, most risk factors tend to "track" from childhood to adult life; cholesterol levels rise progressively.

Worldwide evidence suggests that adult cholesterol values of 160 to 180 mg/dl are associated with both lower incidence of heart disease and better overall health. To achieve such levels, Dr. Kannel says, values of about 140 mg/dl are needed in children to track into adult life.[2]

Several studies have looked at the phenomenon of tracking heart-disease risk factors in children. In a landmark investigation known as the Bogalusa Study[12] scientists found persistence of levels even during the first year of life; in 440 children, levels "tracked"—stayed the same or rose—from 6 months until their first birthday.

The authors of the Muscatine Study[10] wrote that an important reason for concern about elevated serum cholesterol levels in children is the knowledge that after the age of 24, there is a progressive rise. They suggest that every child exhibiting a level of 180 mg/dl should receive dietary intervention. They also cited Austra-

Table 3. PLASMA LOW-DENSITY LIPOPROTEIN CHOLESTEROL (mg/dl) IN ADULT MALES[11]

Age/Years	Average	5%	75%	90%	95%
5–19	95	65	105	120	130
20–24	105	65	120	140	145
25–29	115	70	140	155	165
30–34	125	80	145	165	185
35–39	135	80	155	175	190
40–44	135	85	155	175	185
45–69	145	90	165	190	205
70+	145	90	165	180	185

Table 4. PLASMA HIGH-DENSITY LIPOPROTEIN CHOLESTEROL (mg/dl) IN ADULT MALES[11]

Age/Years	Average	5%	10%	95%
5–19	55	35	40	75
15–19	45	30	35	65
20–24	45	30	30	65
25–29	45	30	30	65
30–34	45	30	30	65
35–39	45	30	30	60
40–44	45	25	30	65
45–69	50	30	30	70
70+	50	30	35	75

lian research with nearly 1,300 children in which 6-year-old children had a median level of 160; at 17 years of age, the median level had gone up to 183.

Even preschoolers show signs of future heart disease. In 5,000 such little ones, the mean serum cholesterol level was 163, changing only slightly from 1 year to 6 years of age.[13] Investigators noted that socioeconomic levels made no difference. Cholesterol levels and subsequent heart disease are equal opportunity killers.

Tracked over an eight-year period, the children in the Bogalusa Study showed consistently similar cholesterol levels.[14] Some lucky ones reduced their levels. But especially the children whose values were particularly high—in the 95th percentile (the top 5 percent)—were likely to remain in that high-risk category.

In another noteworthy long-term investigation, the Princeton School Study, hundreds of children were studied over a four-year period.[15] The authors wrote that "hypercholesterolemic children who tend to "track" in the upper decile may mature to become

Table 5. PLASMA TOTAL CHOLESTEROL (mg/dl) IN ADULT FEMALES[11]

Age/Years	Average	5%	75%	90%	95%
0–19	160	120	175	190	200
20–24	170	125	190	215	230
25–34	175	130	195	220	235
35–39	185	140	205	230	245
40–44	195	145	215	235	255
45–49	205	150	225	250	270
50–54	220	165	240	265	285
55+	230	170	250	275	295

Table 6. PLASMA LOW-DENSITY LIPOPROTEIN CHOLESTEROL (mg/dl)
IN ADULT FEMALES[11]

Age/Years	Average	5%	75%	90%	95%
5–19	100	65	110	125	140
20–24	105	55	120	140	160
25–34	110	70	125	145	160
35–39	120	75	140	160	170
40–44	125	75	145	165	175
45–49	130	80	150	175	185
50–54	140	90	160	185	200
55+	150	95	170	195	215

hypercholesterolemic adults, at increased risk to coronary heart
disease (CHD)."

Other studies have demonstrated that such children do, in fact,
become adults with elevated cholesterol levels. The Beaver
County Lipid Study was a nine-year follow-up of free-living (non-
institutionalized) young adults in Pennsylvania.[16] Averaging 22
years of age, the subjects were first evaluated as seventh-grade
schoolchildren. The tracking phenomenon held, with some individuals later showing cholesterol levels as high as 358 mg/dl.

Our country's two most recent wars provided additional,
though depressing, information. Autopsies were performed on 300
soldiers killed in action in Korea[17]; their average age was 22. In
77.3 percent of the cases, some evidence of coronary atherosclerosis was found. The disease ranged from fibrous thickening of the
artery wall to large, occluding plaques.

Eighteen years later, in an examination of the hearts of over 100
soldiers killed in Vietnam, 45 percent were shown to have some

Table 7. PLASMA HIGH-DENSITY LIPOPROTEIN CHOLESTEROL (mg/dl)
IN ADULT FEMALES[11]

Age/Years	Average	5%	10%	95%
5–19	55	35	40	70
20–24	55	35	35	80
25–34	55	35	40	80
35–39	55	35	40	80
40–44	60	35	40	90
45–49	60	35	40	85
50–54	60	35	40	90
55+	60	35	40	95

Table 8. PLASMA TRIGLYCERIDES IN MALES[11]

Age/Years	Average	5%	90%	95%
0–9	55	30	85	100
10–14	65	30	100	125
15–19	80	35	120	150
20–24	100	45	165	200
25–29	115	45	200	250
30–34	130	50	215	265
35–39	145	55	250	320
40–54	150	55	250	320
55–64	140	60	235	290
65+	135	55	210	260

evidence of atherosclerosis.[18] While those latter numbers are still high, they are lower than those from the earlier study of battle casualties. The authors of the more recent study cite differences in research techniques.

Until 1986, battle autopsies were the only large autopsy studies done on specific groups of individuals, relative to the progress of coronary heart disease. Then came a report published in the *New England Journal of Medicine*[19] that shook the collective consciousness of the medical community. The findings were an outgrowth of the Bogalusa Study already noted.

That research project is an epidemiological study of risk factors from birth through the age of 26 years, in a biracial community in Louisiana. Deaths owing primarily to accidents and suicides provided an unwelcome opportunity to perform autopsies on young people who had died at an average age of 18 years, within a range

Table 9. PLASMA TRIGLYCERIDES IN FEMALES[11]

Age/Years	Average	5%	90%	95%
0–9	60	35	95	110
10–19	75	40	115	130
20–34	90	40	145	170
35–39	95	40	160	195
40–44	105	45	170	210
45–49	110	45	185	230
50–54	120	55	190	240
55–64	125	55	200	250
65+	130	60	205	240

of seven to twenty-four years. Fibrous plaques were found in thirty-three of the eighty-eight subjects autopsied.

The report's authors wrote that "the results show that risk factors for cardiovascular disease are related to even the earliest stages of grossly visible atherosclerotic lesions in the young. The extent of aortic fatty streaks is very strongly related to the levels of both total cholesterol and low-density lipoprotein cholesterol, and tends to be inversely associated with the high-density lipoprotein cholesterol ratio. Fatty streaks in the coronary arteries are significantly related to antemortem levels of very-low-density lipoprotein cholesterol and tend to be associated with levels of serum lipids, other lipoprotein cholesterols, and blood pressure."

This is very sad but very convincing evidence that something must be done to stop the progress of this disease in young children. And as it turns out, this disease has progressed unchecked within families throughout generations.

A report in *Circulation,* the official publication of the American Heart Association, states that children's cholesterol levels cluster with those of their relatives.[20] Mortality due to heart disease before the age of 65 was increased by 2.5 times in grandfathers of children with high levels of cholesterol. The authors wrote that "first-degree relatives of adults with coronary heart disease have a 2.5- to 7-fold increase in the risk of early coronary death compared with relatives of controls."

Simply stated, the higher the cholesterol levels of children in families with heart disease, the greater the parents' risk of developing that same disease themselves. The correlations were particularly strong for levels of LDL cholesterol.

Conversely, the higher the level of protective HDLs, the less the chance of developing coronary heart disease. That was true in the *Circulation* report as well as in the Princeton School Study[21] which showed that in the study group of 301 families, children whose parents have high risk factors for HDL have similarly high factors. The lower the HDL, the greater the risk; the higher the HDL, the lower the risk.

But does the family's diet have anything to do with cholesterol levels? Researchers looked at the diets of 6-year-old children to see.[22] They found that dietary cholesterol intake at age 6 was significantly correlated with serum cholesterol levels. The average serum cholesterol level for children who ate one or fewer eggs per week was 175 mg/dl; two to three eggs weekly resulted in a level of 190; four or five eggs per week brought the blood level up to 198; six or more eggs per week elevated the children's cholesterol levels to 206. Meat intake was similarly correlated.

Studies comparing serum cholesterol levels with dietary habits have been done all over the world, and the results are similar in every instance. In four out of five countries studied by a team of international researchers, a positive correlation was found between the concentration of total cholesterol and the intake of saturated fatty acids.[23] More than 100 boys age 8 to 9 from Finland, the Netherlands, Italy, the Philippines, and Ghana participated. Table 10 compares diet and serum cholesterol levels for those boys.

Certainly other factors are responsible for the development of coronary heart disease. Genetic factors come into play which cannot be measured. In Finland, where high cholesterol levels are found in both sexes, coronary heart disease reaches record dimensions only in males.[24] There the mortality rate of men is nearly five times that of women. The coronary arteries of white males of European origin are particularly prone to atherosclerosis.

One possible, measurable manifestation of this genetic influence may be seen in differing levels of the protective HDL cholesterol. Women and blacks have higher HDLs.[24] Although mortality rates from heart disease for women are now catching up with those of men, it is unlikely that they'll ever match the rates for males because women remain protected for much of their lives owing to differences in hormones. While certain influences such as smoking cigarettes, obesity, and lack of exercise play some role, there remains no explanation for the vast differences noted when comparing sexes, races, or even individuals within given families.

The same holds true for levels of total cholesterol and the detrimental LDL cholesterol. Some individuals have less ability to

Table 10. DIET AND SERUM CHOLESTEROL LEVELS IN 100 BOYS[23]

Country	Weight (kg)	Saturated Fat Intake*	Total Cholesterol
Finland	30 ± 5	17.7	189.63
Netherlands	30 ± 5	15.1	174.15
Italy	30 ± 7	10.4	158.67
Philippines	22 ± 3	9.3	147.06
Ghana	24 ± 3	10.5	127.71

* Numbers refer to percentage of total calories (similar for all boys except for those in the Philippines, where total caloric intake was higher).

handle dietary intake of fat and cholesterol, and their bodies appear to manufacture more of the substance than needed.

As I have grudgingly stated to friends and peers many times, my own brother has been blessed with remarkably low levels of cholesterol in his blood. This is in spite of his diet. My background and his are very similar in terms of childhood experiences, education, and current socioeconomic levels. But while I must be very careful about what I eat, my brother eats whatever he wishes and his cholesterol level remains within safe limits.

There would be no way anyone looking at my brother and me could tell which of us had the cholesterol problem. Tom and I are both about the same height and weight and in similar physical condition. So how can a parent determine whether a child has the tendency toward elevated levels of cholesterol?

The only way is with a relatively painless blood test. Dr. Kannel[2] says a case can be made for universal screening at age 2 and again at age 16. He points out that most coronary attacks occur in persons with more modest elevations in serum cholesterol than would qualify as being due to an inborn error of metabolism; the average cholesterol level in men having heart attacks is a mere 215 mg/dl. In other words, even those with slightly elevated cholesterol levels ought to begin dietary adjustments.

The American Heart Association (AHA) recommends screening all children from families with any history of coronary heart disease. Remember that children whose parents have high cholesterol levels are likely to have the problem themselves. If elevated levels are detected, the AHA recommends dietary changes. They state that "based on the epidemiological risk factor data, a lifelong serum cholesterol differential of only 10 mg/dl"—in other words, 10 mg/dl higher than is desirable—"could be expected to have a substantial effect on risk of coronary heart disease."[25]

Why restrict routine screening to only those children from families with previous heart disease or elevated cholesterol levels? The reasoning is based solely on money. Yes, it would cost some money to determine which children are most likely to develop coronary heart disease as adults. Of all children, perhaps 50 to 60 percent would be considered at risk. But unless we test those kids, we'll never know who is at risk and who is not. Children are routinely tested for tuberculosis before entering school, yet the risk of heart disease from elevated cholesterol levels is much greater than the risk of tuberculosis, especially in this day and age. I agree with the many authorities who believe that cholesterol testing should be an automatic component of pediatric examinations.

Happily, too, the costs of such testing have come down. Supplies for each test are now well under $2, and community programs are being organized to offer the tests at low or no cost.

For people who are found to have cholesterol levels higher than they should, this is the time to do something about it. Those whose levels are more optimal can breathe a sigh of relief and provide a healthful, low-fat diet and environment conducive to maintaining that status.

Following the report on the autopsies done in the Bogalusa Study, Dr. Glueck published an editorial in the same issue of the *New England Journal of Medicine.*[26] He was unequivocal about his belief that, "We should consider measuring lipoprotein cholesterols in all school children, preferably before sexual maturation with its attendant decrease in HDL cholesterol and increase in LDL cholesterol. Since most children have a yearly evaluation by a physician or clinic, perhaps even more regularly than adults, blood lipid sampling would be relatively efficient."

When should you schedule a blood test for your child? The test is quite accurate in reflecting a tendency, even by age 2, toward high or normal levels of cholesterol in the blood. Therefore, since all schools in the nation require a preschool examination by a physician prior to admission, that would be an excellent time to do the test.

Depending on your own preferences, insurance coverage, and financial condition, you can approach the test in one of two ways. You can have a complete lipid profile done. This would tell you the levels of total cholesterol, low-density lipoprotein (LDL) cholesterol, high-density lipoprotein (LDL) cholesterol, and triglycerides. Or, you may wish to have only the total cholesterol level checked; then, if the level is elevated, you can have the more complete testing done.

In some instances, an elevated total cholesterol level may be owing to a high level of protective HDL. If that's the case for your child, of course, you need not be concerned about the total.

If the initial test shows the total cholesterol at a happily low level of, say, 130 or 140 mg/dl, again you need not check any further. But if the initial test shows an elevation in the range of 175 or higher, you will want to know which fraction of the cholesterol is elevated.

Some communities around the country are becoming more knowledgeable and are screening both adults and children. Often paramedics in the local fire department can perform a preliminary finger-prick blood test. Other times hospitals become involved, possibly by sponsoring health fairs.

As time goes on, you will see and hear a great deal more about this topic. It was the subject of an ABC Network News 20/20 presentation hosted by Dr. Timothy Johnson. He reported many of the studies and surveys cited in this chapter. Asked by Barbara Walters at the conclusion of the report whether he had tested his own children, Dr. Johnson said, "I've become a believer in it [testing], and I'm going to do it in my children."

Many physicians still do not realize the importance of testing for cholesterol and of reducing levels to safe values. As a result, the U.S. Department of Health and Human Services of the National Institutes of Health began a program to educate physicians through a booklet called "Cholesterol Counts: Steps for Lowering Your Patient's Blood Cholesterol."

In the introduction to that brochure, the president of the American Heart Association, Dr. Antonio Gotto, Jr., wrote that, "For more than 25 years, the American Heart Association has been urging Americans to reduce their blood cholesterol levels. And the recently concluded Federal study, called the Coronary Primary Prevential Trial, has provided conclusive evidence that Americans can lower their risk of coronary heart disease if they will only reduce their cholesterol to a safe level. . . . Certainly the identification of high-risk individuals with hyperlipidemia and their aggressive treatment must be high priorities for practicing physicians."

The booklet advises physicians who previously believed that average cholesterol levels were *safe* levels. These beliefs are erroneous. The average American's blood cholesterol level is high because the average American is at risk of heart disease.

After your child's test results come in—and it might not be a bad idea to have your own level checked at the same time—don't simply accept your physician's statement that the figures are normal. Ask for the specific numbers. Check them against the tables in this chapter. You want your child's cholesterol to be in the safe range of between 140 and 160 mg/dl. Levels in children are *not* comparable with adult values. Those numbers will rise progressively as the child matures, possibly reaching cholesterol levels that place your child at risk.

Moderately high cholesterol levels *can* be brought down to safe values by relatively simple dietary changes. Higher levels may require special attention and certain dietary restrictions. Very high levels—over 200 mg/dl—will require the assistance of your physician and perhaps a nutritionist. In some cases, drugs can be used very safely to lower particularly high cholesterol levels. Few children, happily, are in that category.

For half the children in the nation, testing need be performed only once during childhood and again in their teens. For those with elevated levels, the test should be repeated annually to see how effective any dietary changes have been.

The next chapter deals with necessary changes in diet, based on the recommendations of the nation's top authorities. Depending upon your child's current cholesterol level, you can determine how stringent your own modifications should be. Then, after a period of at least two months, you can have the blood test repeated to determine effectiveness. If additional lowering is required, you can further modify the diet.

How radical must the diet be? As you will soon read, the changes are relatively simple. It all really comes down to rejecting an unhealthful, fatty diet for one that actually is best for the health of the entire nation. Even then, however, there's still room for an occasional trip to McDonald's!

There is no question, however, that many children with high cholesterol levels today will be adults with high cholesterol levels tomorrow and patients with coronary heart disease some time after that. But *your* child and mine can be free of that major risk factor forever!

4

Fighting Killer Cholesterol

There's no longer any question in any authority's mind that an elevated cholesterol level in the blood dramatically raises the risk of coronary heart disease. Since the beginnings of that disease process can be seen even in young children, it's only logical to consider ways to reduce the level of cholesterol early in life.

Just how extensive those efforts must be depends entirely upon the child's individual situation. Only a blood test can determine the cholesterol level. For most children, relatively minor dietary changes will quickly correct a higher-than-desirable cholesterol count and will place youngsters on the path to a long and healthy life. For some others, however, the treatment will be more extensive.

On the far end of the spectrum, one in one million Americans has a genetic disorder that causes abnormally high amounts of cholesterol to accumulate in the blood. This condition, known as familial homozygous hypercholesterolemia, requires that both parents provide the gene for abnormal cholesterol metabolism, in the same way that it takes both parents to provide the gene for blue eyes in their children. Just as there are far more people with brown or hazel eyes than there are with blue eyes, there are relatively few people with the cholesterol metabolic error inherited from both parents. Those who do have the condition are at serious risk of early heart disease.

Such individuals record cholesterol levels in the several hundreds, with soaring amounts of clogging LDL and little protective HDL. Plaques called xanthoma, which contain cholesterol, form on the tendons and other parts of the body. Pain of angina pectoris occurs early in life as the coronary arteries become blocked. Sudden death by heart attack—myocardial infarction—may result in the teen years or 20s. Even children may be afflicted.

Diet alone has little effect on this condition. Cholesterol-lowering drugs have limited effectiveness. Even coronary bypass surgery provides only limited correction of the problem, since the grafted veins themselves become occluded.

There is hope on the horizon, however. A new form of treatment similar to dialysis for kidney patients can clean the LDL out of patients' blood. The procedure, known as LDL-pheresis, is still very expensive and is considered experimental. Patients relax for three to four hours as their blood flows through an apparatus that first separates the blood cells from the plasma and then filters out the LDL. Happily, only the LDL is affected, with HDL returning in the blood to the patient. One can only hope that the procedure becomes refined soon to make it available to those patients requiring such dramatic efforts.

Moving across the spectrum, the next group of patients are those who receive the cholesterol-defect gene from one parent. This condition is termed heterozygous hypercholesterolemia. Its severity varies from person to person, as seen in charts displaying the cholesterol levels of the population broken down by percentiles. Those in the 95th percentile have the highest levels and are at the greatest risk.

For adults, authorities set the level of 250 mg/dl as being at high risk of coronary heart disease. A level of 220 puts someone at moderate risk. *That means that at least 50 percent of all Americans are at risk of this disease.* The desired levels for adults are between 150 and 180—certainly lower than 200.

To achieve those healthy levels as adults, children have to keep their cholesterol levels down to between 140 and 160 mg/dl. For children, a level of 185 puts them in the 90th percentile; levels of 200 or more put them in the 95th percentile. Corresponding with the adult risk factor of 200 or less, children must have levels of 170 or less. Again, probably half the population of children are, therefore, at current risk of future heart disease.

For those boys and girls with very high levels, diet must be greatly restricted and, in many instances, drugs may be added. The drugs typically used are called resins, and the two most frequent ones are cholestyramine and colestipol, both of which act by binding bile in the intestine and eliminating it in the feces. Since bile is made from cholesterol, as bile is eliminated, cholesterol must be drawn from the blood by the liver, thus lowering blood cholesterol levels.

The safety of those drugs has been shown in many years of use, and, for children at very high risk, the benefits greatly outweigh any disadvantages or side effects. You, your child, and your physician can discuss this option if cholesterol levels are already dangerously high.

But for the vast majority of boys and girls in the United States and elsewhere, rather simple dietary modifications do the job very nicely and effectively. If the blood sample reveals a nice, safe cholesterol level of, say, 140 to 160 mg/dl, or 170 tops, keep doing whatever it is you've been doing—it's working nicely. That doesn't mean, however, that children should eat as much fat as they want; it's still wise to limit the amount of fat in the diet. If the level is above 170, your child is in the 75th percentile, and a few reductions in fat and cholesterol consumption will probably bring the level down quickly and easily. A cholesterol level of 185 or more means that dietary modifications probably will have to be greater. Remember though that at, say, a level of 187, your child's cholesterol level may be high because his or her diet contains many items that can easily be eliminated.

On a very practical plane, a child's cholesterol level does not necessarily indicate the severity of potential future disease, but rather the type of diet the child currently eats. One boy may have a level of 189 mg/dl and another a level of 178. It may be that the first boy consumes a lot more pizza, whole milk, and hamburgers than the second; therefore the same diet may be equally effective for both boys, bringing the levels of both down to safe points. Of course, it'll be more difficult for that first boy, since he'll have more to change in his diet than the second, who is already eating a more healthful variety of foods.

Should everyone modify his or her diet to reduce the amount of fat and cholesterol? Most authorities and virtually *every* medical organization in the United States and around the world say yes—to a point. They agree that the typical Western diet is simply too loaded with fatty foods and too short on fruits, vegetables, and whole-grain cereals.

Even if someone is not at risk of future heart disease, moderate dietary modification in this direction will have likely benefits in terms of total health and possible prevention of other diseases, including cancer and diabetes. Certainly a reduction of total fat alone will help the millions of people who are currently over-weight. Increasing fiber, if nothing else, will eliminate much of the current Western dependence on laxatives. Fewer greasy meals will mean fewer sales of antacid preparations for heartburn and indigestion. And a low-fat dietary pattern based on a wide variety of foods will provide all the nutrients needed for good health, development, energy, and growth.

Should everyone adopt a Spartan, ultra-low-fat diet? Certainly not. First, half of all adults do not have the risk factor of elevated serum cholesterol levels that warrants such drastic restrictions Only a few children are in this category. Bear in mind that for every five children in the 95th percentile, there are ninety-five children with lower cholesterol levels. Second, certain children and adults should *not* under any circumstances drastically alter their diets.

Pregnant women, for example, need extra calories and nutrients, not fewer, to assure a successful pregnancy and a healthy infant. Elderly individuals often consume diets that are marginal in needed nutrients, and they should alter their diets only after consulting with their physicians.

The majority of authorities also agree that children under the age of 2 should not be placed on a low-fat diet, even if their parents have a history of heart disease. In fact, there have already been some problems with zealous parents who, in their desire to avoid future problems for their offspring, have shortchanged their children in terms of nutrients needed for normal growth and development.

Recently there has been an increase in the number of very young children with the syndrome referred to as "failure to thrive." Well-meaning parents, frequently in the higher socioeconomic strata of our society, have fed their children diets that compare in terms of nutrient density with those in Third World countries. The little ones are given only skim milk, very lean meats, and complex carbohydrates. Between-meal snacks are prohibited.

Now, common sense would indicate that this certainly is going overboard. Pediatricians see patients, as a result, who are much smaller in both height and weight than they should be for their ages. When the diet is liberalized, growth quickly returns to normal, and within three months, youngsters no longer exhibit previous symptoms. Almost unbelievably, parents have to be vehemently convinced that it is all right to feed their children foods which they themselves are not permitted.

Because of such extreme experiences, some pediatricians take an overly conservative view. Fearing overcompliance in lowering the fat and cholesterol contents of the diet, they prescribe no changes at all. Some people have complained that such pediatri- cians actually are remiss in their duties, and do not consider the health of their young patients once they leave their care.

The American Academy of Pediatrics currently advises no dras- tic dietary changes for youngsters under the age of 2 years. They believe a diet containing 30 percent of calories derived from fat will be both healthful and efficient in ensuring adequate growth and development. Of course, for many children this still is a re- duction in total fat in the diet, since the average American con- sumes 40 to 42 percent of calories from fat each day. This recom- mendation appears to make a lot of sense for a number of reasons. First, we just don't have enough experience and research to indi- cate how the diet can be safely and effectively altered prior to that age. Second, growth and development occur at dizzying speed during those early years. Third, there's more than enough time to correct an existing problem after the age of 2. And fourth, choles- terol levels during the first few months of life may not be indicative of future levels. So, for the time being at least, we'll restrict our discussion to what can be done for children older than 2 years.

There are experts, however, who believe that younger children may, under certain circumstances, benefit from some of the recom- mendations we'll discuss. They point to children in vegetarian families, who thrive on a diet completely free of animal foods. It would appear that the argument really centers on fears that many parents may deprive their children of necessary nutrients while restricting fat intake.

A leading expert in the area of children's lipids, Dr. Charles Glueck of the University of Cincinnati, spoke on this subject at a meeting of the American Society for Clinical Nutrition in 1986. He said that he wouldn't hesitate to place a child as young as age 3 on a low-fat and low-cholesterol diet as well as on drugs to lower cho- lesterol if the youngster had a greatly elevated level and a family history of severe heart disease.

At the same meeting, Dr. Glueck described the results of his long-term study of seventy-three children with elevated cholesterol levels. Neither drugs nor restricted diet, he said, interfered with normal physical development, sexual maturation, behavior, or intellectual capability. Children with levels above 275 mg/dl were given drugs, while those below that level were placed on restricted diet alone. Cholesterol intake was kept to less than 250 milligrams daily, with total fat less than 35 percent of total calories.

On average, diet alone produced a 9.6 percent decrease, and diet plus drugs resulted in a 12.5 percent decrease in blood cholesterol levels.

In another study, Dr. Glueck found that in boys whose initial cholesterol levels were 200 mg/dl or higher, the average reduction by dietary change was 15.6 percent. Among boys with initial levels of 199 or lower, the levels fell only by 8.3 percent.

Studies in boarding schools provide some valuable insights because the food intake can be controlled and researchers have a better idea of just what is being eaten. Such research has shown that substantial plasma cholesterol lowering can be expected by cutting back on dietary fat and by increasing the ratio between unsaturated and saturated fats. That is to say, previous levels of saturated fats are replaced by unsaturated fats, while the total amount of fat is also reduced.

A great deal of research has been done with various kinds of dietary fats. We'll talk about them in greater detail in Chapter 12, "The Oil of Methuselah," but for the time being suffice it to say that unsaturated rather than saturated fats are preferred in the diet. This does not mean only the polyunsaturated vegetable oils touted on TV, however. Monounsaturated fats such as in olive oil and the fats in certain fish oils also play an important role.

Time after time, in study after study, diets low in cholesterol and saturated fat and high in unsaturated fat produce lower cholesterol levels. Such studies have been done around the world, with cholesterol reductions averaging 11 percent in the United States, 10 percent in Finland, and up to 20 percent in Norway. The job can be done, and done safely and effectively.

An old argument against worrying about children's cholesterol levels maintained that fats and cholesterol early in life prepared an individual for eating foods with high cholesterol later in life. Besides the most apparent counterargument that adults shouldn't be eating those high-cholesterol foods anyway, four studies in humans have failed to show any support for this concept. A person doesn't become "used" to the fat and cholesterol in a diet such that his or her body can metabolize those foods more readily. Whether high-fat and high-cholesterol foods are given early or later in life, the result is the same: elevated cholesterol levels in the blood. If anything, investigations have shown lower blood cholesterol levels in adults who started on low-cholesterol diets as children.

CHOLESTEROL-LOWERING DIETS

We have seen that modified diets can achieve reduced cholesterol levels in the blood. Not only do children reap the immediate benefits of such lowered levels, but also they begin to practice the good habits they will carry through life. The younger the child, the easier it is to establish healthful eating patterns.

In our own family, my son was 7 years old when we found that his cholesterol level was moderately elevated and I began changing his diet. My daughter was only 4 years old at the time. As it turns out, Jenny does not have a problem with cholesterol. But because she's part of the family, she was affected by the dietary changes we made for Ross's sake. Yet, probably because of her age and the lack of firmly established habits, she has had a much easier time with the changes than has Ross.

One might question why the entire family wasn't already on a low-fat, low-cholesterol diet to begin with, since I had my strong family history of heart disease. Certainly I was following such a diet myself. And there were many changes that had influenced the entire family. We drank only skim milk, butter wasn't to be found in the house, and trips to the ice-cream parlor were not as frequent as in other families.

But after Ross's blood test, we knew we hadn't gone far enough. If neither Ross nor Jenny had a higher-than-desired cholesterol level, we wouldn't have become quite so careful. Since his results were on the high side, it was necessary to seriously consider cutting back on fat in the diet.

What did this mean in everyday, practical terms? As I have alluded, neither I nor the majority of health authorities recommend radical dietary change to effectively lower cholesterol levels in children. My own diet, as an adult, is certainly more restricted. And I supplement my diet with the vitamin niacin. For me and for many others who have followed the program, as detailed in *The 8-Week Cholesterol Cure,* the results have been dramatic and potentially lifesaving. But children should not be given large amounts of vitamins, so Ross does not use niacin. Moreover, a child's liver is vulnerable and not fully developed. Since niacin is metabolized by the liver, the vitamin should *never* be given to children.

The program that has been effective for Ross is a gradual reduction in foods high in fat and cholesterol and the addition of those very special foods which have been shown to actually lower blood cholesterol. The star of his diet is oat bran, as described fully in Chapter 11. This program greatly reduces fat and cholesterol, especially when compared to the typical American diet. But the plan is far short of deprivation. In fact, thanks to the many recipes and modifications I've created for Ross, it's hard to tell the difference between the foods we eat and those consumed by most American families.

I have two goals for Ross which can be achieved by the program described in this book. The first, of course, is to lower his cholesterol levels to values that will predict a future free of heart disease. Second, I can hope—and maybe even expect—that he'll stick with the program throughout his life.

We're seeing nice, beneficial changes almost every day in our home. Ross and Jenny both have come to love the many dishes made from recipes in this book. They make requests for "bad" treats far less often. When tasting high-fat recipes elsewhere, they express a preference for our lighter fare. McDonald's and Burger King are places to go play and have an orange juice more often than a meal. It's nice to see my kids growing up with those attitudes. I'm more and more confident they'll become healthy, happy adults who will lead their peers in terms of nutrition and lifestyle by their good example.

THE SPECIFICS . . .

Study after study has shown that dietary changes alone can reduce blood cholesterol levels by about 10 percent. That number will depend, of course, on how closely a person follows a low-fat, low-cholesterol diet. But unless that person becomes a strict vegetarian, larger reductions are unlikely.

Certainly that 10 percent drop is a step in the right direction. If a child learns to prefer low-fat foods early on, it's likely that he or she will continue to opt for such foods in adulthood. For some individuals, that dietary lifestyle can be combined with additional treatment such as niacin. The end result will be a reduced cholesterol level throughout life, and, therefore, a greatly diminished risk of heart disease.

Happily, however, you can expect *more* than a 10 percent cholesterol drop for your child. As discussed fully in Chapter 11, oat bran very effectively reduces cholesterol levels in the blood. Studies have shown decreases of up to 20 percent when this delicious form of fiber is added to the diet. That means that if your child has a cholesterol level of 200 mg/dl, dietary modification and oat bran can bring it down to a healthy 160. It worked for Ross, and it can work for your children also.

How and when do you start?

TALKING AND PLANNING

The first step, of course, is to get that blood test to determine if your child's results are too high. If so, the next step is to sit down with your youngster and talk about it. Remember that the numbers you've just learned are an indication of potential problems in your child's future. Even greatly elevated levels do not pose immediate dangers for children. There is no reason for alarm, and certainly you don't want to frighten your kids.

Pick a nice, quiet time. Even if you have to wait a week or two, it's best to have a time when the phone won't likely ring, when people aren't running in and out, and when neither you nor your child will be tired or irritable.

Calmly explain that you've gotten some information from your doctor that means the family really should make some simple changes in the way it eats. Point out that the changes aren't dramatic, but that they do reflect how lots of people are eating to improve their health.

It's probably best not to go into a lot of details all at once. Take it a little at a time. After all, this is a decision to improve your child's lifestyle, it is hoped, for the rest of his or her life.

There is no reason in the world to upset the child or to make him or her feel that some dreadful disaster has been visited upon the family. You've made a lot of health decisions already, haven't you? Probably you don't allow your kids to eat all the candy they want, since you don't want them to have cavities. You don't let little ones play on busy streets in traffic, and you've probably told them about not talking to strangers or accepting gifts or rides. This is just one more wise family decision you've made.

I remember very well certain restrictions placed upon me when I was a child. Even then I realized, as all kids do, that these warnings and restrictions were "for my own good." And later on, when I was old enough to fully understand, I appreciated my parents' interventions.

I grew up before the days of polio vaccine, and every summer brought fear of that horrible, crippling disease. One of the kids on the block walked with braces, and that made polio very real for us. No one really knew what caused the disease or how to prevent it, but my Dad believed that it was best to avoid crowds of other children during the summer months. So my brother and I were not allowed to go to movie theaters and other such places.

Did such restrictions protect me from polio? I don't think so. But then again I never developed the disease. And as I look back now, I appreciate that my Dad cared enough to try to shelter me in the best way he could. Do I have any feelings of hostility? None at all. I have feelings of love.

A friend of mine grew up as the daughter of a dentist. In her house, candy, soda, and other sweets were tremendously restricted. None of the other kids on the block had to avoid those treats. She grew up to be a dental hygienist, telling others to avoid the sweet snacks as well. She also grew up with very few cavities.

Today she's happy her Dad kept the candy away. She thanks him and thinks of his restrictions with love.

Was she happy about not eating candy when she was a child? Of course not. Was I happy about not going to the movies in the summer? Of course not. Were you happy about various laws and restrictions during your childhood? Probably not.

But there comes a time when a parent has to be a parent. If your child wants to cross a busy street at age 6 or 7, you don't agonize over your decision to say no. It's often much more difficult to say no than to say yes. Saying no is an act of love.

Saying no to fat and cholesterol is an ultimate act of love. It would be easier to ignore the situation and not think about the future. But I love my children and you love yours, and that love makes it all worthwhile.

I go into a lot more detail about counseling kids in Chapter 9. Suffice it to say that the kinds of dietary changes needed to set your child on the path to good health won't traumatize anyone.

If anything, the changes may be more difficult for you and other adults in the family. But remember that nothing teaches like a good example. You can't expect to limit the hot dogs on the table while you indulge in all kinds of high-fat foods yourself.

This is the time to make a commitment for your entire family's good health. There is no doubt that *everyone* will benefit.

ZEROING IN ON THE NUMBERS

Virtually every magazine and newspaper in the country has brought home the message that we should modify our diets for better health. In a nutshell, recommendations include eating less fat in general and less saturated fat in particular. Authorities tell us to cut down on cholesterol, along with sodium, sugar, and alcohol.

Now that all sounds good on paper. But what do those recommendations mean for the individual? The American Heart Association has long recommended that we get no more than 30 percent of our total calories from fat, and that the fat be divided equally among saturated, polyunsaturated, and monounsaturated fats. Those authorities also recommend limiting cholesterol to no more than 300 milligrams daily. Those are general recommendations. For people with a recognized tendency toward elevated blood cholesterol levels, and those with a family history of heart disease, they say to reduce both fat and cholesterol even further.

Do you know how much fat you and your family are currently eating as a percentage of your total calories? I know very few people who do. Those numbers are very confusing and, as a result, practically no one follows the advice very closely.

If someone were to say, for example, not to drink more than two cups of coffee daily, everyone would know what to do; the third cup is out. Those are the kinds of numbers we all need for guidance. And I've developed a way to make your awareness of fat and cholesterol just as practical.

Bear with me for just a little while as I go through some explanation, and within the next few minutes you'll have a dietary program tailored for your entire family. From that point on and forever, you'll never have to worry about percentages or calories again.

But to begin, we have to talk a bit about calories. That's the term used to measure the amount of energy we all need to maintain or grow, and to function in good health. In case you don't know how many calories you need, let me make it very simple—big people first, kids later.

An average adult male requires about 15 calories to maintain each pound of weight. An average female needs about 13 calories. Of course if you are very active, more energy can be burned. Conversely, very sedentary individuals need even less.

If an average large man weighs 200 pounds, he will need about 3,000 calories per day to maintain that weight. If he eats more food, he'll gain weight. If an average woman weighs 120 pounds, she'll maintain her weight consuming about 1,680 calories per day. If she eats more, she'll gain weight. And, of course, if either eats less, he or she will lose weight.

If you now weigh 140 pounds but you want to weigh 120 pounds, feed *only* the 120 pounds. That's 120 pounds multiplied by 14 or 15 calories. The extra 20 pounds will melt away.

The mathematics behind weight gain and loss is equally simple. Each pound of weight gain or loss represents 3,500 calories. That means that if you or I eat an extra 100 calories each day for 35 days, one pound of weight will be noticed on the bathroom scale. Regardless of what kind of weight-loss scheme you use to shed pounds, it all comes down to that simple bit of mathematics.

For children, the picture is different. Table 11 shows on average the amount of caloric intake needed for children at different ages. Kids, of course, are growing and maturing. They're also more active than most adults. All that takes more energy, and allows youngsters to eat more food, more calories.

Take a look at the tables. Look at yourself in the mirror. Determine for yourself how many calories, on average, each member of your family really needs.

Now we're going to figure out how much fat should be included in those calories. For optimum cholesterol reduction, authorities agree that we should limit our fat intake to 20 to 30 percent of our total calories. Here's how to calculate what that really means for your family. We'll use a compromise of 25 percent fat.

Let's say that the child needs 2,400 calories—the average requirement for growth and development for a youngster between 7 and 10 years of age. Next, let's assume that the mother wants to maintain her weight of 120 pounds. To do so she needs about 1,700 calories daily. Those numbers then—2,400 and 1,700—are the total calories for the day. Since we want to limit the amount of fat consumed to 25 percent of the total calories, we simply multiply.

Table 11. ENERGY INTAKE IN CALORIES

Category	Age (years)	Weight (kg)	(lb)	Height (cm)	(in)	Calories Needed
Infants	0.0–0.5	6	13	60	24	95–145
	0.5–1.0	9	20	71	28	80–135
Children	1–3	13	29	90	35	900–1800 (1300 ave.)
	4–6	20	44	112	44	1300–2300 (1700 ave.)
	7–10	28	62	132	52	1650–3300 (2400 ave.)
Males	11–14	45	99	157	62	2000–3700 (2700 ave.)
	15–18	66	145	176	69	2100–3900 (2800 ave.)
	19–22	70	154	177	70	2500–3300 (2900 ave.)
	23–50	70	154	178	70	2300–3100 (2700 ave.)
Females	11–14	46	101	157	62	1500–3000 (2200 ave.)
	15–18	55	120	163	64	1200–3000 (2100 ave.)
	19–22	55	120	163	64	1700–2500 (2100 ave.)
	23–50	55	120	163	64	1600–2400 (2000 ave.)

The data were assembled from the observed median heights and weights of children and young adults as surveyed in the U.S. population. Source: Recommended Dietary Allowances, Ninth Revised Edition, National Academy of Sciences, Washington, D.C. 1980

2,400 calories × 25 percent = 600 calories as fat

1,700 calories × 25 percent = 425 calories as fat

The next step calls for a word of explanation. Carbohydrate and protein provide 4 calories per gram, while fat offers 9 calories per gram. There are 28 grams in 1 ounce of food. Most foods are a combination of carbohydrate, protein, and fat, with calories contributed by each.

To determine how much fat we can consume, we merely divide 9, the number of calories per gram of fat, into the number of calories as fat to be eaten in a given day. In our example, then, we do this calculation:

600 calories as fat ÷ 9 calories = 67 grams of fat

425 calories as fat ÷ 9 calories = 47 grams of fat

Now we know exactly how much fat should be included in our example. The youngster will be able to eat a bit more than 67 grams, while Mom will be limited to just under 47 grams.

Why should we care about grams of fat? Why is this so "simple"? Just look at practically any food label, be it on a carton of milk or a loaf of bread. You'll see a complete breakdown of carbohydrate, protein, and fat. The amount in a given serving is represented in grams. By becoming acquainted with the amount of fat in various foods, you'll quickly start thinking about the amount of fat each person in your family needs.

While 20 percent fat is optimal for good health, you may wish to compromise at, say, 25 percent or so. For those with a very high initial cholesterol level, fat certainly should be restricted to 20 percent of total calories. Those children with less elevated cholesterol counts may need to reduce fat content to 25 percent. Certainly *no* child or adult should consume a diet with more than 30 percent fat. There will also be individual differences in response. If a 25 or 30 percent diet doesn't reduce cholesterol to desired levels, you'll need to further reduce fat content. Ross and Jenny eat a diet with no more than 20 to 25 percent fat, and both are thriving. And both have very desirable cholesterol levels today.

An additional benefit of this approach is that by keeping track of the grams of fat in your daily diet, you'll never have to worry about calories again. Just keep the grams of fat down to your calculated level, and the calories will count themselves. Very important, if you follow this program as well as your children do, you'll never have a weight problem.

To help you start thinking about those grams, in Chapter 20 I've provided a listing of the fat, cholesterol, calories, and sodium content in hundreds of commonly eaten foods, including those notorious fast foods.

No one can be expected to memorize the breakdown of each and every food. But you'll very quickly start to pick up on trends. You'll notice that beef has more fat than poultry and that poultry has more fat than seafood. You can be the final judge as to whether you'll choose the fat in beef one day, and the fat in cheese another day.

As you do your shopping, read those nutrition labels. You'll find fats hidden in the most unlikely places. For example, each hamburger or hot dog bun may contain 2 to 3 grams of fat.

Remember, also, that the total fat for the day shouldn't all come from just one kind of fat. Try to divide the daily allowance equally among the saturated, polyunsaturated, and monounsaturated kinds. The most difficult part will be cutting down whenever possible on saturated fats, which are mostly from animal sources. That means you'll need to replace butter with margarine, for example, and a tuna sandwich for a hot dog or a bologna sandwich.

Milk is an excellent example of how simple changes can cut out a lot of fat. Whole milk contains 8 grams of fat in an 8-ounce serving, while skim milk has only a trace, so certainly you'll want to switch from whole milk to skim milk. In some families that could practically mean culture shock. The trick is to go gradually. First replace whole milk with 2 percent low-fat milk. Next, move down to 1 percent low-fat milk. If you can't find 1 percent milk, mix equal parts of skim and 2 percent. Finally, after your period of transition, go all the way to skim milk. It's well worth the effort. By switching gradually, your family probably won't even notice the difference. You'll also want to use nonfat yogurt. By just eliminating the fat in dairy foods you can vastly improve your family's nutrition in terms of preventing heart disease.

For some foods, there is no low-fat replacement, and you'll just have to cut back on the size of the portions instead. Vegetable oil contains about 12 to 14 grams of fat per tablespoon. There is no low-fat variety to buy. So in your recipes, use half the amount called for or substitute other ingredients when feasible.

We'll talk about fast foods a bit later, but for the moment let me say that you don't have to banish them forever. Again, count the number of times you allow your children to have those fast foods. Then gradually cut back until you've achieved a 50 percent reduction.

By making those kinds of changes—cutting the fat intake in half—you'll reduce your family's fat consumption from probably close to what is the national average (about 40 percent of total calories) to 20 to 25 percent. Counting the number of grams of fat in foods eaten at home can help you get to that point without much difficulty at all.

When thinking of heart disease and cholesterol in the blood, most people talk about cutting down on cholesterol in the diet. Certainly that's good. But the fact is that *fat* is the far more important dietary culprit in raising blood cholesterol levels. Also, by cutting back on fat, especially saturated fats from animal sources, you'll automatically cut back on dietary cholesterol.

Stated simply enough, the only source of cholesterol in the diet is animal-derived food. There is no cholesterol at all in fruits, vegetables, grains, cereals, or bread. Period. Not even a tiny bit. When you cut back on animal foods, you cut back on cholesterol.

You'll want to reduce your children's cholesterol intake from their current level to no more than 200 milligrams per day. The typical daily American diet contains about 400 to 600 milligrams. That may seem like a drastic change in lifestyle, but it's really not. Why? Because cholesterol is only in animal foods. So every time you choose a peanut butter sandwich instead of a hot dog, you've cut out not 50 percent but *all* the cholesterol in that meal. Whole milk has 33 milligrams of cholesterol per 8-ounce glass, while skim milk has only 4 milligrams. See how easy it is?

It's really a lot easier to cut down on cholesterol than on fats. The only huge source of cholesterol found in the typical diet is the egg. Each egg contains about 250 milligrams. Happily, all the cholesterol is in the yolk, with none in the white. That means you can use all the whites you want. I use them in baking, cooking, snacking, even in milkshakes. Most kids don't even like the yolk of a hard-boiled egg; mine are happy when I let them throw it away. We also use a lot of egg substitutes, preferably Egg Beaters, since no fat is added to that product. But mostly we rely on egg whites.

Children in America will be elated to learn that liver—the dreaded, hated liver that lots of Moms want them to eat—is loaded with cholesterol. Do your kids a favor: cut liver out of the diet entirely. That also means eliminating chicken liver, liverwurst, and all other varieties.

Look at the food composition table in Chapter 20, listing cholesterol levels of common foods. You'll quickly learn where it comes from. But I can predict at least one surprise.

Which would you expect to have more cholesterol: beef, chicken, or fish? Probably you'd answer beef. But the fact is that all flesh of animal origin has about the same amount of cholesterol.

The big difference is in the amount of fat in the different kinds of meat. Red meats contain the most, while white meats of poultry and seafood contain the least. That doesn't mean you have to cut out all red meats. It simply means that you should try to prepare beef less often, and have chicken and turkey and seafood more often, planning your meals with lots of variety.

It's always a bit difficult to learn new habits. But before you know it, you'll start thinking in terms of grams of fat and will be automatically cutting down on cholesterol. Even your children will pick up this way of thinking. My little 6-year-old daughter now talks about the grams of fat in foods.

I have only one caution as you begin your noble fight against cholesterol. Don't rush it. Your family's eating patterns have been established over a period of years. Give yourself and your kids time to gradually change those habits.

If you come in one evening and declare an all-out war on cholesterol, radically changing your family's eating habits and wiping out all their favorites, you'll be doomed to failure.

Take it easy. Don't get upset with setbacks. As time goes on, you'll achieve your goals. Start with "kindergarten" changes and soon enough your kids will be graduating from "university" alterations with honors.

SHOPPING TOGETHER

What better way to get your kids involved with the foods they eat than to take them along on shopping trips? View these trips as opportunities to spend a bit of time with your children. Don't drag them along when you're running late and dead tired. Plan times when you can take some additional moments together.

Start by including them in preparing the shopping list. Talk about foods as you drive to the supermarket. When you get there, let one child push the cart through the aisles while another is on a "mission" to get a loaf of bread. Spend some time in the produce section. Let them discover new fruits and vegetables. You'll find that they are more receptive to eating foods they themselves have selected.

Even little children can start to read nutrition labels. In the bread section, let them select the loaf that has the lowest number of grams of fat listed. Show them the difference between whole milk and skim.

I've gone into a lot of detail about preparing the family shopping list in Chapter 14. Talk about it with your kids. Get their input as to the foods they like and the ones they hate.

Each trip to the supermarket should be exciting, something to look forward to. And each should produce something new to put on the table. One nice way to do that is to let your children do some of the selection. If you keep trying new foods, something they reject today may be acceptable next month.

Never lose sight of the fact that this is a long-term, lifetime commitment. You don't have to be perfect during the first week; no one is keeping score of the total fat grams. Let the process develop gradually. Don't discourage your kids or yourself by becoming obsessive about food.

COOKING TOGETHER

Both my children love getting involved in the kitchen. Ross takes tremendous pride in being able to prepare a meal of scrambled eggs or an omelet with toast. Of course he uses Egg Beaters. His friends are impressed. Omelets were his first culinary success; since then he's added a number of "specialties" to his repertoire. And even at age 5, Jenny loved to get her fingers into mixing doughs and batters.

You and I both know that having kids in the kitchen can mean far more work than doing things yourself. But cooking provides a great sense of independence for anyone, and there's no better time to start than in childhood. Now that you want your kids to be more aware of the foods they select, get them to do some of the cooking.

As with shopping, pick some occasions when you'll have a bit of time to work with them. If you have just a little time, tell them. Ask them to do something simple, like washing the vegetables. When you have more time, you can determine a real project.

What could be better than making cookies? The recipes in Chapter 11 let you prepare treats that can actually lower cholesterol levels. How about making a pizza together? Creating a salad bar? Or getting the fixings for taco building? Recipes for lots of kid-pleasing meals also appear in Chapter 18.

EATING TOGETHER

Here's the key to success in good nutrition: eating should be a pleasant experience. If you make a big deal about your kid's diet, day in and day out, you're doomed to failure. Maybe he or she will eat the foods you force today, but this won't lead to life patterns in the years to come. The worst place to lecture about the evils of butter or ice cream is at the dinner table.

For that matter, you don't want to discuss anything that can be disturbing at meal times. A calm atmosphere filled with tasty foods and good conversation is most conducive to "conditioning" your youngsters to eat the foods best for them.

Don't be terribly concerned about food acceptance and rejection, especially on a short-term basis. One day your child will be ready to eat anything; the next, he or she won't want things normally welcomed. Keep trying to introduce new foods, but don't be terribly surprised or hurt when they're rejected.

I remember so well my mother's attempts to get me to eat new foods when I was a child; a pickier eater no mother should ever have. I absolutely refused to eat seafood of any kind. Fish produced a gag reflex. Yet today I enjoy a truly wide variety of foods, and fish are among my favorites.

Within reason, try to prepare foods that children will enjoy. Even schools have come to accept that kids like to eat the same foods over and over again. They just don't seem to get tired of hamburgers, pizza, tacos, burritos, and the like. I've put together lots of recipes for "Food Fit for a Kid," Chapter 18. In addition to those recipes, you'll want to include your own favorites, modifying the ingredients appropriately.

Don't forget that food is meant to nourish and to provide pleasure. It shouldn't be used as either a reward or a punishment. Think about the logic behind that.

If you offer dessert as a reward for eating the day's vegetables, the child must view the vegetables as merely a means to an end. That won't lead to good food attitudes. Moreover, if the child really isn't hungry that day, bribing him or her with dessert will only force the child to overeat, leading to food aversions.

Likewise, don't offer certain foods as a psychological crutch. The child skinned his knee? Don't cry—eat this ice cream instead. It's raining outside? Keep still with this candy. Childhood disappointments? Console her with some cake. It doesn't take a Ph.D. in psychology to recognize that this type of behavior sets up a lifetime of improper food dependencies. It's little wonder we have so many eating disorders today.

The other side of the coin is not to use food as a punishment. It's nonsensical and harmful to say to your child, in effect, "you can't have the food you need to grow and mature because I'm mad at you."

Set the right example. Parents should not use their own food —or alcohol—for purely psychological purposes. That's self-destructive behavior your child doesn't need to learn from you.

And, speaking of setting an example, be sure that you too eat a wide variety of foods. There are so many wonderful foods available to us in this country that you should have no problem selecting many different kinds.

Every once in a while, invite your children's friends to your home to eat. Often the presence of others will stimulate your kids to eat foods they would otherwise reject.

Ideally, you should limit the amount of food you put on the plate or serve at the table. Children can easily become intimidated by portions that are too large—and then they grow up to eat portions that are too large, resulting in weight problems. Little kids like little portions.

What kind of child is most likely to welcome new foods, or foods that are not on the all-time favorites list? A hungry child! Don't let your kids spoil their appetites with snacks eaten too close to mealtimes.

And remember that no child has ever been known to starve to death when food is available. Don't beg, cajole, or plead with them to eat. If they're not hungry, don't force the issue. We're a nation of overeaters, anyway. Relax. Enjoy your food and your family.

"But what if my kids don't like certain low-fat, low-cholesterol dishes I prepare?" you ask. Then they won't eat too much at that particular meal. They certainly won't starve.

As a nation, we've tended to let children have their own way far too often. Many parents act as if they have been placed on earth to be their children's servants. They want to be "best friends" and never disappoint their offspring. This certainly is a distorted view of the way things should be.

As a parent, your ultimate role is to get your children ready to leave home. That principle should apply from birth through the toddler years, childhood, and the teens. You teach your kids to cross the street carefully. You send them to school. You show them how to live their lives in a moral, worthwhile manner. Then they can live a successful, happy life when they leave home and eventually start their own families.

Certainly that thinking belongs in food planning as well. If you gave your children exactly what they prefer at every meal, the day's food might consist of candy, soda, popcorn, cake, ice cream, hot dogs, and French fries. It's your job to provide direction, in a strong but loving way.

Let me digress for a moment to tell you a little story. When I was doing my graduate studies in college I had an Irish setter. During her early puppyhood I was struggling along financially on a small graduate assistantship. There was no money for frills of any kind. Trish got nothing but dry dog food, and she thrived on it.

Then I was appointed editor on the university's information service staff. The position came with assistant professor status and a large increase in salary. I started eating better foods, enjoying a lot more treats, and I shared my good fortune with Trish. I'd buy her hamburger and moist dog burgers and mix them with the dry dog food. After a while, she picked out only the burger and left the dry chow.

The fact is that dry chow is better for dogs. But when I returned to feeding her only the chow, she refused to eat. Because I knew "what was best" for her, I remained firm. Trish lost weight. Her ribs began to show. My neighbors thought I was being cruel. And then she started to eat the chow. She gained the weight back. And she thrived. I'm glad I didn't give in.

Will you "give in" to your children? Probably you won't let their ribs show! We know we can't be that strict with my children. As much as we wish those kids would eat fish and lentil soup and other foods that are good for them, we don't force the issue. I suppose that if there were nothing but fish in the house, they would come to eat it, much as Trish returned to her bowl of dry food. But kids aren't dogs.

We settle for letting my children eat their favorite foods, with fat-reducing modifications, most of the time. Then once in a while I bring in something new and ask them to at least try it. Little by little their tastes have developed for the better. Ross now really enjoys Chinese wok-prepared foods, for example. And he likes a few kinds of seafood. As time goes on, I'm sure he'll expand his tastes, without being "traumatized" at the dinner table.

PARTIES AND HOLIDAYS

I admit that my wife and I feel a bit out of control when Ross goes to a birthday party or when he's invited to dinner at a friend's house. There's just no way that we can have total control over our kids at all times. Besides, we wouldn't want to.

So how do we cope? I hate to sound repetitious, but the idea of lowering fat and cholesterol intake is a lifelong affair. It's a learning process, and as is true with academic tests, your kids and mine will do better at some things than at others.

Don't underestimate your children. Even the very young ones will understand the connection between their health and what they eat. You provide direction in many aspects of life, and now and then your youngsters slip. But for the most part they probably do pretty well. Similarly, you can send your son or daughter off to a party or a dinner and expect that he or she will stay somewhat in control.

The operational word here is *somewhat*. Don't expect any child to say no to everything; it's an unnatural expectation. But if he eats half the French fries, that's an improvement. If she skips dessert, that's more fat uneaten. If he asks for juice rather than whole milk, that's 8 grams of eliminated fat. Look at the positive side of the ledger.

As one nutritionist once said to me, "everything in moderation, including moderation." Once in a while it's perfectly OK to expect your child to forget the diet entirely and just have a good time. It's psychologically healthy to do so.

But that doesn't mean that parties and dinners and holidays should "blow" the diet two or three times weekly. If that were the case, such occasions wouldn't even be treats any longer. And there are a number of tricks you can use to reduce the impact of those treats.

At Easter, my children don't find a lot of candy left by the bunny. Instead, the traditional morning hunt reveals plastic eggs filled with small toys, novelties, and coins. The brightly colored real eggs prepared the night before are enjoyed, but the yolks are tossed in the trash or fed to the neighbor's dogs. The basket contains mostly toys and other gifts. And, yes, there are a few pieces of candy. But only a few are made of chocolate; the rest are sugar candies free of fat.

Christmas cookie making can be a wonderful holiday event. In our house we use egg whites instead of yolks, light corn syrup instead of butter or margarine, raisins instead of chocolate chips. They're delicious, and, even more important, the kids have a terrific time making them and using the cookie cutters to form all kinds of shapes.

Halloween trick or treating poses some dangers far beyond the diet. It's a disgusting social commentary that kids can't innocently accept treats without parental fear of poisoning. Many parents refuse to allow their youngsters to do any trick or treating for that reason alone. But it's so much fun for them, so we let our kids do a parent-supervised tour through the neighborhood. But they're not permitted to eat *any* of the treats along the way.

At the end of the evening, Dawn and I sort through the bag and carefully select the items allowed. In our case, we eliminate not only the unwrapped pieces and those easy to sabotage, but also most of the chocolate and other high-fat candies. Another approach is to count the pieces of booty and trade them for coins or collectors' cards.

Birthday parties present other problems. The menus for kids' parties center on hot dogs, cake, and ice cream. Or else parents arrange to have the parties at places such as pizza parlors or McDonald's. What to do?

First, remember that children go to parties to have fun, not only to eat. So I have no problem at all. I just spoil Ross's appetite before he leaves the house. Most kids are hungry just before such a party; I make him some snacks to be certain that when he gets there he'll eat just a bit of the otherwise forbidden foods.

Is your child invited to a party at a video arcade? Give him or her a few extra quarters to play more games. And, again, make sure you take the edge off that appetite before the party. Your child will be happy to forget the foods in favor of playing the games.

Don't get paranoid about this. Sure, Ross eats food we wish he wouldn't. But it's all part of the larger picture. Whether your kids are young or in their teens, peer pressure and peer approval remain paramount. Older children have the most such pressure. And social development and self-esteem cannot be downplayed. Food is a part of the social scene. Ross and your children will have to learn to deal with it. That doesn't mean perfect compliance each and every day. The end result is still a reduction in the *total* amount of fat and cholesterol in a given day or week or month or year.

What about eating at friends' homes? Dawn and I feel no embarrassment in explaining to the parents of Ross's friends that we limit the fat in his diet. They don't mind at all. They know that Ross is coming to visit, and that night they serve chicken, for example. Or they ask him when they have those dinners they know are on the approved list. A bit of planning goes a long way.

As our kids grow up, they'll be able to make their food selections from a far wider variety than they currently do. By that time they'll know how to make those selections with fat content in mind. It's all a learning process.

Today when I go to a party, I select drinks made without cream or coconut. I choose the lowest-fat items on the hors d'oeuvre table. I munch on pretzels rather than mixed nuts. My children will learn to do the same.

SNACKS HOME AND AWAY

Years ago it was the local drugstore. Today it's often the drive-in convenience market. Every kid in history has a place to hang out with friends. And every kid wants to nibble on snacks. Teach yours to do it right.

In the frozen desserts case, your child can select either a popsicle or sherbet rather than ice cream. When he wants a candy bar, he can avoid chocolate and those products made with hydrogenated fats. When picking out a bag of crunchies, she can forget the chips and have pretzels instead. Sure, it takes a bit of self-discipline. But it doesn't mean total deprivation.

At home, the trick is simply to have healthful snacks available at all times. Popcorn can be made in an air popper, not in oil. Try seasoning it with a sprinkling of garlic powder instead of popcorn salt. Buy some frozen giant pretzels; make them with little or no salt. Dip them into a bit of mustard for real zing; that's the way they were invented in Philadelphia, where they were sold by street vendors. Make lots of granola bars and cookies with oat bran; recipes abound in Chapter 11.

Here's another instance of how you as a parent can make a lifelong contribution to your children's health. Whether child or adult, when the snacking urge strikes, a person grabs the easiest, most convenient foods in the house. Too often those foods are the worst for health.

Certain foods just don't belong in your house at all. Eliminating temptation becomes the easiest path to follow. If those potato chips aren't there, you and your children will have to turn to something else. Here are some alternatives to have on hand for snacks:

- Raisins, dried fruits, prunes—but limit the total number eaten, since they still contain a lot of sugar concentrated in each piece.
- Fresh fruits attractively sliced and arranged on a platter that can be taken to where you are.
- Dry breakfast cereals that don't have a high salt, sugar, or fat content. Pour some into a bowl and let the kids nibble.
- Vegetable sticks such as carrots, cucumbers, squash, green peppers, and celery, with a dip made from nonfat yogurt. See Chapter 18 for recipes.

- Crunchy foods like homemade tortilla chips, bagel munch-ies, and others detailed in Chapter 18.
- Low-fat and nonfat beverages including skim milk, decaf-feinated ice tea, NutraSweet-flavored drinks, and fruit "smoothies."

You'll have an easy time selecting frozen snacks for home use. More and more products are being introduced for the health-conscious shopper. You'll see frozen fruit bars, frozen yogurt, sor-bets, sherbets, and other confections. Look at the ingredient list and nutrition labels before buying to make sure the fat content is low.

Yogurt makes a terrific snack and adds a lot of good nutrition to the diet of everyone in the family. Select the nonfat varieties. Sev-eral manufacturers make excellent yogurts with lots of fruit and flavor. Your kids won't even know that it's good for them.

When it comes to fruits and vegetables, you may say that *your* kids don't like them for snacks—or any other time. But I submit that it's only because those foods haven't been made properly available. A head of cauliflower in the vegetable bin of the refriger-ator is inaccessible for an on-the-spot snack. So is an unpeeled cucumber or carrot. The same applies, more or less, to fruits of different kinds. The trick is to have them easy to grab and eat at those moments when the kids are really hungry. No one wants to spend forever preparing a snack. We tend to reach for what's there right now. Too often that means junk foods.

If you buy grapes or cherries at the store, clean them and put them in a bowl at kids'-eye level in the refrigerator. Peel and slice some cucumbers and carrots, arrange them attractively, perhaps with some green pepper strips, and they'll be gone before you know it. Keep wedges of oranges, apples, and grapefruit in the refrigerator. A sprinkle of lemon juice adds zing and keeps the fruit fresh.

The same kids who won't eat cauliflower and broccoli at dinner will happily munch those veggies as snacks. That also goes for zucchini and even turnips, and just about anything else you can think of. And to make such snacking really festive, add a dip. Com-mercial dips are made with sour cream or mayonnaise or both, so you'll have to come up with your own. The easiest thing, if your kids like it, is to offer a carton of yogurt to dip veggies in. Kids often like weird combinations, like cucumbers and strawberry yogurt. It's also quite easy to make healthful dips with yogurt, cottage cheese, and a few flavorings. See the recipes in Chapter 18, "Food Fit for a Kid."

As an extra benefit from expending a bit of effort to supply your family with low-fat snacks on a regular basis, you, too, will start to eat them, and that means an easier time controlling your waistline.

Snacking should be viewed as a way of supplementing the day's total nutrition as well as satisfying immediate cravings. Why not keep some hard-boiled eggs in the refrigerator? Eaten without the yolk, dipped in a dab of mustard, it's a delicious snack that also provides lots of protein with no fat or cholesterol.

Try a few of these tips, and soon you'll wonder why you ever worried about snacks for your kids. You may wind up feeding much of the neighborhood when your kids' friends find out about your refrigerator. But then maybe they'll tell their parents, and your kids will eat those same kinds of snacks at their homes as well.

GARDENING FOR GOODIES

You take a few seeds, put them into the ground, sprinkle with water, and watch your kids watch the miracle of growth. The lessons that can be learned from the most simple gardening make the effort well worthwhile. First, you'll get to spend a bit of time together. Second, the youngsters can be responsible for weeding and watering. Third, you can teach them a little about plants and how they grow. Fourth, I've never heard of a kid who won't eat what he or she grows.

Those of us who don't have the luxury of living in a year-round gardening climate will be happy to know that gardening can be done indoors as well. A windowsill herb garden can bring a lot of eating enjoyment as well as the fun of watching something green grow during the cold winter months. Chives are easy to grow, and they're delicious when chopped fine and mixed into plain yogurt, for a vegetable dip or a topping for baked potatoes. Basil makes ordinary spaghetti sauce an Italian fiesta. Practically all annual herbs are very simple to grow indoors. Just keep trimming and harvesting, and they'll keep growing.

Not only herbs but also certain vegetables can be grown in such indoor winter gardens. Try radishes and leaf lettuce to make your own salad. With a large enough container of sufficient depth you can successfully grow carrots. If you get really serious about this new hobby, you might consider getting indoor plant lighting.

When you can garden outdoors, expand to other vegetables. Scallions and radishes grow very easily, provide an abundant crop, and kids can enjoy them in salads and for snacks. Green beans require a bit more effort; if you grow pole beans, you'll have to supply some support when the vines start growing. In the spring, leaf lettuce takes off like a weed. For real fun, try planting some melons and squash. The kids will love watching them get bigger and bigger.

What's the best part about gardening? You can't grow Twinkies or candy bars!

SCHOOL MEAL PROGRAMS

The federal government set up the school lunch program, and later the school breakfast program, for two reasons: there was a growing surplus of certain subsidized agricultural products, and many children in the country were going through the entire day without sufficient nutrition. A hungry kid just can't learn. But the programs offer children foods that are very, very high in fat and cholesterol.

That should come as no surprise, since the programs are administered by the U.S. Department of Agriculture. When you pay farmers to produce milk and cheese and butter, you have to find a way to get rid of those foods. The politics behind all of this are disgusting, but they don't really belong in a book of this sort. Suffice it to say that meals served in schools have whole milk, cheese, and other fatty foods in excessive amounts. Expect that half or more of the calories eaten will be fat; that's no exaggeration.

To make things even worse, at the start of the program children were not eating the foods served. Predictably, they left vegetables on their plates. So today's menus feature hot dogs, hamburgers, and pizza—all washed down with whole milk.

The breakfasts contribute similarly to the development of heart disease. While one segment of government, through the National Institutes of Health, tells people to avoid fats and cholesterol, the U.S. Department of Agriculture feeds kids eggs, cheese, and fatty sausages for breakfast.

The first thing you'll want to do is check with your child's school cafeteria. You have a right to ask about the items served. Find out whether your kids can have something other than whole milk; some school districts have switched to low-fat milk. Can your child have another beverage such as orange juice? What's the menu for the week? Can the child buy only one item? Is there a choice?

For the most part, you'll find that you prefer to have your children take lunch to school rather than have them buy lunch or breakfast at the cafeteria. I've come up with a list of foods that Ross and Jenny both enjoy toting to school. Sit down with your kids and talk about such a list for your own house. You'll never have to ask what they want for lunch; just repeat the list over and over.

Some of the foods kids tend to like include cold pizza (made at home with a low-fat recipe), and sandwiches of tuna, peanut butter, low-fat ham and cheese, or turkey. Kids also like to eat unconstructed foods. Give them little bags of carrots, raisins, bits of cold turkey, hard-boiled egg whites, and the like. Augment the sack lunch with oat-bran cookies, granola bars, and pieces of fruit. Perhaps, too, your school will allow your kids to buy a single item from the cafeteria line, such as a piece of fruit.

Beverages can be brought from home or purchased at school. Again, make sure your kids don't drink any whole milk. If no beverages are available or acceptable, freeze a plastic container of fruit juice overnight. By lunchtime, it'll be thawed and still cold.

Most kids like buying lunch at school, and yours may resent having to tote their meals with them. You can overcome that resistance. Find out what their favorite foods are and don't force them to eat foods you just happened to have in the refrigerator. Next, point out that a hamburger at school isn't nearly as good and tasty as one served at McDonald's. Most kids would rather have a McDonald's burger once in a while than school-lunch burgers and the like day after day. And when picking a fast-food restaurant, remember that broiling is better than frying.

Level with them. Explain that it's absolutely ridiculous to carefully plan foods at home only to throw one's diet away at school. Ask them to level with you as well. Do they *really* like those poorly prepared meals? Or is it more a social function? Most kids grin and admit that the food is lukewarm, tasteless, and soggy.

Maybe some day school administrators will recognize the importance of providing high-quality foods that promote health in both the short and long term. But for today, the national school-lunch program is an atherogenic atrocity, contributing to future heart disease.

FAST FOODS: GREASE TO GO

This may come as a surprise, but there's really nothing wrong with fast food per se. The problem is with the kind of foods served in most fast-food restaurants.

Throughout the world, fast food has been available for generations. In Japan, vendors sell noodles on street corners. Hungry passersby stop, and the vendor pours boiling water into a cup of dry noodles for an instant meal. Or the person may choose a bowl of rice with some vegetables. Perhaps a dish of sushi or sashimi in a tiny restaurant might be just what the taste buds call for that day.

In Mexico, the choices are equally healthful. Fish taco stands can be found on any street. Vendors sell fruit in ways not seen in this country. Imagine a peeled mango on a stick, arranged to look like an open blossom. Or maybe a cup filled with a variety of melon chunks. To wash it down, there are any of a number of fruit juices.

Fast food is also a European tradition. The fast food I'm speaking of is food served fast, not the typical franchise foods which originated here in the United States. In Italy, someone in a hurry can stop for a bowl of spaghetti. In Spain, people can enjoy seafoods and vegetables in a number of *tapas,* or bar dishes. The streets of Greece are lined with tiny cafés, with little tables for eating quickly al fresco. In fact, eating out is a way of life throughout Europe. That's particularly true for single men and women, who don't have the time or inclination to do much cooking.

The problem with fast food began in America. The phenomenon started in the 1950s, with a little hamburger stand called McDonald's. The rest is history. At first it was a matter of being an occasional treat. Today, far too many men, women, and children practically live on hamburgers, cheeseburgers, French fries, milkshakes, tacos, fried chicken, and doughnuts. The menus have expanded, and advertising has fostered a multibillion-dollar industry.

Who's to blame? In a way we're all responsible. In many or most households, both parents work, or maybe children are raised by a single parent, with little time allocated for preparing nutritious foods.

Most parents don't even realize the harm they're doing to their children by feeding them those foods. What could be wrong with a hamburger topped with cheese? Isn't that meat full of protein? Isn't the cheese loaded with bone-building calcium? And how about those chicken nuggets? We all know that chicken is good for you. Right?

To make things even more appealing and wholesome, fast foods are sold in an aura of "all-American goodness." Ronald McDonald smiles, and the company contributes to philanthropic medical causes. The restaurants sparkle and management keeps them shining clean and free of any loitering teens. TV shows us images of Americans of every age, sex, color, and walk of life—all of them apparently thriving on burgers and fries.

Currently the fast-food industry is fighting what they view as a real threat. Critics want fast foods to have nutrition labels, informing consumers as to just what is in those foods. You can find such labels on the majority of foods in the supermarket, so why not on the fast foods? What does the industry have to hide? Plenty.

Arby's talks about the lean beef used in sandwiches, but conveniently forgets the fat content of the toppings. McDonald's paints a rosy picture of Chicken McNuggets, but fails to tell us that those little balls are formed with chopped chicken skin and chicken fat and then drowned in an ocean of beef tallow. The result is a meal that's 60 percent fat. Until recently no one realized that French fried potatoes are cooked in beef tallow at the vast majority of fast-food restaurants. The industry would prefer that you naïvely consume those foods while thinking about the healthful potato, not the killer fats.

In Chapter 20, I've listed many of the fast foods available in the major outlets. Take a look at what we're feeding our kids. The McDonald's Big Mac provides 33 grams of fat and 86 milligrams of cholesterol along with 1,010 milligrams of sodium, all wrapped up in 563 calories. That's a real attack, all right. How about some nice, healthful fish? Long John Silver has just the ticket: three pieces of fish with an order of fries—a "mere" 63 grams of fat. Don't forget that most of that fat is saturated, ready to go to work clogging arteries.

It's enough to make you sick. That's why I was so shocked and horrified to read an article in *American Medical News,* a publication of the American Medical Association, with the headline "Hospitals Diversifying With Fast-Food Restaurants." They reported that fast-food restaurants "have replaced visitors' cafeterias in two Pennsylvania hospitals." The Children's Hospital of Philadelphia "houses a McDonald's restaurant in its lobby." The reason is very simple: money. The hospital receives a percentage of the income from the franchise. A hospital spokesperson said it's "quite heavily used by both employees and visitors," and that parents can bring their patient-children down for Big Macs.

I wrote a letter to the editor of the publication, pointing out that "the article omitted mentioning one notable benefit: tacitly approving of such atherogenic fare will ensure a supply of future patients for the cardiology wards." Needless to say, they didn't print it.

In my own diet, fast foods have been greatly restricted. The best item on the McDonald's menu is orange juice. The salad is OK, but you have to be careful with the dressing. Actually, I don't miss the food very much; it's certainly not gourmet fare. But what about the kids? Of course I'd prefer that neither Ross nor Jenny eat those foods, either. But that's not the real world. So, again, it's a matter of compromise.

Before I started tinkering with Ross's diet, he ate with his friends at McDonald's, Del Taco, Burger King, and Pizza Hut. Surely it started as "once in a while," but it began to escalate. Sound familiar? And he was eating lunches at school with more burgers and pizzas and fried chicken.

Today Ross takes his lunch to school in a bag. He misses the school lunches in the cafeteria, but to even things out, I allow an occasional trip to McDonald's or the like. By "occasional" I mean once every two weeks or so. It's not a perfect solution, but it cuts way back on the total fat consumption in his diet.

I've also provided some guidance as to the foods to be selected. At McDonald's, Ross orders a "happy meal" with hamburger, fries, and a Coke. No cheese on the burger. The fat content comes to about 20 grams. And I really prefer that he have the Coke rather than the milk, since he can have skim milk at home. It saves some fat and gives him a treat. When Ross and Jenny crave fried chicken, they eat it at Burger King rather than McDonald's or Kentucky Fried Chicken. Burger King's Chicken Tenders are made with actual chunks of chicken breast rather than bits and pieces and skin and fat, and they're cooked in vegetable oil.

In Mexican fast-food shops, refried beans are made with lard, and the taco shells are deep-fried and fat-laden. Instead of burritos or tacos, my kids get an occasional Del Taco treat of a taco salad, which contains more lettuce than beef.

But not all fast food requires such strategic planning. There actually are places that offer good, low-fat, nutritious meals—and kids like them. Denny's, a nationwide chain, serves a number of menu items that meet reasonable guidelines for reduced fat and cholesterol. They even have a small brochure at the register, which lists the cholesterol counts of different foods. Options include a chicken-salad pocket lunch, French dip, tuna and turkey sandwiches, and lots of side dishes that are really low in fat. You can also order an omelet made with Egg Beaters. And you can choose skim milk. Thanks, Denny's.

Another place where we can feel comfortable is Pollo Loco Chicken, one of a number of competitive restaurants cropping up. They serve barbecued chicken that's been marinated in fruit juices, accompanied by corn tortillas, rice, and salsa. Side dishes include both fruit and green salads. We pass on the refried beans, since they are made with lard. Here in the West we also have Carl's Jr., for an excellent broiled chicken sandwich.

Some restaurants today make a real effort to provide heart-healthy foods. They mark specific menu items with the American Heart Association's heart symbol to show that the food complies with AHA standards.

A lot of people have said that they'd like to see a fast-food restaurant offer good food. The D'Lites chain of fast-food places seemed just the ticket. Based in Atlanta, D'Lites offered vegetarian pita-bread sandwiches, diet cheeseburgers, and frozen yogurt. At first the chain was successful, with locations primarily in white-collar areas. Then an overambitious expansion program pushed them to financial ruin. Let's hope they make a comeback.

Ultimately, public tastes will have to change in order for the restaurant industry to offer the kinds of foods I'd like for my kids and myself. Competition now really forces them to sell the foods that most people want to buy. Numerous taste sessions have been conducted by major chains in trying to develop lower-fat foods and foods cooked in vegetable oil rather than beef fat. Time and again the taste panels have prefered the flavor of artery-clogging foods. And that's what continues to be sold.

COPING WITH ADVERTISING

Tobacco companies can no longer advertise on radio and television, and their products have been branded with no-nonsense warnings from the surgeon general. Unfortunately that's not true for foods that place the public at just as high a risk of heart disease.

To make matters worse, the majority of the population continues to believe the ads that tell them how wonderful those fat-laden foods are. Even before we learned how deadly the cigarette habit is, no one ever advertised that smoking was healthful. But companies of all sorts are on TV telling your kids and mine that they should eat hamburgers and French fries, Twinkies, cheese, and sugary breakfast cereals.

You should also know that the makers of many of those artery-destroying foods have managed to gain a substantial foothold in the schools, with their programs of so-called nutrition education. The National Dairy Council has infiltrated school systems across the entire nation and tells kids how healthy they'll be if only they eat lots and lots of butter, cheese, ice cream, and sour cream. They get away with it because the programs were started decades ago in cooperation with the U.S. Department of Agriculture, long before we knew about the link between diet and heart disease.

The promotional materials produced by the National Dairy Council are colorful, well designed, and market tested for effectiveness. While there is no question that dairy foods belong in a healthful diet based on the four major food groups, it is irresponsible to fail to note the crucial role played by fat and cholesterol in the disease process.

Why don't they advocate skim milk and low-fat or nonfat dairy products? Because dairy farmers are paid for their milk on the basis of its fat content. If they get money for that fat, they have to sell it. Any tactics are permitted, even if it means compromising the health of our children.

So how can we as parents compete with advertising and so-called education? No question about it; this is a tough one. It calls for talking with your kids about the realities of life. Not all those products advertised on TV are good. We live in a country that places great value on its freedom of speech. Not all the movies advertised are good for kids to see—many aren't fit for anyone. How many of the products advertised—food and otherwise—don't get into your home? Talk to your kids about how people make decisions when they buy food. We all place our votes at the cash register.

The fact remains, and children should quickly learn, that companies are willing to sell products for the sole reason of making money. It's up to us not to let them get away with it with *our* lives and health!

If your children are receiving nutrition education in school, find out what's being taught. Then talk with them. Explain that some of the people who make those educational materials have a vested interest that's more important to them than kids' health.

Discussions with your children early on will help them learn the facts of life. You'll find that they really enjoy talking about advertising. If nothing else, you'll establish a healthy line of communication.

SPECIAL FOOD NEEDS

Are there any reasons for certain children—or adults, for that matter—to include more than a minimal amount of fat and cholesterol in their diet? What about kids who are very active in sports and athletics? What about the differences between girls and boys? The answer is that no one needs more fat.

Let's first consider the athletic child, regardless of age. A long time ago, coaches used to tell their athletes to eat lots and lots of protein—pounds of steak and gallons of whole milk. Unfortunately that bit of "myth-information" continues to float around locker rooms.

We live in a very sophisticated age. Scientists have carefully studied the needs of athletes in order to have them perform to the very limits of their genetically endowed abilities. We even have a scientific specialty of exercise physiology. And athletes are very willing to be studied and experimented upon.

Much landmark research has been done at Ball State University in Muncie, Indiana. The director of their Human Performance Laboratory is Dr. David Costill, a man who has an enormous reputation worldwide in this field. He set off to determine what foods are best for a competitive athlete, such a world-class runner, a college star, or an Olympic contestant. The group that sponsored the study—the dairy industry—would have liked to see the results demonstrate the need for additional fat in the athletic diet. But research results did not justify additional fat.

Dr. Costill concluded, and his results have been reported widely, that the athlete must have the same nutrients as everyone else. Yes, physically active people need more calories. But those calories are best supplied not by fat but by additional carbohydrates. Pasta, bread, cereals, and fruits and vegetables should provide the energy needed for performance, he said.

There is no room for the argument that anyone need consume more than 20 to 30 percent of their total calories as fat. In fact, as one's caloric needs increase, the percentage derived from fat ought to drop rather than rise.

The only specific nutrient scientists agree that athletes need more of is water. During exhaustive physical exercise, the fluid loss is significant and should be replaced—with water, not with any of those specially formulated drinks with minerals added. That replacement should take place during practice and competition as well as after. Again, coaches haven't picked up on this information as well as they should have, and many still deprive athletes of water. The result can be dehydration.

Is there any difference between the needs of boys and girls? Sure. But those differences don't extend to the diet. Boys and girls both need the same nutrients. Both have growing and developing bodies.

It is true that boys can often eat more calories without gaining weight. Teenage girls have different metabolic rates and less lean muscle tissue, and as such need far fewer calories than boys of the same age. But young boys and girls have the same caloric needs unless the girls—or rarely the boys—do less exercise. And, of course, a very athletic girl may well need more calories than a boy of the same age.

The problem that does emerge, however, is that girls' diets may be less than optimal when it comes to certain nutrients. They often do not consume enough calcium and iron, and sometimes not enough vitamin C. The culprit is a poor diet, with emphasis on fast foods eaten with friends rather than on a balanced selection of foods. Studies have shown that not even women medical students' diets contain enough calcium and iron. Girls need adequate calcium to ensure proper bone growth and to lessen the chance of osteoporosis in later years. The denser a girl's bones are in youth, the less likely that the bone-demineralizing disease will be a problem when elderly. Yes, girls need more dairy foods; but they don't need butterfat. All the necessary calcium can be found in nonfat and low-fat varieties. Fruits and vegetables supply vitamin C, along with needed fiber. Enriched breads and cereals contain iron, although as girls begin to menstruate they may well need an iron supplement. But then, as discussed in Chapter 10, "Children's

Nutrition," it's probably a good idea to give all children a high-quality vitamin and mineral supplement.

The bottom line is that the requirement for fat is quite low. We can all, children included, do with far, far less fat than the average American consumes. A 20 to 30 percent fat diet based on a variety of foods does a fine job of nourishing everyone while also protecting against heart disease.

There is no question that in the future we will view high-fat and high-cholesterol foods with as much disdain as we now give tobacco. Will everyone in the future consume a healthful, low-fat diet? Probably not. People continue to smoke even though they know the habit can kill them. But your children and mine can be protected, starting right now.

RESULTS OF THE FIGHT

Throughout the medical literature, results of efforts to lower blood cholesterol levels in children have been about the same. Studies have been conducted in all parts of the world. The conclusion is that reducing the fat and cholesterol intake of youngsters typically causes the cholesterol level in their blood to fall by about 10 percent, more or less.

In each of those instances, however, most effort was made to get certain foods *out* of the diet rather than to put other foods *into* the diet. The program that's worked very well for Ross and for other children, and for many adults as well, has been to cut fat levels in the diet and also to increase the foods which have a role in actively lowering blood cholesterol levels.

As we'll discuss in Chapter 11, the major food for lowering cholesterol levels is oat bran. Certain beans can also do the job. That's because both have soluble fiber, which gets cholesterol eliminated by the body.

We began to work with Ross's diet when he was age 7½. At that time, his cholesterol level was 181 mg/dl, a number indicating reasonable concern that he would be a future candidate for heart disease. At first we gradually began to cut back on the most obvious foods: egg yolks, McDonald's and Del Taco fare, fat-containing candies, potato chips, and other fatty snacks. Only nonfat and low-fat dairy foods got into our refrigerator. That was phase I of my efforts on Ross's behalf. After six months, his results showed a 5 percent reduction, down to 172.

During phase II, we began cutting back further on trips to fast-food restaurants. Ross began carrying his lunch to school, and I started baking oat-bran treats for snacks. Ross's cholesterol level was lowered by another 6 percent, down to 161.

In phase III, Ross began to regularly consume more oat bran. He now eats about 2 ounces daily, either as hot cereal or in baked goods. That's not a very difficult thing to do, as Ross really enjoys those foods. The reward was 12 percent reduction, this time down to a very comfortable level of 141.

Altogether, then, the total reduction was 22 percent from the original level. That's well above what would be expected for a child with dietary intervention alone. The bottom line is that Ross is well on his way to controlling his blood cholesterol level and changing his destiny in terms of heart disease risk.

Certainly cholesterol is just one of the risk factors of heart disease, although most authorities agree it is the major one. I'm also working on the other risk factors—at least the ones I can change. I can influence Ross's decision not to smoke or do drugs as he gets older. I can limit the amount of sodium in his diet in case he has a predisposition toward high blood pressure. I can be sure he gets plenty of exercise and maintains an ideal body weight. And I can try to affect his behavior in terms of stress. Those factors are discussed elsewhere in the book in greater detail.

During the 1960s, when I was going to college, the slogan was "Make love, not war." Today we've declared war on cholesterol. But we're doing it as an act of love.

5

Not Just Baby Fat

Picture a cute, gurgling baby with pudgy cheeks, chubby thighs, and rolls of flesh at the wrists that give the impression of bracelets: the image of infant health? Until fairly recently most people thought so. They chucked the little one under the chin and remarked at what a good eater Mom was raising. Mother beamed, fed the child the next bottle, and proclaimed with confidence that the baby fat would disappear. Unfortunately, we recognize now that the overweight baby becomes the overweight child who, in turn, becomes the overweight adult. Baby fat is nothing to smile about.

In his editorial in the *New England Journal of Medicine*, weight-loss expert Dr. Theodore Van Itallie stated strongly that "evidence is now overwhelming that obesity has adverse effects on health and longevity." He said that overweight is clearly associated with hypertension, hypercholesterolemia, noninsulin-dependent diabetes mellitus, and an excess of certain cancers and other medical problems.

More than thirty-four million Americans tip the scales at over 20 percent above their desirable weight. The National Institutes of Health (NIH) has declared that such obesity is "a biologic hazard" which ought to be treated as aggressively as any other disease. The NIH panel investigating the phenomenon of obesity in this nation has linked overweight with many of the major causes of death, and has said that at least 40 percent of all cases of high blood pressure in whites could be prevented by controlling weight.

The chairman of that NIH panel, Dr. Jules Hirsch, said "Obesity is a killer. It is a killer just as smoking is."

Studies have shown that obese people have three times the normal incidence of high blood pressure and diabetes, an increased risk of heart disease, a shorter life span, and much higher than expected rates of respiratory problems and cancer. And while the medical cutoff for clinical obesity is 20 percent over optimum, even slight gains can increase risks.

Fat cells in overweight children are both more numerous and larger than those in normal-weight children. Pediatric-onset obesity represents the greatest number of individuals who will go on to be clinically obese. Later in life treatment is far more difficult.

In addition, overweight children can suffer socially. When shown pictures of lean and overweight children, other kids opted every time to play with the lean boys and girls. Shown pictures of both overweight children and others with physical disabilities, the children actually said they'd rather play with handicapped children than those who were overweight. While this may be a sad reflection on the value we place on appearance, it is nevertheless undeniable that an overweight child is more vulnerable than a slender child to loneliness and feelings of not belonging.

Writing in the *Annals of Internal Medicine,* Drs. Artemis Simopoulos and Van Itallie put it another way: "In the United States, the weight associated with the greatest longevity tends to be below the average weight of the population. . . . Overweight persons tend to die sooner than average-weight persons."

So, of the two cultural stereotypes, the skinny kid is far better off than the chubby baby with rolls of fat. But, one might suppose, doesn't that baby fat just go away as the child grows older?

The famous Bogalusa Study threw cold water on that idea. To use their word, there was a strong tendency for "tracking" in lean, obese, and very obese children. That is to say, skinny kids tend to stay skinny, and chubby children remain on the heavy side—all the way to adulthood.

More than 2,000 children were examined in 1973, in 1976, and again in 1978. They were tested for body weight, lipid profiles, and blood pressure. There were boys and girls, blacks and whites, representing a range of socioeconomic levels.

Obese and very obese children had significantly higher systolic blood pressure. As a group, the overweight kids had lower levels of the protective HDL and significantly higher levels of the harmful LDL cholesterol. To make things worse, triglyceride levels were up for the heavier children.

Following the youngsters through the years, researchers found that 86 percent of overweight boys and 80 percent of overweight girls became overweight adults, with overweight defined as 20 percent over normal. The words normal, ideal, and desired are used interchangeably in referring to weight.

Both heredity and environment are important factors in determining weight. Family influence is tremendous. If both parents are obese, there is a 70 percent chance the child will be obese as well. If only one parent is obese, the odds of the child being overweight drop to 40 percent.

If overweight begins before puberty, individuals have 1 chance in 4 of being normal weight later on in life. They have only 1 chance in 30 if they continue to be overweight after they leave puberty. But, Dr. Van Itallie reports, "It is good news that body fatness responds to environmental conditions and is demonstrably controllable by many people who are concerned about their physical appearance."

Here again, you and I have the ability to control a major risk factor in the development of heart disease. The time to start controlling body weight is during childhood. The time to start for *your* children is today.

One of the first things to consider is cutting down on television viewing time. Simply stated, TV is fattening. Kids in America spend three, four, even five hours a day gazing at those flickering images. During those long hours they scarcely move, let alone do any exercise except to grab another snack. And along with the cartoons and cops and comedies comes a liberal dose of advertising. It's hard to think about fruits and vegetables when you're invited to gorge on Cookie-Crisp cereal, Hostess Twinkies, and hot dogs guaranteed to plump when you cook them. They don't tell you that those franks will also plump your kids.

Researchers looked at data collected on more than 11,000 youngsters nationwide. They found that the ones who watched the most TV tended to be the most obese. Even more frightening, the kids who were normal weight but who watched a lot of TV became obese in the years to come. Another "tracking" study, this one reported in the medical journal *Pediatrics,* indicated a closer correlation between television viewing and weight.

What to do? First, try to wean your children of the tube by setting certain times for viewing, and establishing limits on the number of hours per day and per week. For many Americans, not only children, television becomes addicting. They sit in front of the set to watch a given show, and don't stand up again until it's bedtime.

The same goes for the kids. They turn on the tube on Saturday morning to watch a particular cartoon, and before you know it, they're glued to the TV for many hours. No exercise gets done, few calories get burned, and young muscles don't develop.

By having their viewing time limited, children at any age start to make decisions. They select one program over another. They decide to watch no TV on a given day in order to watch a bit more on another day when something special will be shown.

The next step is to talk to your kids about the food advertising they're exposed to. Explain the facts of life—about how TV ads sell things that may not be good for people to eat. In a frank and open discussion, even very young children will admit that eating cookies and marshmallows for breakfast isn't such a great idea.

You might want to explain that it costs a vast amount of money to advertise on television. The profit margin for selling bananas and apples just isn't as high as it is for highly processed foods such as cereals. Take the kids on a field trip to the supermarket and show them which cereals cost the most money. They're the ones advertised on TV.

As discussed in greater detail elsewhere in this book, teach your children to read food labels. Those foods that sound so good on TV have labels that read like horror stories.

All of us love to nibble when watching TV. But the habit of eating meals in front of the set can lead to overweight. More attention gets paid to the program than to the food being eaten. As a result, a person eats more than he or she would otherwise. By all means, limit the number of times a meal is consumed with the TV as company. Make it a treat rather than a habit. Perhaps once a week, say on Saturday morning, wouldn't be bad.

There are many ways your child can learn to eat less, if necessary, and to eat better. The National Recreation and Park Association has become involved in a major program to improve children's fitness. They suggest these simple rules for making kids the boss of their eating and drinking:

1. Enjoy your food, but keep your mind on the job. It's nice to have a conversation while eating, but don't do anything else until the meal is finished. This means not only not

watching TV, but also doing homework and other activities. Eating should be an activity in and of itself. It's a good habit to start developing early in life.

2. Eat slowly and chew each bit of food. Think about the flavors of your foods. Food tastes better when you eat it slowly.
3. Don't cook or serve more food than needed. And don't be afraid to leave small amounts of food on the plate.
4. Plan what you're going to serve or eat well in advance. That way you and your children won't grab the most convenient —and frequently the most fattening—food when hunger strikes.
5. Don't let people push or bully you into eating sugary, salty, and fatty foods.
6. Don't keep fattening foods around the house.
7. Limit consumption of candies and chocolates, and don't give such candies as gifts.
8. Don't shop when you're hungry—or when your children are hungry.
9. Don't eat as a consolation prize. As a parent, don't provide food to make your child feel better when things aren't going so well.
10. Get into the habit of selecting sweet fruits instead of sweet candies.
11. When thirsty, drink water. Keep chilled water in the refrigerator.

Think about some of these simple rules. Take number 3, for example. Did your parents tell you to eat every last bite because of the starving children in China? Are you instilling the same ideas in your children? Put less food on the plate, so you won't feel bad about waste. Then let the kids ask for seconds, or be satisfied with a little less.

Look again at rule number 5. Peer influence is increasingly important throughout childhood, and has a tremendous impact on a child's eating habits. Talk to your children about their food needs and show them how to take the leadership role in their peer group. Don't bully or push your own children into eating more than wanted.

Dessert frequently becomes a reward for cleaning the plate. How terrible! For the child to get calories, he or she is forced to eat more calories. That just doesn't make sense at all, even when trying to get the child to eat some fresh vegetables.

The better way is to provide those vegetables when the child is "starving to death" and will eat anything that won't eat him or her first. Keep a platter of fresh, raw vegetables in the refrigerator for just such occasions.

Which brings us to rule 9. Ask any psychologist and you'll get the same reply: overweight individuals often use food for consolation. The heavy boy who doesn't get picked for the team stays home with a box of candies. The man rejected for a job or passed over for a promotion may gorge himself to cover the hurt. And the process begins in childhood. Don't be the one to initiate your child into that kind of thinking by using food to console him; by the same token, food should not be used to reward your child for good performance. Think of alternative ways of celebrating such occasions. The most obvious options are purchased items, from toys to clothes to jewelry, depending on the age of the child. But this can lead to a type of materialism that's not far removed from the oral-fixated desire for food itself. Instead, give something of yourself.

Be honest with yourself. When was the last time you took some of your time and gave it freely to your child to do something he or she wanted to do? Certainly you spend time together merely by living in the same house. But what about special moments? Do you and your child enjoy fishing together? Do you relish a trip to the art gallery? Every family is different; think of the special ways you could spend special time with your children. It's a gift that gives both ways.

Up to this point, I've been discussing ways to keep weight under control. The time to think about weight problems is before they happen. But what if your child is already one of millions of boys and girls who are overweight?

Researchers use a variety of means to determine obesity; it's not only a matter of how much the child weighs. One such means involves measuring the skin thickness on the back side of the upper arm, the triceps skin fold. When a person holds the arm up, the skin hangs down and can be measured with a caliper. But for the most part, you can determine visually whether your son or daughter is above his or her ideal weight.

In addition, a pediatrician will measure height and weight during an annual examination. Talk with your doctor. Find out how your child compares with national norms. If your doctor says your child is in the 90th percentile for weight, that means only 10 percent of the population weighs more. If the child is in the higher percentiles for that age, this is the time to do something about it.

For those trying to bring a child's weight back down to desirable levels, the rules are the same as those for lowering cholesterol. But you'll simply have to be more strident about enforcing them.

By all means, do *not* attempt any of the quick-weight-loss diets developed for adults. In the first place, a child is not an adult and has special nutritional needs which those fad diets almost never satisfy. Second, the child gained that weight slowly but surely, and the increased metabolism of childhood helps burn it off just as certainly. Third, you want to develop sound eating habits that your child can carry throughout life and which are the *only* way to ensure long-term weight control.

The same nutritional needs discussed in Chapter 10 apply to the overweight child. It's simply a matter of reducing the total number of calories while keeping the nutrients coming in. That's not really hard to do. The same fat in the diet that leads to increased risk of heart disease also leads to overweight. So the same fat reduction recommended for all children will help your child reduce weight also.

I would be less than honest if I were to say that the job of keeping your child at an ideal weight is as easy in one family as it is in another. The unfortunate fact is that genetics plays an important role. Some families are more prone to being overweight. The children of overweight adults are more likely to be overweight than their peers from slender families. The jobs of weight control and weight reduction are more difficult, yes. But they are far from impossible.

Start by keeping track of what your child consumes during a given week. Keep a daily diary of everything he or she eats or drinks. You'll probably be unpleasantly surprised when you look at the tally sheet. Even without calculating the calories for each item, you'll quickly see where the problems lie. Count the number of McDonald's hamburgers or other fast-food meals during the week. How many high-calorie, high-fat desserts were served during the seven-day period? Were snacks primarily potato chips, candy, and cookies? Was every meal, or many of them, accompanied by buttered breads and vegetables or heavy sauces? Did whole milk and shakes constitute a goodly number of the beverages?

Next, decide which of those weight-raising occasions can be replaced. If you merely cut the number of visits to McDonald's and Kentucky Fried Chicken in half, you'll eliminate a vast amount of fat and a large number of calories. Replace the offending snacks with more healthful choices, and there will go a lot more fat and calories.

Talk with your pediatrician or family physician about the number of calories your child should consume on a daily basis for normal growth and development. I've given a general overview in Chapter 10, but you may wish to go into more detail with your doctor, tailored to your own child's needs.

If your child is greatly overweight, it's a good idea to consult with a nutritionist or dietitian, who can provide one-on-one advice. Make sure, however, that the person agrees with the overall concept and desirability of reduced fat intake. Unfortunately, not all dietitians are well informed and convinced that heart disease is largely a preventable situation that begins in childhood. They are interested only in a dogmatic approach based on antiquated training, which stresses many of the high-fat foods now known to be detrimental. I've been to many meetings of such individuals and have seen them stuffing themselves with high-fat foods while praising the nutrients they contain. The result, of course, is an overweight dietitian.

On the other hand, there are many well-informed professionals who can help you and your children adjust your dietary habits in ways that will facilitate weight loss and ultimate weight control. Again, talk to your doctor for a recommendation. I do stress, however, that this may not be necessary for most individual cases. You may very well find—and I believe this will probably be the case—that simply following the dietary recommendations in this book will allow for a safe, gradual weight reduction at the same time as blood cholesterol levels diminish.

For all children, more exercise means more calories burned. For the child who is already at ideal body weight, this means more foods can be eaten to balance the calories lost. Those extra foods should be complex carbohydrates in the form of additional breads and cereals, fruits, and vegetables rather than more fatty foods. For the child wishing to reduce weight, increased exercise helps in two ways: calories burned mean weight actually lost, and stepped-up activity increases the child's metabolism, allowing better, more efficient utilization of food energy.

Your child may be eating more than needed, owing to psychological disturbances you may or may not know about. Childhood stress is discussed in more detail in Chapter 7, and this must be at least considered in dealing with the overweight child. As a parent, you are in the best position to judge whether pressures and problems are being soothed by doughnuts and Twinkies. You may well be able to reduce some of that stress once you know what troubles your child.

Be careful, however, not to create an exaggerated attitude toward weight control. It's not your child's fault that he or she is overweight; don't instill guilt that can become a lifelong problem. Stress that maintaining optimal body weight is primarily for health rather than cosmetic reasons. You don't want to replace an overweight problem with anorexia.

Eating disorders have become virtually epidemic in the United States, especially among teenage girls. Anorexia nervosa has been the subject of countless magazine articles and even television dramas. Victims of this disorder never feel satisfied with their bodies, they completely shun food, and they rely on a variety of bizarre and unhealthful methods of weight reduction. The problems of anorexia and other eating disorders such as bulimia have grown to such an extent that clinics have been established solely to deal with these individuals. Many authorities believe the underlying reason for this epidemic is our society's distorted emphasis on being slender. While you cannot get rid of all the advertisements portraying thin models as the ideal, you certainly can avoid bringing additional stress into the family.

As in all things, moderation must prevail as the most healthful approach to life. As a parent you want your child to eat a moderate amount of a wide variety of foods, to engage in pleasurable physical activities, and to view life as a wonderful experience.

One of the benefits of following the anticholesterol program in this book is that by greatly reducing the amount of fat in the diet, you virtually eliminate the problem of obesity. If an adult begins eating a low-fat diet, he or she will gradually become slender. But the situation is even better for children, since their metabolic rates are higher and they are capable of using calories more efficiently. By starting kids off on a low-fat lifestyle, parents can assure that obesity won't be a problem for them later in life.

My Jenny has inherited a family tendency toward chubbiness. As a toddler, Jenny started getting more than a little chubby. Now that she is eating the foods available in the house—in other words, eating like her brother and me—Jenny doesn't have a weight problem at all. And she's proud of it! She knows that the good foods we eat keep her slender and healthy. That's a lifestyle she can live with.

There are, of course, many influences determining weight. The higher the education and income levels, the less likely females will be overweight. Just the reverse is true for males. However, for both sexes, obese individuals are unlikely to attain the highest incomes in their professions.

There are also racial implications. Black females are the heaviest, while black males are the leanest people in our society. But one wonders whether cultural aspects are more important than racial or genetic. Japanese men and women tend to be lean, as do many other Asian peoples. But the Chinese often are quite heavy. It's no surprise to learn that fat content is higher in Chinese cuisine than in other types of Oriental cooking. In fact, it's considered a compliment to serve "honored guests" meals with particularly high levels of oil. When my family visits a Chinese restaurant, I ask that the chef prepare the dishes with as little oil as possible.

Whether eating in restaurants or at home, never praise or allow gluttony. Children who begin to gain excess weight are unlikely to outgrow the trend.

Take a moment to compare your child's height and weight with the averages shown in Tables 12 and 13 here. Has your boy or girl been consistently higher than average for weight over the years? Don't think they'll outgrow the trend.

I heard one mother say with blithe confidence that her son tends to "blimp out" for a while, then add height, then "blimp out" again. Obviously each surge in height results in a slenderizing effect. But what happens when the last height increase ends? It doesn't take much to figure out that the next "blimp out" may be permanent.

Kids tend to eat more, or to eat less, from time to time. Those cycles seem to correlate to periods of growth. Let your child follow his or her own biological tendencies. Don't feel that he or she must eat the same amount day in and day out. It's OK to not eat so much every day. Don't encourage overeating.

If your child is currently overweight, the odds are in his or her favor that, if intake of calories—especially of fat calories—drops, weight will normalize over time. In this case, time is on their side.

Table 12. WEIGHT AND LENGTH OF CHILDREN FROM BIRTH TO 3 YEARS, WITH 3-MONTHLY INCREMENTS

WEIGHT (in pounds)

Age	Distance*			Age	Three-Monthly Gains		
	5th P	50th P	95th P		5th P	50th P	95th P
Boys: 0–3 Years							
Birth	5.9	7.5	9.1	4 wk.	0.4	4.8	8.0
1 mo.	7.3	9.4	11.1	3 mo.	3.6	5.7	8.2
3 mo.	9.8	13.4	16.0	6 mo.	2.0	4.6	6.6
6 mo.	14.7	18.0	21.3	9 mo.	1.5	3.4	5.1
9 mo.	16.8	21.4	25.1	1 yr.	0.9	2.3	3.9
1 yr.	18.7	23.3	27.8	18 mo.	0.7	1.5	2.5
2 yr.	23.3	28.3	33.3	2 yr.	0.7	1.5	2.2
3 yr.	27.1	32.5	37.9	3 yr.	0.5	1.1	1.7
Girls: 0–3 Years							
Birth	5.3	7.3	8.8	4 wk.	0.7	3.5	6.8
1 mo.	6.6	8.3	9.8	3 mo.	3.2	5.1	7.2
3 mo.	10.2	12.4	14.4	6 mo.	2.1	4.2	7.2
6 mo.	13.4	16.7	19.8	9 mo.	1.5	2.8	5.2
9 mo.	15.3	19.8	24.1	1 yr.	1.1	2.3	3.6
1 yr.	17.4	21.7	26.0	18 mo.	0.5	1.5	2.6
2 yr.	22.3	27.1	31.9	2 yr.	0.3	1.3	2.2
3 yr.	26.3	32.3	38.3	3 yr.	0.4	1.0	1.9

LENGTH (in inches)

Age	Distance			Age	Three-Monthly Gains		
	5th P	50th P	95th P		5th P	50th P	95th P
Boys: 0–3 Years							
Birth	18.4	19.8	21.1	3 mo.	2.9	3.9	4.9
1 mo.	19.9	21.4	22.9	6 mo.	1.9	2.7	3.5
3 mo.	22.6	24.0	25.4	9 mo.	1.2	1.9	2.6
6 mo.	25.1	26.7	28.3	1 yr.	1.0	1.6	2.3
9 mo.	27.2	28.7	30.2	18 mo.	0.7	1.3	1.9
1 yr.	28.4	30.2	32.0	2 yr.	0.5	1.0	1.5
2 yr.	32.1	34.6	37.1	3 yr.	0.6	0.8	1.0
3 yr.	35.3	37.8	40.3				
Girls: 0–3 Years							
Birth	18.3	19.5	20.7	3 mo.	2.7	3.7	4.7
1 mo.	19.5	21.0	22.5	6 mo.	1.6	2.6	3.6
3 mo.	22.2	23.6	25.0	9 mo.	1.1	1.9	2.7
6 mo.	24.6	26.1	27.6	1 yr.	0.5	1.5	2.5
9 mo.	26.3	27.9	29.5	18 mo.	0.4	1.25	2.0
1 yr.	27.6	29.4	31.2	2 yr.	0.6	1.0	1.4
2 yr.	31.6	33.8	36.0	3 yr.	0.6	0.8	1.0
3 yr.	35.3	37.5	39.7				

* "Distance data," i.e., average measurements attained at various ages. P = percentile. From F. Falkner: *Pediatrics*, volume 29:467–74, 1962.

Table 13. HEIGHT AND WEIGHT OF CHILDREN AGED 4–12 YEARS, WITH ANNUAL INCREMENTS

Ages (yr.)	Height (in inches)			Weight (in pounds)		
	5th P	50th P	95th P	5th P	50th P	95th P
Boys: 4–12 Years						
4	38.3	40.8	43.3	30.0	36.1	42.2
5	40.3	43.4	46.4	33.0	40.3	47.6
6	42.8	45.9	49.0	36.0	44.7	53.4
7	44.8	48.1	51.4	40.3	50.9	61.5
8	46.9	50.5	54.1	44.4	57.4	70.4
9	48.8	52.8	56.8	48.0	64.4	80.4
10	50.6	54.9	59.2	51.4	71.4	91.4
11	51.9	56.4	60.9	53.3	78.9	102.5
12	53.5	58.6	63.7	60.0	86.0	113.5
Girls: 4–12 Years						
4	38.1	40.7	43.3	28.8	36.1	43.4
5	40.6	43.4	46.2	32.2	40.9	49.6
6	42.8	45.9	49.0	35.5	45.7	55.9
7	44.5	47.8	51.1	38.3	51.0	63.7
8	46.4	50.0	53.6	42.0	57.2	72.4
9	48.2	52.2	56.2	45.1	63.6	82.1
10	49.9	54.5	59.1	48.2	71.0	95.0
11	51.9	57.0	62.1	55.4	82.0	108.6
12	54.1	59.5	64.9	63.9	94.4	124.9

Annual Height Gains (in inches)			Annual Weight Gains (in pounds)		
Age (yr.)	Boys	Girls	Age (yr.)	Boys	Girls
4	2.8	2.8	4	4.4	4.4
5	2.6	2.7	5	4.5	4.4
6	2.5	2.5	6	4.8	4.4
7	2.4	2.25	7	5.5	5.3
8	2.4	2.3	8	6.4	6.4
9	2.3	2.3	9	7.0	7.6
10	2.1	2.4	10	7.0	9.4
11	1.7	2.5	11	6.8	10.6
11½	1.6		11½	7.4	
12	1.9	3.1	12	8.4	12.6

From F. Falkner: *Pediatrics*, volume 29:467–74, 1962.

Another mother I know started limiting her son's carbohydrate intake. How ridiculous! Those complex carbohydrates such as breads and pasta provide excellent nutrition, accessible energy, and little if any fat. She was really surprised to learn about the calorie differences in foods.

One gram of carbohydrate provides 4 calories. One gram of fat provides 9 calories. Fat is a concentrated source of calories. Every time you substitute a gram of carbohydrate for a gram of fat, you save 5 calories. That really adds up in no time at all.

Take one more example. Suppose that, as part of your cholesterol-lowering efforts, you're going to stop using butter. If you use vegetable-oil spray on a nonstick pan, you save 12 grams of fat—about 100 calories—for every tablespoon of butter not used. More about such matters when we go shopping, in Chapter 14.

My Jenny is only 6 years old as I write this, and yet she knows that certain foods are better than others. She recognizes that food is good for her and she enjoys eating; I don't fear future anorexia nervosa. But she also knows that, more than too much food, the wrong food can make her chubby and unhealthy. She's proud that she isn't chubby anymore, and I'm mighty proud of her!

Give your kids an edge in life by helping them to be slender. They'll thank you for it throughout their lives.

6
Today's Sedentary Child

We hear a lot about the American fitness revolution and how men and women all over the country are jogging, swimming, doing aerobics, and working out with weights and machines. But when Mom and Dad lace up their Reeboks and head out to the health club, the kids stay home playing video games and programming the computer. Today's kids are starting off on sedentary lifestyles earlier than ever before.

Personally, I don't think it's anybody's fault. We tend to believe that children just naturally run and play. That's the way it always was. Most of us remember how we played all kinds of games and were involved with sports throughout our childhoods. Parents have begun to concentrate on their own physical fitness, assuming that their sons and daughters are just fine.

At the same time, we've become proud of accomplishments on the computer. Instead of swimming and horseback riding, kids at summer camp are likely to learn how to program the Apple. And if given the choice, children likely opt for a session at the video arcade rather than an hour of playing catch in the park.

To make matters worse, no one seems to walk, run or bike ride as a form of transportation. If no one is available to provide a car ride, children often would rather wait thirty minutes to catch a bus than walk fifteen minutes to their destination.

The benefits of exercise for adults have been well documented, as we'll see a bit later in this chapter. And we're beginning to note the advantages for children as well.

Coronary heart disease is rare in African populations. Total serum cholesterol levels remain low while protective HDL levels are high. Looking at children ages 10 to 12, researchers in South Africa learned that lifestyle plays a major role.

Comparing black African children with their white counterparts, the scientists concluded that both dietary and activity patterns of rural African children seem close to optimal for the inhibition of atherosclerosis. Black boys and girls run and walk far more, and their diets are much lower in fat and higher in fiber.

In the study, African boys' HDL levels averaged 66 mg/dl, while white boys' levels were 58. Black African boys who walked more than six miles a day displayed HDL levels of 70. Compare that with the HDL levels of white boys in the United States, with an average of 56.

When scientists looked at total serum cholesterol, they found that black African boys averaged 135 mg/dl, while their white counterparts totaled 167, about the same as American boys at 164. In terms of risk of heart disease, those differences are significant. The incidence of heart disease among black Africans is rare, while that of their white counterparts compares with the American statistics.

Certainly a genetic component comes into play, but the effects of diet and exercise cannot be denied. To look at the effects of an exercise program on heart-disease risk factors in children, researchers studied sixteen children with one or more risk factors. Children included in the study had serum cholesterol levels of 190 or more, blood pressures of 135/80 or higher, and weight at least 15 percent above normal.

The children met three times weekly for an extensive exercise program that lasted twelve weeks. They warmed up for fifteen to twenty minutes, then walked, jogged, and played games for forty minutes or so. At the end of each session, the kids could swim for another thirty minutes; most chose to do so. The level of exercise was designed to increase and maintain heart rates to 75 percent of maximum.

At the end of the twelve-week period, serum cholesterol levels decreased from an average of 194 to 183. Bear in mind that the decrease was the effect only of exercise. Dietary changes could be expected to further reduce those levels. Blood pressure measurements also fell significantly, as did weight.

These results show that the exercise program was certainly worthwhile. The researchers noted that such training regimens have to be rigorous enough to achieve desired benefits.

These were kids who, understandably, did not do a lot of exercise prior to the study. At least five of them needed constant pushing and a lot of supervision to keep them going. It was not easy to motivate the children, but the effort paid off.

These studies are not unique in the medical literature. More and more investigations have demonstrated the benefits of getting children to begin strenuous exercise programs. In every instance, total blood cholesterol levels fall, HDL counts rise, weight is reduced, and blood pressure comes down.

At the University of Michigan, a program called "Fitness for Youth" was begun in 1983. For one year, 1,000 boys and girls from kindergarten through sixth grade did thirty minutes of aerobic exercise twice a week. They also learned about nutrition, specifically about the need to eat more fruits and vegetables and to cut down on fatty foods. At the end of the year, improvements were noted across the board: serum cholesterol levels and blood pressure were reduced, weight came down, and their bodies were stronger and leaner. The "Fitness for Youth" program has now gone nationwide to provide these benefits to others.

How badly out of shape are our children? National studies give the kids failing grades.

Thirty years ago President Eisenhower became alarmed about the physical condition of our nation's youngsters. He formed the President's Council on Physical Fitness and Sport to correct the situation. During the following years, efforts were made to step up awareness of the importance of fitness. Every ten years a study determines the current status. The 1985 study showed that our youth's fitness has reverted to levels not seen since before the Vietnam War.

George Allen, the council's chairman and former coach of the Los Angeles Rams and Washington Redskins, has said: "The best-kept secret in the United States today is youth fitness, or lack of it. Kids have no endurance, no strength, and very little flexibility."

The most recent study was designed by the Institute for Social Research at the University of Michigan. It was the largest of its kind ever conducted in the United States, sampling nearly 19,000 boys and girls, ages 6 through 17. They came from 187 schools across the nation, in 57 school districts.

Nine standard tests were included in the study, including bent-knee sit-ups, pull-ups, a fifty-yard dash, and walking/running. Results were alarming.

The 14- to 17-year-old girls did worse in eight of the nine events than had the same age group ten years earlier. Forty percent of boys 6 to 12 years old couldn't do more than one pull-up; one in every four couldn't do even one. Seventy percent of girls age 6 to 17 couldn't do more than one pull-up; more than half were unable to do a single one. Forty-five percent of boys 6 to 14 years were unable to hold their chin over a raised bar for more than ten seconds; 55 percent of girls couldn't do it. Half the girls 6 to 12 years couldn't run a mile in less than ten minutes; 30 percent of the boys failed that test as well.

Obesity in teens has increased by 40 percent during the past two decades, the study revealed. More than 20 percent of teens from age 12 to 17 are 20 percent overweight.

According to George Allen, commenting on the study results, American children would rank about twentieth by nations worldwide. He points out that many schools have no physical fitness programs. Only one-third of our youngsters have daily physical education classes. Compare that with 90 percent in 1964.

Federal and state funds have been cut for many health programs, and physical fitness has been no exception. To make matters worse, parents seem less interested in physical education than in any other aspect of their childrens' education. Sure, you ask about how your child is doing in math and spelling. But do you inquire about his or her progress in PE? Probably not.

Many authorities believe that the lack of emphasis on physical fitness and sports has also contributed to our nation's problems with alcohol and drug abuse. Kids in elementary schools are routinely tempted, and all too many succumb to peer pressures. It's difficult if not impossible for a kid who has been abusing alcohol and drugs to perform well in sports.

Moreover, we still don't know what inactivity will mean with regard to long-term physical development. But what we already know is bad enough.

Does encouraging children to begin a life of exercise and fitness pay off in the long run? Until very recently, fitness buffs only had testimonials as proof. They spoke of how terrific they felt and the exhilaration they experienced during running and so forth. But there wasn't any hard evidence to prove scientifically the benefits of exercise.

Three separate studies have now provided definitive proof that regular aerobic exercise does indeed improve the health of the heart. These studies used animals rather than people, for the very simple reason that animals could be sacrificed so their hearts could be examined.

One study using pigs was done at the University of California at San Diego. The pig's heart and circulatory system are very similar to that of humans. In this study, Dr. Colin M. Bloor artificially blocked a coronary artery in eighteen pigs. Nine animals were then strenuously exercised on a treadmill for five months; the other nine did no exercise. At autopsy, the hearts of the exercised pigs showed twice the development of collateral vessels supplying blood to the heart.

Let me explain. When an artery is blocked, no blood can get through. Collateral vessels can form a kind of natural bypass around the blockage, providing the needed blood flow. A good system of collateral vessels can sometimes prevent a heart attack and can lessen the likelihood of death, should a heart attack occur.

If this kind of improvement could be demonstrated in animals with impaired circulation to the heart, just think how much benefit exercise would achieve for children.

In a second study, physical exercise was shown to protect against sudden cardiac death. This research was conducted by Dr. George E. Billman at the University of Oklahoma Health Sciences Center in Oklahoma City. He and his associates used dogs that had previously had heart attacks. Some were given exercise and others were not. After just six weeks, all the dogs were put on the tread- mill for testing. None of the exercising dogs showed any cardiac rhythm disturbances or signs of weakened or malfunctioning hearts, while seven of the eight nonexercising dogs showed those signs. Your children currently have no cardiac problems. Think of the protection regular exercise can provide for them.

How about the potential harm of exercise for those with high blood pressure? Dr. James Scheuer, director of cardiology at Montefiore Hospital and Medical Center in New York, addressed that issue in a study with rats having high blood pressure. Ten rats were put on a program of regular swimming, while another ten remained sedentary. Cardiac function returned to normal in all of the rodent swimmers.

High blood pressure frequently is found in today's sedentary children. Think of the enormous benefits of starting your children on the excellent habit of regular strenuous exercise.

A study reported in the *Journal of the American Medical Associ-*

ation predicts low coronary-heart-disease risk for those who habitually exercise. Dr. Ralph S. Paffenbarger and his associates studied nearly 17,000 Harvard University graduates. They found that the risk of heart disease correlated directly with whether men were currently and regularly exercising. Even those who were university athletes but who stopped exercising after graduation were at risk. But the men who engaged in strenuous exercise were protected.

Interestingly, the benefits of exercise were said to be "independent of contrary lifestyle elements—smoking, obesity, weight gain, hypertension, and adverse parental disease history—in affecting coronary heart disease incidence." That's not to say that you should look the other way if your children begin to smoke or gain weight, but it shows the strong protective effect of exercise, even for those with such bad health habits.

Dr. Paffenbarger made some even more positive statements in a subsequent report in the March 6, 1986, issue of the *New England Journal of Medicine.* In that landmark article he said that those who regularly exercise throughout their lives add from one to more than two years to their lives. Those are average numbers, with some individuals expected to tack on ten or even twenty years of living. Put another way, Dr. Paffenbarger said, every hour spent exercising will be returned in an hour of added life, plus an extra hour as a dividend. You just can't beat that kind of investment for your children—or for yourself.

What can you do to start your child off on a lifetime of exercise and physical fitness? First, become aware of his or her current state of fitness or lack of it. Too many parents take certain things for granted. We may feel that while our child sits around quite a bit at home, he or she exercises regularly at school or in the park or playground.

Try to be objective in your observations and evaluations. Your family, as a whole, may be less than fit and quite sedentary. For example, what kinds of toys does your child play with? What kinds of activities are preferred? If your child plays only with sedentary toys such as dolls or cars and trucks rather than balls and jump ropes, there may be a problem. The same holds for preferring only to watch TV, play video games, and draw or read. Certainly all those things are fun and some are a crucial part of a child's development. But if such inactive pursuits become the only activities, your child probably is far from physically fit.

If this is the case, don't overreact. But do encourage your child to go outdoors and play actively. One certain way to achieve this is to play with him or her yourself. When was the last time you asked for a game of catch? How about taking a long walk together? Later you can increase the distance and maybe start doing a walk-jog that can lead to regular runs together.

Take a look at your child's appearance. Be objective about that "baby fat." Is your child lean and trim or overweight and flabby?

Observe energy levels and attitudes. Does your child balk at suggestions to engage in active play? Is he or she tired frequently without reason? Don't expect overnight improvements. It took a few years for your child to become sedentary and out of shape, and it'll take more than a few days to become active to the point of enjoying it.

The younger your child is today, the easier it will be to initiate a program of regular exercise. It's never too early to begin. Your YMCA may very well have programs for children still in their infancy. Community programs are springing up all over the country. It takes a bit of effort, but the rewards—both long- and short-term—are overwhelming.

One potential problem with structured activity programs for children is the pressure from parents to perform and compete. It doesn't matter whether your kid is the best or most aggressive going down the slide, running around the gym, or winning in Little League. This is the time to instill *pleasure* in exercise. The fastest way to kill that pleasure is to force a child to meet your expectations. Don't start whistling the theme from *Rocky* too soon!

On the other hand, perhaps it may be time to praise physical and athletic performance as much or as often as you do academic achievement. Most families have ways to reward high scholastic endeavor, but few recognize a child's sports milestones, even if that means just *doing* something.

The ancient Greeks considered the whole person in education. Academic and physical education received equal attention. Keep that as your standard, too.

You can get an accurate picture of your son's or daughter's physical fitness with the following tests. Together they measure strength, flexibility, and stamina. Give your child the test now, then see how he or she progresses. There is no absolute judgment on performance here. You want to know how well your children do today, and then see how much they improve. Both you and your children will be encouraged by even some small progress over time.

TEST 1: BENT-KNEE SIT-UPS

Sit-ups are an excellent way to measure abdominal strength and endurance. Doing them with bent knees protects against injury to the back. Never force a child to do "just one more." Let progress come naturally.

Have the child lie down on his or her back, with knees bent, on a soft surface such as a carpeted floor or exercise mat. Arms should be crossed, with hands on opposite shoulders. Tuck the chin into the chest. Hold down the child's feet and ask him or her to bend forward—while exhaling—until the elbows touch the thighs. Inhale on the way back down. Score in terms of how many sit-ups can be done in a sixty-second period.

TEST 2: SIT AND STRETCH

Here's a great way to measure flexibility. You'll need a box twelve inches high and a yardstick. Place the box against a wall and position the yardstick on top of the box. Have the child take off his shoes and sit on the floor with his feet against the box. Position the yardstick so that the nine-inch mark is even with the child's heels, the lowest numbers extending toward him or her. Now have him reach forward along the yardstick. He or she should make three stretches forward, then you should measure the distance reached on the fourth try. This test gauges hamstring and back flexibility. As the child exercises more, flexibility will increase. You'll see it in the numbers reached.

TEST 3: STANDING LONG JUMP

All you'll need for this is a tape measure or yardstick to measure the jump. Have the child stand at the starting line with feet apart and arms behind the trunk of the body. Then he or she should jump three times by bending the knees, squatting down, and then explosively leaping forward as far as possible. Measure the best try.

TEST 4: CHIN-UPS

This test requires a bit more preparation than the others. You may wish to go to a park that has a chinning bar. Or maybe you'll consider installing a rod outdoors between two branches of a tree or indoors in a door frame. Then have the child grasp the bar with knuckles turned away and fingertips toward him or her. Count the chin-ups done.

TEST 5: WEIGHT SUPPORT

Using the same chinning bar from the previous test, have the child hang from the bar as long as possible and time it. This measures the ability to support body weight.

TEST 6: ONE-MILE RUN

The ability to run a mile in a given amount of time is a good way to gauge stamina and cardiovascular fitness. Measure a track or distance to equal one mile. Have the child warm up by doing a few minutes of rapid walking or jogging. Then clock the time in minutes and seconds it takes to complete the mile. Don't be surprised if the child needs to walk part of the mile, alternating walking with running. Soon he or she will run the entire distance, and the time will improve quickly.

Researchers found that children who were badly out of physical condition required a great deal of motivation and encouragement. Left to their own devices, the children would not have continued the exercise program which proved to benefit them greatly. Remember this when you begin working with your own child.

Remember, too, that failure is a very poor motivator. The child who is unable to perform well will not want to do more and will find every excuse to avoid exercise sessions. Be lavish with your praise and ignore the child's shortcomings. Ignore the nine times he drops the ball and praise the one time he catches it. Point out how much improvement there has been since the last time. Show her how she can run faster, or jump farther, or stretch more than when she began.

Think of as many ways as possible to include physical activity in your lives. Bike riding is a great family activity. How about a nature walk through the woods? Or maybe a game of volleyball on the beach rather than just sitting on the blanket listening to the radio. Sometimes it's absolutely necessary for you to drive your children to various activities. But there may well be times when they can walk or ride their bicycles.

You may also want to check out the physical education program at school. Talk to the instructor and find out what kinds of activities are being performed. Ask how your child is doing.

If you have some time available, consider volunteer work. That might involve coaching a local team, helping out at the YMCA, or assisting in the PE program at school. Not only will you get things going, but you'll also show your child how important you think exercise really is.

That brings us to the next point. Set a good example for your children in exercise as in other aspects of life. It's hard for them to believe exercise is important if they see you sitting all weekend long reading the paper and watching TV. Physical activity provides tremendous relief from daily stress. And you'll appreciate the improvement in physical image. Consider this an opportunity to get into a program of physical exercise yourself. The same benefits you want for your child apply to yourself as well.

As is true for all aspects of preventive health care, exercise must be a long-term, lifelong part of your routine. Both you and your children should come to enjoy exercise. After a while, it becomes as addictive as runners say, when they describe the "high" they experience while jogging several miles.

Both good and bad habits take time to develop. No one gets hooked on smoking from the first cigarette or on alcohol after drinking the first beer. Habits are developed gradually. Promise yourself that you'll stick with an exercise program for just a few months. Do it at least three, and preferably five, days a week. At the end of that time, neither you nor your children will want to quit. And you'll be well on your way to cardiovascular fitness, reducing a major risk of heart disease.

7
Today's Stressful Child

We live in a fast-paced, hectic, acquisitive society. Never before have we had words such as "Yuppie" in our everyday vocabulary, with its connotations of self-centered, materialistic behavior. We live in a "me" generation. The family is frequently undermined by the need for two-parent incomes or divorce. Not only do we seldom stop to smell the roses, but we scarcely take time to even notice them.

With that as background, it comes as no surprise that stress levels in society have never been higher. And to make it even worse, there appears to be a distinct personality type literally programmed to self-destruct.

Several years ago Drs. Meyer Friedman and Ray Rosenman coined the phrase "Type A personality" to describe the person who is rushed, aggressive, competitive, and achievement or goal oriented. These people never have enough time to get through the impossible list of tasks they set for themselves. They never take satisfaction in their efforts, continually seeking greater challenges in a carrot-on-a-stick manner. They exhibit what's been called a "free-floating hostility," or anger, that comes to the surface whether in traffic jams or in family settings.

This syndrome of traits has also been called the coronary-prone behavior pattern. Individuals exhibiting certain characteristics have been shown to be at far greater risk of coronary heart disease, heart attack, and death.

There's little question in most authorities' minds that the Type

A personality is a major risk factor in heart disease. And we're learning that such behavior patterns, just like elevated cholesterol levels, begin early in childhood and continue throughout life.

The link between the Type A personality and heart disease has to do with stress. Stress does part of its damage by actually elevating blood cholesterol levels.

A classic study was performed with accountants two weeks before and two weeks after the April 15 deadline for filing tax returns. Anyone who's ever filled out a tax form can relate to the pressures experienced by accountants during that time of year. Researchers found that the accountants' cholesterol levels were greatly elevated before the filing deadline. Those levels dropped after the deadline passed. No question about it; stress elevates cholesterol levels.

But while stress may be a temporary thing related to a current situation or dilemma, for the Type A personality stress is unrelenting. The Type A person perceives stress where there need be none, and has little ability to cope. So cholesterol levels remain high, lining the arteries with occluding plaque buildup.

But the problem isn't just limited to adults. Scientists involved in the Bogalusa Study looked at the lipid profiles of children 10 to 17 years of age. Some of the kids tested out to be Type A personalities, and others were classified as Type B personalities (free of most of the characteristics we've been discussing). Sure enough, the Type A kids had about 10 mg/dl higher readings than their Type B counterparts—a significant difference.

Personality type has also been linked to high blood pressure. Remember that high blood pressure, like cholesterol levels, tends to "track" throughout childhood and on into adulthood. And the Type A personality trait grows and grows in intensity. As it does, the blood pressure keeps going up, creating another major heart disease risk factor.

And there's more. Dr. Friedman reports that Type A behavior may not only elevate the plasma cholesterol, triglycerides, and a number of vital chemical reactions in the body, but may also enhance the clotting of blood and the sludging (thickening) of red blood cells. What does that mean? A heart attack may occur when a clot forms in the blood and is unable to pass through the artery. The more occluded the artery, the more likely the clot will block the flow of blood, and the heart then receives no life-giving oxygen. As red cells become "sludgy" they precipitate the clotting problem.

Researchers at Stanford University studied Type A children in a three-year-long effort. They surveyed 700 youngsters in grades five, seven, and nine. The more intense the Type A behavior pattern, the more common were sleep disturbances. During a three-month period, those high Type A kids suffered many more headaches, sore throats, colds, flus, and allergies than other children. Interestingly, often the high Type A youngsters—and their parents —would ignore the symptoms, perhaps because they occurred so frequently. In any case, the Type As wouldn't miss school because of those symptoms; they would just go on. And, I suppose, they would grow up to "tough it out" by going to the office and perpetuating the problem.

Although this book focuses on the distinct problem of heart disease, it's worth noting that other researchers believe the stressful Type A personality has further implications. Depending on the person and on his or her individual genetic constitution, such behavior patterns may affect the body in other ways—chiefly by attacking the weakest link in the chain. For those with an already weak heart, it might lead to a heart attack. Others might suffer from respiratory ailments or gastrointestinal diseases.

Perhaps the most frightening manifestation of stress in children and adolescents is seen in our nation's newest immigrants, the Asians. We hear a lot about how the Vietnamese, Japanese, and other Orientals coming to this country quickly adapt and go well beyond survival to all-out success. Children who arrive on our soil unable to speak a word of English are within a short time winning spelling bees, receiving awards in science fairs, and earning scholarships to prestigious institutions of higher learning. But there's a price that's paid.

Those children feel tremendous pressures at home to succeed. It's a matter of family prestige and honor. When the child cannot live up to family standards and expectations, the result can be disastrous. The suicide rate of these sad children escalates each year. And those who do survive have compromised their immune systems and their total health.

Regardless of race, children under stress and developing the Type A behavior patterns simply are unhappy. By the very definition of the syndrome, they can't enjoy accomplishment for the simple reason that before the first task is even completed another is self-assigned—a better grade, a higher score, a more prestigious award, greater recognition. Sometimes they can't please their parents, and soon they lose the ability to please themselves.

After years of intensifying these behavior traits, it's no surprise that many Type A men and women find it hard, if not impossible, to change even after experiencing a heart attack. After returning from the hospital, many coronary victims exhibit a new kind of anger: their bodies have let them down, their expectations of themselves have been dashed. Yet Dr. Friedman has been able to recondition the thinking processes of many such men and women through his rehabilitation efforts in San Francisco.

I think it's much better not to wait until it's almost too late. I've started to work with both Ross and Jenny so they'll be a bit more "mellow," and you may well want to do the same with your kids. Ross definitely exhibits some of those Type A traits. Perhaps it is genetic; we'll discuss that a bit later.

But what are the characteristics that define the coronary-prone individual? And what can we do to change them?

Most of the research in this area has concentrated on middle-aged men, since they were the first to be identified as a group at risk. Looking at some of those characteristics can give us insights into our own children. And perhaps we can see a bit of ourselves which we as role models reflect on our kids.

Dr. Friedman identifies two components as diagnostic indicators of Type A behavior. The first is time-urgency. Some of the physical characteristics displayed by time-driven people are tautness in their facial muscles, expressing tension and anxiety; rapid horizontal eye movements, which occur during ordinary conversation; and jiggling knees and finger tapping. You'll notice rapid eye blinking. Speech patterns tend to be choppy and rapid, as though they can't get their words out fast enough. In some cases the tongue clicks in contact with front teeth as the person speaks.

When interviewed by professionals administering behavioral tests, the Type A personality will interrupt a question with the answer when the question seems too long; there is no time to waste. Haven't you noticed that behavior in friends (or perhaps a spouse—or perhaps yourself)? It's hard to get a word in edgewise when speaking with a Type A person.

The Type A individual will often report doing at least two things at once. He or she rarely gives undivided attention to anything or any person, because his or her mind is racing along on many tracks. Everything—eating, working, even playing—is done fast and efficiently to a fault. The Type A person must always be on time. He or she finds it difficult to simply sit and relax. And even when friends and relatives tell such a person to "slow down," it's still full speed ahead.

The second component of Dr. Friedman's classification is hostility. Once again, we see the set facial muscles often distorted into a grimace or belligerent expression. The hostile person may have one or more facial tics. Laughter can often be aggressive in tone. Such individuals resort to clenching fists and pounding tables to make their points clear. The Type A person may threaten violence vocally or may use obscenities. Spouses often complain of verbal abuse, of insults and demeaning statements. And, if asked even months afterward about a situation that angered the person, the Type A individual will dredge up his or her rage. When interviewed, the Type A personality becomes hostile if challenged. He or she will state opinions about various subjects as absolutes, with an "I dare you to differ" attitude.

This hostile personality become easily aroused when kept waiting. Traffic poses a particular problem, as does waiting in a supermarket checkout lane or at an airport. Such individuals express distrust of others, find flaws in peers and associates, and openly disdain altruism. The Type A plays to win, at practically any cost, whether in a game or at work. He or she won't even let kids win, not even once in a while.

Does this sound like a nice person? Even the most extreme Type A personality is actually proud of this behavior. That's what's gotten him or her along so far in life, it's claimed. That's the basis for success.

Nonsense. The Type A personality often is far *less* efficient than others. He or she is unable to delegate authority, for example, and unable to take a moment to fairly assess a situation before acting. The Type A is unable to work effectively with others, and unable to chart realistic goals and expectations.

I've gone into some detail describing the Type A personality to help you recognize these traits in your children, adolescents, or perhaps in yourself or your spouse. Let's look, now, at ways of measuring the Type A behavior pattern in children. We'll see the same kind of competitiveness, impatience, anger, and aggression. It's scary.

One of the principal workers in this area has been Dr. Karen Matthews of the University of Pittsburgh. She started out by developing a diagnostic tool, a questionnaire to be filled out by teachers working with children. Ask yourself some of these questions about your own children:

1. When the child plays, is he/she competitive?
2. Does the child work quickly and energetically rather than slowly and deliberately?
3. Does the child become impatient when having to wait for others?
4. Does the child always or almost always do things in a hurry?
5. Does it take much to make the child angry?
6. Does the child interrupt others to a greater extent than expected for the age group?
7. Is the child a leader in various activities?
8. Does the child easily become irritated?
9. Does the child perform better when competing with others?
10. Does the child like to argue or debate?
11. Is the child patient when playing with others who are slower?
12. When working or playing, does the child always try to do better than others?
13. Can the child sit still for extended periods?
14. Is it more important for the child to win than to have fun at games or in school?
15. Does the child tend to get into fights?

I could add other questions to Dr. Matthews' list: Does the child truly take satisfaction in achievements? Is victory over others flaunted? Does the child take a few moments to reflect on the achievement, or does he or she immediately go off to another task or challenge? Is there ever a sense of serenity and contentment at "a job well done"?

The next step in Dr. Matthews' study was to correlate the answers to her questionnaire with observed behavior. Children were placed into a room where they were asked to trace a star on paper. The tracing assignments grew increasingly difficult, and the children exhibiting Type A behavior were more likely to become irritated. Next the researchers played a car-race game with the children, hand pushing a toy car along a track drawn on the floor with a piece of tape. The researchers didn't try too hard to push their cars fast. Type A children tended to "beat" the researchers more dramatically, by greater margins, than Type B youngsters.

Finally, children were given the opportunity to choose from and to play with a number of toys. There were puzzles, cars, coloring books, and a plastic punching-bag doll. You guessed it. The Type A kids headed straight for the doll. They punched it, kicked it, yelled at it. The play was purely aggressive.

Which toys would your children play with? Oh, of course it's just fine to play with the punching-bag doll now and then. But would the choice *always* come down to the opportunity to beat and punish the doll? Can you start to see how such children are developing traits that can lead to lives of illness, disease, and unhappiness?

Now let's look at some of the work done with adolescents. By the time children are in their teens, they exhibit traits similar to those of adults. Reporting her work in the journal *Psychosomatic Medicine,* Dr. Judith Siegel explained how the types of questions asked of those aged 13 to 18 were geared to content of replies rather than to facial expressions. In other words, adults may say one thing while their facial expressions reveal another attitude. Younger people are rather more honest in their answers, and thus the content of their answers is sufficient. The questions asked also eliminated situations that were unlikely to be encountered by younger persons.

In adult studies, two factors seem to predict actual heart disease: competitive drive and impatience. Those traits can also be seen in adolescents. Does the adolescent show hostility and irritation in response to frustration? Does he or she try to hold in emotions? Is anger a frequent emotion? Does he or she cry when frustrated? When waiting in lines, is the adolescent impatient?

Research has also shown that college students are especially sensitive to threats of loss of control. Does the young man or woman prefer to work alone? This may show a strong need to remain in total control over a situation. Is he or she unlikely to remain at home or in bed when feeling ill? Again, the loss of control owing to being bedridden comes to light. Such behavior patterns continue on into adulthood, as men and women refuse to take vacations, take large workloads home with them each night from the office, work on weekends and holidays, and are unable to delegate authority. They do it all themselves, frequently saying that no one else can handle it, while all the while stating frustration with being unable to get it all done.

Adolescents also begin to display indications of what has been called "hurry sickness." Does the adolescent do everything as fast as possible, instead of in a relaxed manner? Do you notice that his or her mind wanders when you speak about something? Is there a tendency to "bite off more than can be chewed"?

You'll notice that there are distinct similarities to the characteristics of the Type A behavior for adults, adolescents, and younger children. Anger, hostility, impatience, a sense of frustration, hurry, and competitiveness mark those destined to develop a major risk factor for heart disease.

What causes Type A behavior? One major question that remains only partially answered is whether the behavior is part of one's genetic endowment or the influence of environment.

Dr. Karen Matthews reported that there are distinct resemblances in Type A behavior between twins and their parents. Testing for a number of typical traits, she found a genetic component for the hard-driving, competitive aspect of this pattern. Twins with identical gene patterns exhibit similar behavior patterns—far more so than ordinary siblings, thus negating some influence from environment.

Dr. Matthews also looked at the environmental issue. She and her colleagues observed mothers assisting their sons on three tasks designed to elicit child-rearing practices. The mothers of Type A children gave their children fewer positive evaluations following the tasks than did the mothers of Type B children. And Type A children were pushed to try harder more often than Type B children.

Evaluating such research becomes a matter of "the chicken or the egg." Do mothers push Type A children because they feel those kids are more likely to be achievers? Or do the children's behaviors modify their parents' attitudes?

The actual environment also seems to play a role in the development of the Type A behavior. When students from rural and suburban schools were tested, rural students felt less time-urgency, although they were no less competitive or achievement oriented than suburban children. Why?

The researchers speculated that the rural students are working in a particularly well-defined arena, with definite and attainable goals. They are, for example, more likely to follow in the footsteps of their parents, and thus they don't have to give too much thought to the future. On the other hand, suburban students have goals that are more open ended and whose attainment is more uncertain.

Dr. Meyer Friedman brings up an even more visceral, thought-provoking concept: the relation between heart disease and what he calls unconditional love. The pioneer in Type A behavior research finds that heart attack patients found to exhibit hostile, hurried traits lacked a 100-percent commitment of love from parents. He defines unconditional love as that which is given freely, without strings. It's not earned in any way.

Thus a hug from a parent and a fervent statement of love for "no good reason" is more nurturing than a hug given for achievement of some task. Not that we shouldn't praise our children's accomplishments. Rather, let's all try to love our kids completely, even when they're not doing something brilliant.

Dr. Friedman believes this is dramatically true for girls. When they don't receive that unconditional love from their fathers, they become overly competitive and driven to achieve goals which they believe, unconsciously, will please those parents and thus "earn" their love.

Perhaps by this time you have some distinct misgivings about all of this. You might have been saying all along that without drive and competitive spirit your child won't be able to accomplish career goals. How can she excel? How can he go on to college?

Certainly those concerns are valid. Like most fathers I want my children to "succeed" in life. It will be terrific if they both go to college and have wonderful, fulfilling careers. But it's very possible to be both successful and happy. In fact, being happy is no doubt more important. And, yes, the Type B person, or the "modified" Type A, *can* also go on to greatness. In fact, such an individual might even have an easier time doing so.

To make my point, let me draw an absurd comparison. Let's say, just for the sake of discussion, that your Type A child wants to be a neurosurgeon, lawyer, architect, and actor. Not one of those careers, but all of them. We might as well throw in major league baseball player for good measure. What are the chances of success? Practically zero. Yet that is precisely the kind of expectation the Type A personality tends to have: to do far more than humanly possible. The first step toward healthful behavior, then, is to start being able to define clear and attainable goals.

Zeroing in a bit closer and still using this silly analogy, let's say your child now wants only to be a baseball player. But he wants to play all the positions—not pitcher or fielder or catcher, but all the positions. Impossible you say? He has to be one of the team? Exactly. So, learning early on how to work with others is important.

But silly examples aside, the bottom line of success is happiness. Yet so many driven, competitive, hostile Type A men and women attain financial and professional success without ever being happy. There's always another rung on the ladder to climb. They're never content. And, as we've discussed, these behavior patterns may well contribute to heart disease and even premature death. So what can we do to direct our children toward a more peaceful, contented way of life?

The first step is to become a good role model. When you are in the car with your kids, do they hear you yell and swear at other motorists? Do you become impatient at a red light? Do you get upset that you'll be a few minutes late for an appointment because of the traffic? Your kids are learning your Type A behavior.

Granted, it's not easy to change. The traffic where I live is notorious for snarls and congestion. But I've beaten it. I don't let it get me angry any longer. I simply leave a few minutes earlier than I'd have to if there were no traffic. If I'm alone, I bring along a magazine to read if I arrive a few minutes early. If I'm with the kids, I have a bit of extra time with them to shop or chat.

While waiting in supermarket lines, I've been working with the kids to show how it's really not so bad to have a moment to oneself. It gives one a bit of time to think or just plain mentally relax.

As a parent, take a few moments to think of the times in your life when you get irritated, upset, hostile, angry—all those terms for the behavior of the Type A personality. Do it right now; there's no sense in putting it off. Now what can you do about those things?

Next, what are you doing to relax so that you're not constantly in a state of stress? Do you ever have a quiet moment? Your children will notice if you never take time off from your work or if you're constantly upset and stressed.

By all means, the place to start is with yourself. Then take a look—a close look—at your children. Do so in a calm, objective manner as though you were studying someone else's kids. Do you see some of the traits we've been talking about? Does your 4-year-old easily get frustrated with a toy? Has your 7-year-old been crying in anger because of arguments with friends? Is your 14-year-old getting upset about exams to the point of having stomachaches? It's time to do something about it.

Happily, one way to eliminate this risk factor is the same as that for another: exercise helps tremendously to ease the stresses and anxieties of life. Why not make a decision to be an active family? Whatever you choose, the best activity is the one you can stick with on a regular basis.

How about spending other family times together? When was the last time your family went on a picnic? Or picked up the newspaper to see what's happening around town and made some plans? If you wait until you "have time," you'll never get around to it. You have to make time. Get tickets to see the circus, or choose a day to go to the zoo. How about a weekend at the beach or in the woods? It doesn't have to be expensive.

Does your son belong to the Cub Scouts or Boy Scouts? Is there a troop in the neighborhood? How about Brownies or Girl Scouts for your daughter? Do it together. Become involved with their activities.

The Mormons have a wonderful tradition, actually a part of their religion, called family night. One evening a week is designated as such, and it is spent playing musical instruments, games, and charades or doing various arts and crafts. How about a family night for your family? Don't just announce it out of the blue. Talk it over and plan it; say that next Monday evening you'll all spend some time together—not watching TV! Plan some activities.

There's also a place for some quiet time in your family. The child who sees his or her parents truly contented in the evening as they read books is more likely to develop into an adult who doesn't need constant frenzy for stimulus. If you have a hobby, share it with your kids. Maybe your child would like to build a model airplane or ship with you. That's a nice way to learn not to get frustrated when the parts don't fit just as nicely as you'd like. Or maybe your child would enjoy learning to crochet with you.

Next, consider the role of spirituality in your family. Even if you are not a religious person and find it impossible to place your faith in a deity, you can talk with your children about values on a higher plane. Values must be learned early, and having a spiritual outlook can help the individual place everyday frustrations and stresses in perspective.

Begin with the most simple of concepts: the Golden Rule. That's certainly the opposite end of the spectrum—the Type A mentality would define it as "doing unto others before they have a chance to do unto you." As you talk with your children about such matters, you just might find that you, too, have become more relaxed.

Start to develop a good sense of communication within the family. Find out what's happening in your children's lives and how you might be able to help. Start when they're little, and you'll be well rewarded as they grow into open, responsive adolescents.

There's a bumper sticker that reads "Have you hugged your kid today?" There's no such thing as too many hugs and kisses. Children thrive on affection. They need it to grow and develop into happy adults. And, with what we now know about Type A behavior, they need it to be healthy as well. Some families find hugging hard to do, depending on traditions going back for generations. But everyone can make a conscious effort to bestow those hugs and kisses more generously.

Go up to your children and give them a big hug and kiss, saying vehemently that you love them. If they are surprised by that, you know you haven't been doing it enough! Hugs and kisses should be a routine part of every day. Nobody outgrows the need for them. Not even you.

Pick some peculiar times for those hugs and kisses—like after a Little League baseball game, when your son has struck out every time at bat and his team has lost. Or when your daughter has messed up the bathroom while playing "dress up" with her friends.

Instead of getting mad at your child for a grade that's lower than you expect at school, try giving a hug and a kiss. "What's that for?" he or she might ask. "Because I love you and I know you're trying your best." Or, "Because I love you and I know you'll try your best next time."

Many physicians I've known over the years have testified to the value of the laying on of hands in the practice of medicine. It provides a sense of comfort and protection. Even the oldest patients welcome a touch. Your children deserve all the hugs and kisses you can give them.

In my family we have found a way of coping with stress that helps us a great deal. It started as my perfect, never-fail cure for hiccups. A lot of people laugh when I first tell them about it, but then they quickly become converts. And my latest convert is my son, Ross. One evening he got the hiccups after dinner, when we had some company over to the house. A few people in the group had previously experienced my renowned cure, and chuckled when I suggested that Ross try it. My brother Tom, for whom the cure has worked beautifully in the past, didn't think it would work for a little kid.

I took Ross into his darkened bedroom, left the lights off, and closed the door behind us. Ross was hiccuping wildly by this time, but was intrigued by the attention and the promise of something out of the ordinary. I instructed him to squat down on the floor in a cross-legged position.

Then, in a very slow and calm voice I coached him in deep breathing, yoga-style. "Close your eyes," I told him. "Relax. Put your hands gently on top of your thighs. Now breathe deeply, taking in as much air as possible until your lungs can't hold any more. Hold your breath and slowly, very slowly, let the air out. As you inhale, feel your body fill with air such that your back goes upright and your shoulders are thrown slightly back in an arch. Now again slowly, very slowly release the breath. And when you think all the air is out, blow three times through your mouth to clear out that little tiny bit left. Repeat the procedure several times," I said. Each time, I spoke of how the air was filling his chest and how much it was like a balloon, filled to capacity and then completely empty. Then, without any previous indication that it was true, I said, "Ross your hiccups are gone." And, sure enough, they were.

Now what does a cure for hiccups have to do with preventing future heart disease? The answer to that lies with Ross's comments after the cure was revealed to him. He wasn't so surprised that the hiccups were gone; he had expected that. But the added benefit was totally unexpected. Ross's eyes widened. He smiled broadly and said, "Wow, I feel terrific! Like I just woke up from a nap. I feel all relaxed! Can we do that again?"

The notion of deep breathing as a means of relaxation is an ancient concept. It goes back hundreds of years in a number of cultures, the most famous being the Hindus with their yoga and breathing exercises. It's the basis of all meditation programs, and meditation is now recommended by psychologists, physicians, nurses, and other health professionals who have seen the benefits for their patients.

And it really works. If you're starting to mutter that this is just too much for you to even think about doing in your family, let me say that I'm far from a "hippie," sitting around with incense and candles burning. Try to relax this way just once, and you'll see the tremendous value that deep breathing offers.

Of course there might be a bit of giggling when you first suggest it. But don't cave in. Just as you say to your kids that you want them to taste something at the table to see if they like it, suggest that they give this activity one try.

Take the phone off the hook. Turn off the TV and radio. Darken the room to a soft glow. Sit on the floor and go through a session as the leader. Here's a sample "script" you might want to follow in your own words:

> *Close your eyes and keep your back straight. Put your hands on your thighs, with palms up. Feel your neck become limp as your head rolls forward.*
>
> *Take a deep breath, drawing air in through your nostrils. When your lungs are full, take just a bit more air. Now hold the air inside and keep your back straight. Hold it. Hold it.*
>
> *Now release the air slowly through your mouth. As the air escapes, feel your shoulders go forward and your back slump. When you feel that all the air is gone from your lungs, push three more times to expel the little bit of air left in.*
>
> *Slowly, now, take the air back into your lungs and feel your back straighten. Drink in all the air you can.*
>
> *Continue to breathe in slowly. Hold it, then let all the air out. As you concentrate on your breathing, picture yourself walking along the beach. The waves are gently washing up on shore. The water is warm, and you step into the water and walk along as the water splashes around your ankles. . . .*

With a bit of practice, you'll come to enjoy these relaxing moments together. Concentrate on breathing and "guide" the others through mental images of other pleasant surroundings, such as walking through the woods, watching a snowfall on a bright winter evening, sitting in front of a fireplace as the embers glow and the logs crackle.

Your sessions of breathing and relaxing should be somewhat regular. But you may also wish to rely on such sessions when things get a bit tense for one reason or another, either for one or all of you.

As time goes on, have the children become the "leaders" who guide the family group through the breathing and guided imagery.

You'll be surprised at how well even the smallest child can do the job. And you'll be readying your children to do such breathing on their own.

In our family those breathing sessions now take place on a fairly regular basis. And Jenny also has come to enjoy these little "mini-vacations." When we've been under a bit of pressure, when emotions run high, that's the time to say, "let's do a little breathing, shall we?"

Whether you are concerned about heart disease or not, it's always nice to have a safe, effective, convenient way to relax. It sure beats taking Valium! I hope Ross and Jenny will continue to do their breathing for many years to come. And the nicest thing is having Ross or Jenny remind *me* now and then to do some deep breathing. We *all* benefit.

By heeding the old saying, "Take time to stop and smell the roses," you and your children can reduce or even eliminate one of the major heart-disease risk factors.

8

Fighting the Other Factors

Many factors contribute to the future development of heart disease. As important as it is, cholesterol levels in the blood represent just one of those factors. Other risks include smoking, high blood pressure, stress and behavior, obesity, physical inactivity, increased age, sex, and genetic history. Much of this book deals with diet and cholesterol because the issue has a number of ramifications. Two of the risk factors we haven't yet discussed are smoking and high blood pressure, both of which play significant roles in heart disease. Yet both can be controlled. In the case of smoking, the risk can—and should—be completely eliminated.

The statistics on smoking are more than a little scary. Recent figures indicated that 350,000 people in the United States die each year as a direct result of the habit. That's a higher death toll than claimed by alcohol, illegal drugs, traffic accidents, suicide, and homicide combined.

Of course, smoking has a direct cause-and-effect relationship with lung cancer and emphysema. And every coach can tell you what it does to endurance on the athletic field. Those factors are reason enough for adults to stop the habit and for parents to discourage it in their offspring. But what about the relationship between smoking and heart disease?

Simply stated, cigarette smoking increases the risk of heart disease by five times. When you combine the risk factors of elevated cholesterol levels with cigarette smoking, the dangers escalate dramatically. And there appears to be a link between them. Dr. Charles Glueck worked with nearly 1,000 children aged 12 to 19. His findings were straightforward: smokers had average "good"

HDL levels 6.1 mg lower and average "bad" LDL levels 4.1 mg higher than comparable nonsmokers. Think of what those numbers mean in terms of the risk ratio between total cholesterol and HDL!

As you've learned, "bad" LDL cholesterol tends to deposit in the arteries, while "good" HDL cholesterol remains circulating in the blood, offering a protective effect. The result of the clogging process, of course, is a gradually diminished interior diameter of the arteries. Little by little the lumen of the artery gets smaller, allowing less and less blood to pass through. Eventually that lumen is so small that a blood clot can shut down the flow entirely, and the person experiences a heart attack.

And cigarette smoking has been shown to have yet another direct effect on the size of the artery's diameter. Obviously, the larger the lumen the better the blood keeps flowing. In a study at Johns Hopkins University, researchers looked at thirty-one men aged 20 to 66. None of the men had any sign of coronary artery disease. Of the thirty-one men, nine had never smoked. The coronary arteries of the nonsmokers were, on average, 61 percent larger in cross-sectional area than the arteries of the twenty-two men who were current or former smokers.

The implications are obvious. While it's terrific to stop smoking, it's far better never to have smoked.

But the disturbing fact is that more teens are smoking every year. Of the more than 54 million smokers in this country, over 3 million are teenagers. And for the first time in history, more girls are smoking than boys. Sadly, as more adults are quitting the habit, children are starting.

The reasons kids pick up the first cigarette haven't changed over the years. They begin to experience peer pressure to start smoking somewhere between ages 12 and 14. And at that age it's a lot harder to say no to friends than to parents. It's also a time in life when adolescents feel the need to rebel. What could be more rebellious than "outlaw" smoking? And, of course, teens feel immortal.

Teens who smoke are most likely to have friends who smoke. And it's probable that they come from families who smoke. In a very real way, these kids are practically programmed to start the habit. Parents smoke in front of them from infancy. Like father, like son. There's no social stigma—at least not until recently. And advertising continues to portray a glamorous image of the smoker.

The actors in those ads are seldom old and feeble—and they never appear to be wheezing and coughing.

If you, as a parent, still smoke, it's time to quit. Do whatever it takes. Go to a clinic, get hypnotized, try gum substitutes—anything. It can be done. Even my wife did it, and I thought she never would. Both my kids and I complained for years. She was even limited to smoking in just one room in the house—actually a room somewhat separated from the rest of the house. But she wouldn't or couldn't quit.

Then one summer I took the kids for a week at a lake in the mountains. My wife isn't an outdoors person and prefers to stay home and read. For months, she now tells me, she had planned that during that week, while we were all out of her hair, she would quit. She'd even told some of the other teachers she works with.

And it worked! She spent the week keeping herself busy with one thing or another, going to read at the library where smoking wasn't permitted and doing anything she could to keep her mind off the cigarettes. Was it difficult? Of course. Does she still miss them? Yes, now and then. But the urge to smoke lessens in both frequency and intensity as time goes on.

One year later, when the kids and I returned from a repeat jaunt to the lake, the three of us toasted Dawn's twelve-month success rate. We're all very happy to live in a smoke-free house.

Studies have shown that children living in homes with smokers experience more lung illnesses than kids with parents who don't smoke. Coughing parents spew their germs into the air. And kids are forced to breathe the second-hand smoke. Isn't it time to make your house smoke free?

If you're not quite ready to give up the cigarettes, at least don't smoke in the house or in the car with your children. In fact, you might even make an announcement that you won't smoke at home and that you won't allow anyone else to do so, either. Isn't that hypocritical, you might ask? It's both a very honest statement of love for your children and an admission of your inability to quit. Admitting your addiction can be an educational experience for your youngsters.

There are some parents who allow their children to smoke in the home. They say that they know they'll smoke anyway, so this is a more honest approach. Nonsense. Say no to smoking in the house. Admit that you know they'll smoke outside the house even though you'd prefer they didn't. But don't give *any* kind of approval.

Anything you can do to help your kids to quit the habit or to make sure they never start is just fine. Bribe them if necessary. Make it a wager, perhaps.

A man I know tells the story of how he smoked as a teen. His dad saw him one day, and bet him that he couldn't quit smoking and not smoke until he was 21. The bet was for $100 many years ago—money worth working for. And it worked. He never smoked another day in his life.

This is a matter of life and death. Talk to your kids about it. Reinforce what they're learning at school. Do everything and anything you can to push this insidious, life-threatening habit out of your family.

The same goes for "smokeless" tobacco such as snuff or chewing tobacco. This is a brand-new problem that's been springing up around the country. Teens view athletes who use such tobacco products as role models, and feel that no health hazard exists. A well-publicized case showed the error of such thinking when a very nice-looking, snuff-using boy developed facial cancer which first disfigured him, then took his life. Of course, that story can't be in the newspapers and on TV every day. But the images of "chawin'" baseball players can be. And the dangers go beyond cancer. As with smoking, smokeless tobacco releases nicotine into the bloodstream. This, in turn, has serious long-term effects on heart disease development.

Like many others, I find it appalling that our nation can spend millions of dollars on research and health care, and other millions subsidizing an agricultural crop that kills 350,000 citizens yearly. If you feel the same way, write a letter to your congressperson. In fact, talk with your children about it. Sign the letter together. Perhaps they could even do a school project on the subject. They would then be taking a leadership role, and thus reinforcing their own resolve not to smoke.

A far less obvious heart-disease risk factor is that of high blood pressure, also termed hypertension. As was the case with cholesterol levels in the blood, blood pressure levels were seen to "track" in the studies done in Bogalusa, Louisiana. Kids with normal blood pressure levels were normal year after year, while those with elevated readings continued to show higher pressures.

Hypertension appears to be a hereditary disease, but there is much that can be done to control it, even with children. First, there's a major relationship between high blood pressure and obesity. As hypertensive individuals lose weight, the blood pressure level goes down. Second, those who become involved in regular programs of physical exercise also experience improvement in blood pressure levels.

The third factor is that which we've heard so often: overuse of the salt shaker. There now appears to be no doubt that large amounts of sodium in the diet have the potential of developing the disorder in those predisposed to it. That is to say, people who have the genetic trait will develop hypertension faster and more seriously if they consume a lot of salt and other sodium-containing foods.

How many people does this affect? Some estimates are that as few as 10 percent of the population is influenced by sodium intake; others maintain it to be somewhat higher. In either case, the number is certainly smaller than those whose fatty diets are reflected in terms of high cholesterol levels, though the implications are significant.

In Japan, people who consume large amounts of sodium in their diet exhibit a far greater incidence of hypertension. While the Japanese diet is traditionally low in fat, it is often high in salt.

As with all health-care matters, the place to start control of blood pressure is in your doctor's office. Your pediatrician or family practitioner will know what your child's blood pressure should be. Explain that you're interested in knowing the actual numbers and how they relate to the total population.

If the doctor tells you your child's blood pressure is higher than average for his or her age and sex, this is the time to start doing something about it. Remember that the condition "tracks" through life. It won't go away. And there are no symptoms. That's why hypertension is referred to as the silent killer.

Especially if your son or daughter has the beginnings of hypertension, it's best to start limiting the use of salt and salty foods, as well as those containing other forms of sodium. And even if the blood pressure is currently normal, there's no reason not to at least cut back on the amount of those foods.

How much is enough and how much is too much? Everyone needs a certain amount of sodium; it's one of the essential electrolytes in our bodies. The mineral plays an important role in regulating body fluids and, as we've noted, has an effect on blood pressure. But it's pretty hard to have a sodium "deficiency." Virtually all foods available to us in the average diet contain some amount of sodium. But just the amount occurring naturally in dairy foods would be sufficient for our needs.

The Food and Nutrition Board of the National Academy of Sciences's National Research Council estimates that an "adequate and safe" intake of sodium for healthy adults is 1,100 to 3,300 milligrams a day. That's the amount found in one-half to one-and-a-half teaspoons of salt. But most of us consume more than twice that amount—anywhere between 2,300 and 6,900 milligrams a day is a more common range.

That's why virtually all health authorities have recommended some moderation in sodium intake. Most people can consume salt and other forms of sodium without a problem. Sodium in itself does not *cause* hypertension; rather, it contributes to its development in those who have the predisposition.

The taste for salt is one of the four basic tastes: sweet, sour, bitter, and salty. Some tastes come naturally—such as that for sugar—and others are acquired—such as that for bitterness. Salt is somewhere in between. While some children show a preference for salty foods almost from the beginning, there's no doubt that we learn to enjoy salt more and more as we grow. And the more we eat, the more we want.

Interestingly, as we cut back on salt consumption, the threshold of taste decreases. That is, as we eat less salt, we find smaller amounts increasingly satisfying. People who have drastically cut back on salt discover that after just a short time they find previously bland foods to be salty.

The place to start conditioning the child's palate, and thus helping to protect against a potential risk factor for heart disease, is at the table. After a while no one will notice that the salt shaker is no longer on the table. Then you can gradually cut back on the amount of salt you use in cooking. You'll notice that in many recipes the use of salt is optional; look at the directions for making hot cereals, spaghetti, noodles, and the like.

As with all your dietary manipulations for the family, don't get carried away with this one. Easy does it. Don't instigate family mutiny against the whole program by suddenly and drastically changing the way food tastes.

Is it necessary to start buying no-sodium, no-salt, or salt-restricted foods? That really depends on your own family's condition. And you should, by all means, talk with your doctor about it. To tell a child he or she can't have a pickle, right after denying him or her bacon and eggs, may be overdoing it. If, on the other hand, your family has the tendency toward hypertension, there are an increasing number of foods prepared commercially with you in mind. And to get a better idea as to the quantity of sodium in commonly eaten foods, take a look at the table in Chapter 20.

Cutting back on sodium, in any case, does not completely eliminate the threat of high blood pressure. But combined with weight control and increased physical exercise, it can help a great deal. Being aware of the potential for this disease is the most important aspect of your involvement at this time. That way you can regularly—annually—keep track of your child's progress. He or she can be made aware at the appropriate time, so as to assume self-responsibility later on.

The influence you have now on your children's health is similar to other influences you have on their lives. Just as you warn them about talking to strangers, start early to warn them about the dangers of smoking. And just as you instruct them to be careful when crossing streets, teach them about healthful eating habits.

All these things are done out of love. And by fighting all the risk factors possible, you greatly improve your child's odds of having a long and happy life. That's a nice legacy to bequeath.

9
Talking with Your Kids

When I first learned that Ross's cholesterol level was higher than it should be, I mentioned it at a dinner my wife and I were hosting for some friends. They asked what I planned to do about it, and my first response was that I'd speak with Ross.

There was a very interesting reaction. Virtually everyone at the table said there was no reason to "scare" a child with the information. They said they'd prefer to simply make changes in the family diet without comment.

I was appalled. Especially since one of my guests was a nurse. I pointed out that kids with conditions such as diabetes are carefully instructed and are encouraged to take an active role in their own care. Other kids have other kinds of restrictions and they, also, are given reasons for such restrictions.

Should a parent talk with a child about cholesterol? I don't think there's any question about it. Should "scare" tactics be used? Of course not.

Let's think about some parallel situations. Should a parent tell a child not to get into a car with a stranger? Of course. But there's no need to provide graphic examples of children who did so and were abused, mutilated, and killed.

In terms of personal hygiene, we teach children to wash hands before dinner, to brush and floss teeth regularly, and so on. But, again, there's no need to frighten the kids. You don't tell them about the hordes of germs waiting to infect them with every disease known to man. You don't describe the horrors of dental abscesses, periodontal disease and surgery, or the excruciating pains that could be inflicted by Doctor Agony the Dentist. Do you? Of course not.

In my household, health has become a way of life. So let's make some comparisons here. From a very early age, children in religious homes learn about God, about the church the family attends, and about its doctrines. The parents feel that it's never too young to begin religious instruction and to carry that throughout daily family life. But most of these parents stress the positive aspects of religion: the love of God, the benefits of following the Golden Rule, the ultimate goal of one's eternal reward. Regardless of creed, the positives prevail. Few parents (I hope and pray) raise children in an atmosphere of fear of eternal hellfire and damnation.

Similarly, positive aspects of health must be stressed. The issue of diet, cholesterol, and heart disease can certainly be discussed with even very little children. The youngest kid knows that he or she has a heart beating in his or her chest. Just as you explain that daily tooth brushing and flossing are important to keep teeth healthy, you can explain that good foods are important to keep the heart healthy. And even the youngest child will understand the importance of a healthy heart.

But don't rush into this or into any other such discussion about health. Years have gone by; a few more days won't hurt. Pick a time when both of you are relaxed and not pressured to do something else. View it as an opportunity to really talk. Many parents don't do that enough.

On the other hand, don't make a big production out of it, either. Don't announce your proposed "summit meeting" three weeks in advance, for example. Just ask if your son or daughter has a moment to chat. Then sit down and talk.

Explain that the doctor has told you about the blood test, and that the cholesterol level is a bit higher than it should be. Stress the notion that he or she is perfectly healthy—*there is no heart disease*. You simply want to keep it that way.

That's a very important consideration, and I cannot stress it too much. An elevated cholesterol level during childhood is merely an indicator of a developing risk factor—one of a number of risk factors that come along later in life. It does *not* indicate existing heart disease.

This is very different from other health conditions. In diabetic children, a true disease state exists. It's very important that diabetic children learn about their disease, how to use insulin, how to adjust their diets very carefully, and why it's important to follow medical recommendations to the letter. There's little margin for error. And such kids soon learn how they feel when they "go off the program." The same applies to children who have definite food sensitivities. They eat this food or that and they break out in hives, develop a fever, display allergic symptoms, or whatever.

Your child is perfectly healthy, and you simply want him or her to stay that way. At the same time, you have to understand from the very beginning that you're not going to achieve 100 percent cooperation. There isn't a kid in the world who will say, "That's it, I'll never have another pizza, ice cream, or any other food high in fat." That would make him a "Stepford Child," straight out of science fiction.

And, believe me, having that occasional pizza or ice cream won't kill your child. As time goes on, and the learning and conditioning processes continue, your child will gradually modify his or her lifestyle. Give all the love and support you can. And don't despair that all is lost when a slip takes place. That's part of growing up. For all of us.

Most kids like to be leaders, or at least try to be. In this respect, your kid can definitely be a leader, one of the avant-garde in a revolution against heart disease, with an ultimate victory of overall health. Your child should know that.

Explain that the foods you're going to serve are part of an overall plan to optimize good health now, as well as for the future. Diet has been implicated in a wide variety of illnesses besides heart disease, such as diabetes, cancer, obesity, hypertension, allergic reactions, and structural problems like osteoporosis. In each case, the recommendations are the same: a low-fat, high-carbohydrate, high-fiber diet that includes a wide variety of foods.

You'll want to explain that some foods are worse than others, and that you'll gradually begin phasing the worst ones out. Other foods are particularly healthful, and you'll gradually begin phasing them in. Stress the word *gradual*.

If your kids are currently drinking whole milk, making the change to skim milk in one day will meet with loud complaints. Make the change gradually. Start with low-fat (2 percent) milk. Let the family drink that for a month or so. Then switch to a 1 percent low-fat milk. Not all communities offer the 1 percent milk, so you may want to mix equal amounts of skim and 2 percent milk. Then after another month or so, switch to skim milk. Your kids will get all the nutrients they need, and, like my children, they'll get completely accustomed to the nonfat, skim milk.

Are there some family favorites your family simply "can't live without"? Instead of serving them, say, every week, make those treats every two weeks, then once a month, and so on. Gradually begin altering recipes to reduce their fat content. Your shopping list should reflect those gradual changes from now on.

It's also important to explain that, while certain foods won't be offered as frequently, other foods will come along to take their place. Frozen yogurt, for example, or exotic fruits.

Getting back to the business of leadership, there's no doubt that in the future many families will become more nutrition conscious. Most kids today are learning that cigarette smoking is a dumb thing to do. That certainly wasn't true thirty years ago, when I was in high school. Talk to your child about how it's just as dumb to eat foods that have been proved to increase the risk of disease as it is to smoke cigarettes which have been proved to increase the risk of disease. On a positive note, explain how a diet free of those disease-related foods is associated with the best growth and achievement of potential.

Talk about how athletes around the world are eating the same way. World-class runners, swimmers, tennis players, and other stars have already recognized the winning ways of a low-fat, high-carbohydrate diet.

Since you believe that this dietary approach is the most healthful, you'll want your entire family to follow it—yourself included. One of the best ways to sabotage your success with this endeavor is to be hypocritical about it. For many reasons, this diet is best for every member of the family, whether or not their cholesterol levels are elevated. The same goes for the exercise aspects of the program, as well as for the relaxation techniques.

Obviously your discussions will vary with the age of your children. You might encourage those in elementary school to talk about foods during show-and-tell periods. Have them bring some foods along to show how to read the nutrient label. High school students might be encouraged to participate in a science project related to diet.

In either case, explain that you'll be preparing brown-bag lunches rather than giving money for school lunches. There might be some resistance to this. Talk about favorite foods that might be included, and remind them of past complaints about "lousy food that shouldn't be served to prisoners" or long cafeteria lines.

If there's a day that a particularly enjoyable lunch is to be served, let them buy it. Remember that you're shooting for a lifelong effect, not an overnight transformation.

As children grow older, peer-group influence becomes more and more important. It's tough to say no to friends who want to go out for fast food after school or following a game. Work those problems out with your children. Suggest that they select restaurants that offer a choice between high-fat foods and more healthful alternatives. Or provide guidance as to foods lowest in fat, as shown in the table in Chapter 20.

Similarly, when the family goes out together, find places in your community that offer foods you want to consume. Instead of Häagen Dazs, try some of the frozen yogurt establishments. Set an example by ordering a pizza with half the normal amount of cheese and more of the vegetable toppings. Eventually you may be able to enjoy a pizza with your family with no cheese at all. It can be done. I do it all the time.

It's also time to start finding ways to celebrate events other than with food. Go to the theater. Enjoy a concert. Play miniature golf. Go bowling. There are lots of things to enjoy together.

On the other hand, don't fall into a frequent parental trap. Some moms and dads start feeling guilty about the "deprivation" being foisted on their kids. Health authorities have long noted this in families with diabetic children. Those kids turn into little tyrants, demanding everything and getting everything. Parents tacitly or openly voice feelings like, "I wish it were me." That's foolish, and it does children absolutely no good.

Remember that the dietary changes you're bringing into the family are in keeping with the best advice of health authorities all over the world. You're not depriving your children of anything. Rather, you're giving them a better chance for a long, healthy, and happy life. Feel no guilt. Feel proud.

Can you imagine feeling guilty about telling small children not to play in traffic? Do you feel sorry for teenagers because you tell them not to drink and drive?

Get in touch with your own feelings. You may have a few too many pounds around the middle or on the thighs. In following this lowered-fat approach, you'll easily shed those pounds. As you do, smile and tell the family about it. Be proud of that manifestation of this way of eating. Point out how it's been months (or whatever time) since you've had to take an antacid tablet for indigestion (which was caused by all the fat previously in your diet).

One of the best places to talk about all this is in the kitchen. Whether you have boys or girls, there's no reason not to start them off on the road to the independence of being able to feed themselves. And it's never too early to begin.

Both of my children make their own omelets, and they're proud of the fact. When you're teaching them how, point out that the Egg Beaters they are using is a product free of cholesterol because only the whites are included. Show them how to spray Pam on a nonstick pan, so the eggs will cook without sticking. If they're making a cheese omelet, tell them that Borden's Lite-Line has far less fat than standard slices of cheese.

Work with the kids to make all sorts of blender drinks. Fruit, nonfat yogurt, skim milk, cocoa powder, and other ingredients mixed and matched can be poured into the blender and whirled with a bit of oat bran. Talk about each of the foods. Compare notes on your latest inventions.

As I suggested earlier, take the kids with you now and then to do the grocery shopping, and have them participate in the selection process. But don't overdo it, either. We've all known former smokers and other converts who become zealots, badgering everyone and anyone in sight to make the same change. You don't want to fit into that category, do you?

When someone quits smoking, that's it. Gradually the person learns to live without the habit. There are no more packs to buy. No more ashtrays to empty. It's a black-and-white situation. Not so with food. You're changing habits, not quitting. So food remains a major part of your life, with meals and snacks planned and eaten every day. Little by little you can change, for yourself and for your children. If one meal isn't so terrific, remember that it's only one meal. There will be thousands more.

Don't make a big deal of it. Don't yell and scream. There will come a time when your children will leave home forever. They'll take with them many if not all of the values and morals you've instilled through the years. We've all heard about children raised in very strict households who react against every restriction placed on them once they're on their own. You don't want that kind of backlash.

You do want children who have been given the advantage of learning about the importance of a good diet. And who believe in that diet. It's a slow process, and it starts when you talk with your kids.

10
Children's Nutrition

The controversy regarding efforts to reduce children's blood cholesterol levels boils down to the issue of nutrition. No one really argues that heart disease begins in childhood and that cholesterol reduction is beneficial. But some pediatricians fear that parents will not feed their children properly.

In their zeal to protect their children from future illness, parents have sometimes gone too far. During the growing years youngsters need a large number of calories and nutrients. Certainly kids thrive on the standard Western diet, which is high in fat, because the foods eaten are densely packed with calories. It's no surprise that American children are larger than those in Third World countries. So when parents dramatically slash fat intake and restrict children from eating many foods, the growth rate can be jeopardized. Some children actually experience stunted growth and fail to thrive. An article in *Pediatrics* in 1987 reported the case histories of seven families in which parents greatly restricted the diets of children under the age of two. Fat was tremendously reduced as were total calories. Parents even diluted formula to reduce the fat content. Snacks were not permitted. The seven children failed to thrive, and were well under the norm for height and weight. Confronted with this, parents remained reluctant to change their children's dietary patterns; some actually needed counseling. When diets were liberalized, children quickly returned to normal growth.

But parents of such children were following rigidly restricted diets, such as that recommended by the late Nathan Pritikin. In his book, Pritikin admits that children probably will not grow to their maximum stature if raised on his diet. A diet that starts children off on a healthful path does not necessarily have to be so stringent.

Let's put that into some perspective. The typical American diet contains about 42 percent fat, in terms of total calories. The American Heart Association recommends that the entire population reduce its fat intake to about 30 percent. At the other end of the spectrum, the Pritikin diet and similar others call for deriving only 10 percent of total calories from fat. Even for adults, this level of deprivation ultimately results in a gaunt, even an emaciated appearance. For children it actually could be dangerous, in terms not only of stunted growth but also of vitamin and mineral deficiencies.

So what we're looking for is a compromise—a diet that provides the calories, protein, and other nutrients a child needs while it cuts back on *excess* fat and cholesterol.

The American Health Foundation urges a larger reduction in fat intake than does the American Heart Association—to a 20 to 25 percent level. Authorities advocating the 30 percent fat approach admit that they do so because they believe it's easier to achieve. Those in favor of greater fat reductions cite better results in terms of expected longevity and reduced risks of heart disease, cancer, obesity, diabetes, and other illnesses.

As an adult, I follow a 20 percent fat plan. It's part of a complete program that also includes water-soluble fiber to lower blood cholesterol levels and niacin supplements. I believe children should not be given such vitamin supplementation because their bodies are still developing. (Niacin, a B vitamin, is metabolized by the liver, and in children that organ is not completely developed, making it vulnerable to overloading.) For me, the program works dramatically well. As spelled out in my book *The 8-Week Cholesterol Cure,* this diet has resulted in dramatic blood cholesterol reductions for me and for thousands of others.

As a parent, I feed my children a diet that contains about 20 to 25 percent fat. I also prepare many foods with oat bran, which is rich in water-soluble fiber. It really comes down to cutting back on the number of times my kids go to fast-food restaurants, the way they eat lunch at school, and the kinds of snacks and foods they eat at home. But there's no question that my kids get all the calories and nutrients they need. They're healthy, happy, and thriving. My recommendations are not for an ascetic, deprived diet like that in a Third World country, but rather they are for a healthful, robust diet filled with the wonderful foods of our nation's bounty.

There has been so much information and misinformation about nutrition during the past few years that it's no surprise many people are confused as to what really constitutes a healthful diet. But the basics really haven't changed that much over the years, and nutritionists still recommend a wide variety of foods that provide all the nutrients a person needs for growth and maintenance. To demystify the science of nutrition and to put it into practical terms for feeding your family, let's first look at the nutrients we all need.

In a nutshell, nutrition is the process by which food and everything else we eat becomes part of our bodies and affects our health and growth. All food consists of chemicals working together, interacting with the substances in our bodies. In a very real way, then, it's foolish to refer to a food as "organic," since all foods are composed of organic chemicals. And it's just as meaningless to call one food or another "natural," since they all come from nature and, again, are all composed of chemicals.

We can broadly categorize those food chemicals as protein, carbohydrate, fat, vitamins, minerals, and water. Those are the chemicals we call nutrients. Each has its own function while working in close, often inseparable harmony with others. All together, there are about fifty specific nutrients. But that doesn't mean we need to be aware of all fifty in the foods we purchase and consume.

Over the years, nutritionists have determined that if our diets have sufficient amounts of ten so-called leader nutrients, we'll get plenty of the others. That's because certain nutrients go hand-in-hand with each other. The foods that contain the leader nutrients automatically provide us with all the other nutrients. You probably won't have any difficulty identifying those leaders, so let's look at each one in a little detail.

PROTEIN

Here's the nutrient that takes first prize in popularity. It's usually named first in importance. Yes, it's absolutely true that we need protein throughout our lives to build and maintain body tissues which are constantly being replaced; to manufacture hemoglobin in the blood so it can carry oxygen to the body's cells; to form antibodies to work in our immune system to fight off infections from invading foreign proteins such as viruses and bacteria; and to produce enzymes and hormones that regulate bodily functions. If we eat more protein than we need for those requirements, the body can use it as an energy source as well. Unlike some of the other nutrients, it cannot be stored in the body. We have to eat protein on a regular basis. But that's not a difficult task at all.

The fact is quite the opposite. Most of us in the Western World consume protein far in excess of what we really need. There are many reasons for this. Protein is one of our "favorite" nutrients; everyone is aware of it, and most people make an active effort to get it into their diet. Next, protein comes in foods that we enjoy eating; this is particularly true in affluent nations such as ours, where we can pick and choose among meats, fish, eggs, poultry, seafood, and many other foods rich in the nutrient. Actually, both animal and plant foods contain abundant protein, and it would be difficult *not* to get enough unless one were on a particularly stringent diet.

But we've developed an almost cultlike worship of protein. Coaches tell their athletes to eat more protein. Health food stores advertise protein supplements. And the food industry promotes its foods on the basis of its protein content. In fact, some authorities believe we eat too much protein. When we consume more than is needed, it is used for energy rather than body-building and tissue replacement. This is not only inefficient, but it places an additional burden on the kidneys, which have to break down the nitrogen by-products of protein metabolism. Whether or not we eat too much protein, there is no doubt we get enough.

What our children's bodies—and ours, too—require are the eight indispensable, or essential, amino acids which are the "building blocks" of protein. We can get them either together in one food or by eating a variety of foods that contribute various amino acids. When we get those eight, our bodies can construct complete profiles of the total twenty-two amino acids in our tissues.

How do we know if we're getting enough protein? As I've already stated, almost everyone in the Western World consumes far in excess of a sufficient amount of this body-building nutrient. The Recommended Dietary Allowance for protein is 45 grams. How difficult is it to get that much? An 8-ounce glass of milk has more than 8 grams. For the youngster drinking three glasses daily, that's more than half the day's requirement. A 3½-ounce serving of turkey breast has more than 28 grams. Look at the nutrition labels on the foods you buy, and you'll see that almost all your foods contribute to the day's total of protein and more.

CARBOHYDRATE

The carbohydrate category of nutrients consists of both simple and complex carbohydrates, determined by the size of the chemical molecule. The bigger the molecule, the more complex the carbohydrate.

Simple carbohydrates include the sugars: sucrose or table sugar, honey, molasses, glucose, fructose, lactose, and so on. Ultimately, the body breaks them all down to glucose, which is used as fuel for the cells. While sugar has gotten a lot of bad publicity, and it's true that sticky candy can cause dental caries, for most individuals and certainly for children the simple sugars supply energy that can be put to good use.

The complex carbohydrates are the starches in our diet. That broad category includes breads, cereals, pasta, and so forth, as well as carbohydrates from fruits and vegetables. Most nutritionists today advise us to eat more carbohydrates, especially those made from whole grains. Thus they place greater emphasis on getting calories from this group than from protein and fats. That's because the fiber content of these foods has been proved to help us stay healthy in many ways.

Dr. Denis Burkitt first reported the benefits of eating more fiber after studying the health of African tribesmen. A diet rich in fiber has subsequently been shown to improve regularity, lessen the risks of colon cancer, and help in the prevention and cure of such conditions as diverticulitis.

I'll describe fiber more thoroughly later in this chapter. For good health, you'll want to include both soluble and insoluble fibers in your family's diet. In Chapter 20, I have a table listing the amounts of carbohydrate and fiber found in various foods, so you can get a better idea of where to find that fiber and in what amounts.

FAT

While you want to cut back on the total amount of fat nutrients you consume, you do need some each day for good health. Fat supplies indispensable or essential fatty acids, carries the fat-soluble vitamins, and is an integral aspect of the metabolism of all food. It is a component of cell walls, it cushions vital organs, and it provides insulation. Fat also stores energy to be used at a later time.

We can find fat in both vegetable and animal foods. All fat, chemically speaking, is formed as chains of carbon atoms. Each of these carbon atoms is capable of attracting a hydrogen atom. If all the carbon atoms have hydrogen atoms attached, the molecule is said to be saturated. The saturated fats are the principal culprits in clogging the arteries. While most saturated fats come from animal sources, certain vegetable oils also contain highly saturated fats, including palm oil, palm kernel oil, and coconut oil. If the fat molecule has room for one more hydrogen atom, the fat is said to be monounsaturated. Foods rich in the monounsaturated fatty acids include olives and olive oil, peanuts and peanut oil, cashews, and avocados. Finally, if the molecule has many spaces unfilled by hydrogen atoms, it is said to be polyunsaturated. Soybean oil, corn oil, and most other vegetable oils are in this category. Some manufacturers may add some hydrogen atoms to those oils to give them greater shelf life; as such, they are called partially hydrogenated.

We continue to learn about the role of fats in the diet and their effect on heart disease. At one time, medical authorities believed that adding more polyunsaturated fat to the diet caused a lowering of cholesterol levels in the blood. We now know the benefit comes from replacing saturated fats with unsaturated fats, rather than by increasing the total. All fats in the diet should be consumed in moderation.

Specific information about oils in the diet and their selection in the supermarket is provided elsewhere. Suffice it to say that authorities continue to recommend that we decrease the total amount of fat, the amount of saturated fat, and the amount of cholesterol in our diet.

Cholesterol, as we've already learned, while not a nutrient for which a minimum is set in the diet, is essential in the human body. We need it to manufacture hormones, produce the bile acids used in digestion, build cell membranes, and develop nerves. Yet the body makes its own supply, and you can live very nicely without any cholesterol in the diet at all. The substance is found only in animal foods, in muscle tissue as well as in fat. No cholesterol is contained in any vegetable-based food.

VITAMINS

There are thirteen vitamins recognized as necessary for good health. Each has a specific role in the body, and the lack of any given vitamin results in a deficiency disease. The Recommended Dietary Allowance established for each is based on the amount needed to prevent that particular deficiency state. For example, without enough vitamin C in the diet a person would develop scurvy, a condition marked by bleeding gums. Giving the vitamin to a deficient person or laboratory animal results in a return to normal. Thus the RDA for each vitamin refers to the minimum amount needed. On the other hand, it would be very difficult to get too much of each vitamin from the foods we commonly consume, if we are eating a balanced diet containing a wide variety of foods. In addition, many if not most men and women in the United States supplement their diet with pills and tablets.

It's worth a bit of discussion. For very young children, pediatricians recommend various supplements. Iron and fluoride are typically low in the infant's diet. In later childhood, the majority of parents give their children a vitamin supplement to be certain they get all the nutrients needed. I provide these for my own children, and believe they can be nothing but helpful. I purchase a supplement that includes iron which, as I discuss later, can often be lacking in the diet. I see no reason not to supplement the diet throughout life.

That's not to say, however, that all types of supplementation can be helpful or, on the other hand, that some are not harmful. First, there appears to be no reason whatever for providing children with any single-vitamin or single-mineral supplement. Very large doses of such nutrients can, in fact, be detrimental. Second, we should understand the difference between the two types of vitamins. Water-soluble vitamins are quickly excreted in the urine and must be taken in via food or supplements on a regular basis. The fat-soluble vitamins, however, are stored in the body's fatty tissues. As a result of this storage ability, a person can definitely ingest too much of the fat-soluble vitamins, including vitamins A, D, E, and K. This certainly would be a danger for parents feeding their children cod liver oil, which is rich in vitamin A and D. It's certainly *not* true that if a little is good, a lot is better.

Jenny asked me if it's true that people turn yellow if they eat too many carrots. As I told her, yes that could happen, but only if someone ate *massive* amounts of carrots, which are rich in beta-carotene, the precursor of vitamin A. In a balanced diet with lots of variety it's impossible to overdose on vitamins in the foods we eat.

Now for a glance at the thirteen recognized vitamins:

Vitamin A helps build cells in the body, is necessary for seeing in dim light, and prevents certain eye diseases. We get this nutrient in vegetables, including carrots, sweet potatoes, and green leafy vegetables as well as in enriched foods such as cereals. It's easy to meet the RDA for this vitamin: just ½ cup of sweet potatoes contains 150 percent of the RDA.

Vitamin D aids in building bone tissue by absorbing calcium from the digestive tract. We get all we need from fortified milk and other dairy foods, from fish oils, and from sunshine. Vitamin D deficiencies are completely unknown in this day and age.

Vitamin E protects vitamin A and unsaturated fatty acids from destruction by oxidation. While deficiencies can lead to sexual dysfunction in adults or lack of sexual maturation in youngsters, there is plenty of this nutrient in foods including vegetable oils, green leafy vegetables, whole-grain cereals, and wheat germ.

Vitamin K is the last of the four fat-soluble vitamins, and is essential in the clotting of blood. Deficiencies are virtually unknown since, in addition to the nutrient's availability in vegetables and other foods, the body produces its own supply in the digestive tract.

Vitamin C (ascorbic acid) may not cure the common cold, but it is vital in forming the substances that literally hold the cells and the body together. It also hastens the healing of wounds and increases resistance to infection. You can find this nutrient in a wide variety of fruits and vegetables, and it's also added to many fortified foods.

Vitamin B_1 contributes to the functioning of the nervous system, promotes a normal appetite, and aids in the use of energy by the body. Foods rich in this nutrient include nuts, fortified cereal products, and lean pork such as ham. We need just a bit of this nutrient, also known as thiamine.

Vitamin B_2 promotes healthy skin, eyes, and vision and aids in the utilization of energy. Milk, yogurt, and cottage cheese are excellent sources of this nutrient, also known as riboflavin.

Niacin (nicotinic acid) is a B vitamin which promotes healthy skin, nerves, and the digestive tract and also is a part of energy utilization. Natural sources of niacin include meats, fish, and poultry, as well as peanuts and fortified cereal products.

Vitamin B_6 assists in red-blood-cell regeneration and helps regulate the use of protein, fat, and carbohydrates. It's found in various meats, soybeans, lima beans, bananas, and whole-grain cereals.

Vitamin B_{12} helps maintain nerve tissue and is absolutely essential in production of functioning red blood cells. Only animal foods supply this nutrient, and strict vegetarians are advised to use a supplement. Major sources include fish, shellfish, meats, milk, and other dairy foods. Infants are born with about a six-month supply of vitamin B_{12} and thus require no supplementation. After six months, normal foods provide enough of the nutrient.

Folic Acid (folacin) assists in maintaining nerve tissues and blood cells. You'll find it mainly in green leafy vegetables, nuts, and legumes. Since many children do not eat enough of such foods, a one-a-day vitamin supplement will fill in the supply.

Biotin is another B vitamin but does not have a specified RDA at this time. Playing a role in regulating carbohydrate metabolism, biotin can be found in most fresh vegetables and in milk and meats. For most children, there is no problem with deficiencies or even inadequate amounts.

Pantothenic Acid also currently has no established RDA. Helping in general nutrient metabolism, this nutrient comes in whole-grain cereals and legumes.

MINERALS

Recommended Dietary Allowances have been established for six minerals: calcium, phosphorus, iodine, iron, magnesium, and zinc. In addition, there are nine other minerals which are needed in lesser amounts and which are considered to be supplied by the same foods offering the six major minerals. In general, minerals are required for body-building and regulatory functions.

Calcium requirements begin at birth and continue throughout life to ensure bone health and for regulatory functions in the blood serum. Major dietary sources of calcium are milk and other dairy foods. Certainly there are other sources, including sardines and bone-containing salmon as well as various leafy green vegetables, but since these foods are frequently not eaten on a regular basis, especially by children, they are not a reliable source of calcium. In many Hispanic families, corn tortillas made with slaked lime are a staple of the diet and provide an excellent source of the bone-building mineral.

For best utilization by the body, calcium must be supplied in the presence of other nutrients, including vitamin D, phosphorus, and magnesium. For this reason, dairy foods remain the best source of the nutrient. Happily, we can get all those nutrients without the fat, simply by selecting the low-fat or nonfat dairy foods.

Iron combines with protein and vitamin B_{12} to make hemoglobin, the red substance in blood cells which allows oxygen transport to all parts of the body. The body continuously turns over its iron supply, so there's a need to continuously replace it. Dietary sources of iron include beef and cereals, especially fortified products. Milk is a very poor source of iron, and some children who consume large amounts to the exclusion of other foods may develop iron shortages. Vegetarian children may also be short on iron intake. And those of us limiting the amount of red meat we feed our children will need to be concerned about this nutrient. That's why I select a vitamin supplement for my children that includes iron.

Babies are born with a built-in supply of iron that lasts about six months. Then the mineral runs out and all too many little ones are left with a diet that does not supply enough of this nutrient. After four months, most pediatricians advise giving infants an iron-fortified supplement. Anemia can develop without enough iron, but it's very easy to avoid by simple supplementation.

Phosphorus combines with calcium to form bone tissue and assists in a number of regulatory functions. Sources include milk and other dairy foods, meat, fish, poultry, eggs, whole-grain cereals, and legumes. Soft drinks also supply a great deal of phosphorus. In the U.S. diet, there's no chance of phosphorus deficiency, and some authorities contend we consume too much. How to cut back? The choice is obvious: cut out the soft drinks rather than the milk.

Iodine helps to regulate the rate at which the body uses energy and prevents the formation of goiter by producing the thyroid hormone. Dietary sources include seafoods of all sorts and iodized salt. Goiter is virtually unknown today, largely because of iodized salt. In addition to the normal sources of iodine, a considerable amount is found in milk, owing to current farming techniques.

Magnesium aids in metabolism and assists in the functioning of nerve and muscle fibers. Sources include legumes, whole-grain cereals, milk, meat, seafood, nuts, eggs, and green vegetables. It's apparent from such a listing that this nutrient is easily obtained in the normal diet.

Zinc becomes part of several enzymes and insulin, the hormone which allows the cells to use glucose as fuel. In some children the pancreas produces insufficient amounts of insulin, resulting in diabetes. Zinc is found in meat, eggs, oysters and other seafoods, and whole-grain cereals.

Copper plays a role in the formation of red blood cells and is involved with iron storage. We still don't know just how much is enough in the diet, but copper is available in a wide variety of foods including seafood, meat, eggs, legumes, whole-grain cereals, nuts, and raisins.

WATER

Left in the desert, a person could live quite a long while without any food. But without water, death would be quick. Yet this absolutely essential nutrient is the last thing on the minds of even nutrition-conscious parents. While theoretically it is possible to drink too much, few of us, young or old, consume enough water on a daily basis.

Water accounts for one-half to three-fourths of the body's entire weight. We need it for production of tissue, and children just won't grow without enough. Water acts as a solvent in the body, regulates body temperature, and carries nutrients to cells and wastes away in the urine. Water is the principal component of blood. It helps us digest food, and our bodies require the fluid for a wide variety of chemical reactions necessary for life.

We lose water every day in a number of ways. Of course a great deal is used to produce urine and to flush out wastes. Both perceptible and imperceptible water loss occurs through sweating. And feces contain a large amount. All this fluid must be replaced daily.

As youngsters get involved with sports, water loss can become significant. Too often coaches are ill-informed and advise their young athletes not to drink water while practicing and playing. This has had tragic consequences, resulting in heat stroke and even death in otherwise healthy young people. The solution is to provide enough water to drink and to strongly encourage athletes to drink it regularly.

How much is enough? Again, it's hard to drink too much. The old advice of eight 8-ounce glasses daily remains sound. Part of the total can, of course, be reached with juices, soft drinks, and milk. Some coaches suggest special electrolyte-balanced drinks, but authorities remain adamant that the best drink still is water. There's no thirst quencher quite like it.

Does your community provide fluoridated water? The role of fluoride in retarding the development of dental caries by strengthening the enamel of the teeth has been well established. In drinking the recommended amounts of fluoridated water, youngsters can greatly diminish the number of cavities they might otherwise expect. If your water supply does not contain fluoride, your dentist can recommend a prescription-only fluoride supplement either as drops or as tablets that your kids can dissolve in the mouth or chew at bedtime.

FIBER

Although it can't really be called a nutrient as such, fiber has gotten a lot of attention recently. In the U.S. government's *Dietary Guidelines for Americans,* one of the recommendations is to eat foods with adequate starch and fiber. The authors of that document point out that the American diet is relatively low in fiber, and explain that dietary fiber is a term used to describe parts of plant foods which are generally not digestible by humans. There are several kinds of fiber with different chemical structures and biological effects. Because foods differ in the kinds of fiber they contain, it's best to include a variety of fiber-rich foods. These include whole-grain breads and cereals, fruits, and vegetables.

Why don't Americans eat enough fiber? During the past century our diet has changed a lot. We eat far more refined and processed foods. During those stages of refinement and processing, a lot of the food's natural fiber—the portion we used to refer to as roughage—is lost. In addition, the majority of people eat fewer foods that are rich in fiber. Instead of an apple, they reach for a candy bar. To a large extent it's a matter of convenience. But there's also the aspect of habit. Once you and your family get into the healthful habit of selecting fiber-rich foods, you'll wonder how you did without them.

While it has no nutritional value in and of itself, fiber performs several functions vitally important to good health. To better understand those functions, you must know that there are two basic types of fiber.

Insoluble fiber does not dissolve in water. Chemically, it belongs in the categories of cellulose, hemicellulose, and lignin. Those fibers give plants their stability and structure. They are not affected by the digestive process, and they pass out of the system almost completely intact. You'll find insoluble fiber in wheat bran, whole grains and legumes, and most fruits and vegetables.

Soluble fiber, on the other hand, dissolves in water. It includes the gums, pectins, and mucilages that break down during digestion. Water-soluble fiber binds to the bile acids in the gut, which are manufactured from cholesterol. The bound bile acids are eliminated through the bowel, requiring the manufacture of more cholesterol, and thus the cholesterol stores in the body gradually diminish. Insoluble fiber has no such effect.

Foods rich in soluble fiber include apples and other fruits, some of the leafy greens, dried beans and peas, barley, rice bran, oat bran, and oatmeal. Oat bran is such an important source of water-soluble fiber that I have a whole chapter devoted to it and its marvelous ability to lower cholesterol levels (see Chapter 11). I stress the use of oat bran for two reasons: while other foods also contain water-soluble fiber, they don't have as much as oat bran; also, none of the other foods has oat bran's versatility as a cereal, as a flour substitute for baking, and many other cooking uses.

But fiber has other important roles in maintaining good health as well. Insoluble fiber's ability to absorb water promotes more frequent bowel movements and softer, larger stools. This allows waste products to pass through the intestines more quickly, thereby reducing exposure time to potentially harmful substances such as carcinogenic agents. Soluble fiber, on the other hand, delays food absorption, allowing a more even flow of nutrients through the body. You feel fuller and more satisfied after eating a meal rich in soluble fiber. By all means, you'll want to increase the amount of all fiber, both soluble and insoluble, in your family's diet.

GETTING THOSE NUTRIENTS

Now that we've taken a look at the nutrients in food and their role in the growth, development, and maintenance of the body, you may be getting a bit confused. How, you might ask, can I remember which foods supply what nutrients? How can I possibly do my shopping by trying to supply all those nutrients every day for my growing children?

Well, it's a lot easier than you might think. While it's good to know a little bit about the nutrients we've been talking about, there's no need for you to memorize them. The nutritionists have taken the work out of nutrient shopping. By carefully studying the nutrients found in a wide variety of foods, they long ago established some basic guidelines that still hold up very well today. Simply enough, certain categories of foods are particularly rich in certain nutrients. And those nutrients are frequently accompanied by others. So by eating specified amounts of good food categories, you and I and our children can be assured of getting all the nutrients we need throughout our lives. Sometimes called the four food groups, other times referred to as basic food groupings, by any name the system works the same way. The only difference is that today our selections from those groups are different from those of the past because of what we know now about the dangers of excessive fat and cholesterol in the diet. But happily we can get all the nutrients and calories we need without the fat.

Details on how to do your shopping by way of the four food groups are spelled out in Chapter 14, "Shopping with the Kids." You'll learn how to make your selections from the milk group, the protein group, the fruits and vegetables group, and the cereals group. The milk group supplies calcium in such abundance that no other category of food can compare. And along with that calcium you get a number of other nutrients as well. Similarly, the foods in the protein group—meat, fish, poultry, eggs, and dried beans and peas—supply the vast majority of body-building amino acids in the diet, but also provide other nutrients. Fruits and vegetables are the major suppliers of vitamins A and C, but they come loaded with other nutrients and fiber as well. And the grain and cereals group gives a wealth of vitamins, minerals, and fiber.

The rule is to select a wide variety of foods from each of these food groups every day. That rule has also been expressed in the government's *Dietary Guidelines for Americans* and has been issued by every government in every nation that has looked at its citizens' nutrition. In Japan, for example, the nation's health authorities recommend eating at least thirty different kinds of foods each day. At first that might seem like a very difficult thing to do, but when you think about it, it's not at all impractical. A salad, for example, contains a number of vegetables. Stews can be made from a long list of ingredients. And the most interesting meals are those consisting of a number of dishes rather than just one or two items. In other words, it's time to abandon the idea of meat and potatoes as the basic American diet.

Each of us, whether we're 6 or 60, needs the same nutrients. Each of us can find those nutrients by selecting foods from the basic food groupings. The only difference is in how many calories we each need, thus affecting the number of servings and the sizes of those servings. Now let's look at how this system of selection works throughout the life cycle.

NUTRITION IN THE PRESCHOOL YEARS

Virtually every nutrition and medical authority agrees that the best food for the first six months of life is human breast milk. Nothing can compare with its nutrient content, and there's no substitute for the human interaction between mother and infant. If breast-feeding is impossible or completely impractical, commercial formulas can provide adequate nutrition. Undiluted cow's milk is not a substitute for human milk and should not be fed to infants during those early months. Supplements may be needed and should include vitamin D, fluoride, and iron. Solid foods may be added after 6 months of age, with cereals given first, then fruits and vegetables, and finally meats. At first little ones will need pureed foods, but will soon graduate to junior foods as their chewing abilities develop. No more than one quart of milk belongs in any infant's daily diet. While cow's milk is an excellent source of nutrients, it can never be viewed as a complete diet unto itself. When too much milk is allowed, supply of other nutrients is inadequate, since the milk replaces other foods. Milk is a particularly poor source of iron, and children fed excessive amounts of milk at the expense of other foods often develop anemias. By all means, discuss with your pediatrician your child's nutritional needs during the first formative months.

While a certain amount of controversy exists in this regard, the majority of health authorities believe that no dietary manipulations should begin before age 2 in terms of fat and cholesterol restriction. Some do maintain that fat reduction is perfectly acceptable even for such young children. And a small minority even maintain that a completely rigid vegetarian diet supplies the essential nutrients. However, for practical purposes it appears prudent to initiate a fat-restricted dietary approach beginning at age 2.

One reasonable argument against any dietary manipulation during the first and second years of life is the tremendous growth that occurs during these twenty-four months. The spectacular growth started the first year slows down during the second year, and then continues to slacken in the coming years. Children ordinarily then grow a little less than five inches during the second year and a bit more than three inches annually for the rest of the preschool years. A typical child might gain up to fifteen pounds in the first year, five to six pounds in the second year, and slightly more than four pounds a year after that until school begins. You'll want to know not only how your child compares with the average but also how his or her height and weight rates by percentile. That is to say, is the child in the top 10 percent by weight but only average for height? To make those comparisons throughout childhood, consult Tables 12 and 13 on pages 84–85.

Recommended Dietary Allowances for preschoolers have been set by the Food and Nutrition Board of the National Academy of Sciences' National Research Council to account for nutrient needs for proper growth, development of bones and teeth, average activity levels, increasing blood volume, and dozens of other physiological considerations. An attempt has been made to provide estimates for average caloric needs, but these obviously differ from child to child, just as they do for adults. The rule of thumb in determining whether caloric intake is optimal is to see that weight remains within acceptable limits for that particular age. The old joke in which a man says he's not too fat—just too short—may be funny but it's not a laughing matter for children who can be on a dangerous path to obesity in later life.

As a general principle, RDA levels slowly increase as the child grows. Iron requirements diminish, the need for vitamin D remains about the same, and vitamin A minimums increase just a bit. As bones grow, the calcification process calls for more calcium, phosphorus, magnesium, and fluoride. See Table 14 on page 141 for RDA levels for children at various stages of development.

But how to satisfy those nutritional needs in youngsters? Again turn to the four food groups. Preschool children need 1 to 3 cups of milk daily. They can also substitute some of the milk with cheese or yogurt. Remember that the nutrients in dairy foods remain the same regardless of fat content, so after age 2, there's absolutely no reason not to feed youngsters low-fat and nonfat products.

Table 14. RECOMMENDED DAILY DIETARY ALLOWANCE (Revised 1980)

	Age (years)	Weight (kg) (lbs)		Height (cm) (in)		Protein (g)	Fat-Soluble Vitamins			Water-Soluble Vitamins							Calcium (mg)	Phosphorus (mg)	Magnesium (mg)	Minerals		
							Vitamin A (μg R.E.)	Vitamin D (μg)	Vitamin E (mg α T.E.)	Vitamin C (mg)	Thiamine (mg)	Riboflavin (mg)	Niacin (mg N.E.)	Vitamin B6 (mg)	Folacin (μg)	Vitamin B12 (μg)				Iron (mg)	Zinc (mg)	Iodine (μg)
Infants	0.0-0.5	6	13	60	24	kg × 2.2	420	10	3	35	0.3	0.4	6	0.3	30	0.5ª	360	240	50	10	3	40
	0.5-1.0	9	20	71	28	kg × 2.0	400	10	4	35	0.5	0.6	8	0.6	45	1.5	540	360	70	15	5	50
Children	1-3	13	29	90	35	23	400	10	5	45	0.7	0.8	9	0.9	100	2.0	800	800	150	15	10	70
	4-6	20	44	112	44	30	500	10	6	45	0.9	1.0	11	1.3	200	2.5	800	800	200	10	10	90
	7-10	28	62	132	52	34	700	10	7	45	1.2	1.4	16	1.6	300	3.0	800	800	250	10	10	120
Males	11-14	45	99	157	62	45	1000	10	8	50	1.4	1.6	18	1.8	400	3.0	1200	1200	350	18	15	150
	15-18	66	145	176	69	56	1000	10	10	60	1.4	1.7	18	2.0	400	3.0	1200	1200	400	18	15	150
	19-22	70	154	177	70	56	1000	7.5	10	60	1.5	1.7	19	2.2	400	3.0	800	800	350	10	15	150
	23-50	70	154	178	70	56	1000	5	10	60	1.4	1.6	18	2.2	400	3.0	800	800	350	10	15	150
	51+	70	154	178	70	56	1000	5	10	60	1.2	1.4	16	2.2	400	3.0	800	800	350	10	15	150
Females	11-14	46	101	157	62	46	800	10	8	50	1.1	1.3	15	1.8	400	3.0	1200	1200	300	18	15	150
	15-18	55	120	163	64	46	800	10	8	60	1.1	1.3	14	2.0	400	3.0	1200	1200	300	18	15	150
	19-22	55	120	163	64	44	800	7.5	8	60	1.1	1.3	14	2.0	400	3.0	800	800	300	18	15	150
	23-50	55	120	163	64	44	800	5	8	60	1.0	1.2	13	2.0	400	3.0	800	800	300	18	15	150
	51+	55	120	163	64	44	800	5	8	60	1.0	1.2	13	2.0	400	3.0	800	800	300	10	15	150
Pregnant						+30	+200	+5	+2	+20	+0.4	+0.3	+2	+0.6	+400	+1.0	+400	+400	+150	h	+5	+25
Lactating						+20	+400	+5	+3	+40	+0.5	+0.5	+5	+0.5	+100	+1.0	+400	+400	+150	h	+10	+50

Source: Food and Nutrition Board, National Academy of Sciences—National Research Council

Some children are allergic to milk at an early age; most will outgrow this sensitivity. And other children, especially those of Oriental, African, Mediterranean, and Middle Eastern ancestry, may be intolerant to the lactose or milk sugar found in milk. For such children alternatives to milk will be required to provide calcium. Your pediatrician will provide guidance.

For the protein group, preschoolers need from four to five servings daily, with a serving being 1 ounce of meat, fish, or poultry; 1 egg or its substitute; or ½ cup of dried beans or peas. Those servings of protein-rich foods supply all the body-building amino acids youngsters need. Choose low-fat varieties.

During the preschool years, children need at least two servings of vegetables daily. A serving at that age means ½ cup. This is the time in life to instill a willingness to at least try a wide variety of vegetables and to eat at least a tiny bit of the vegetables served at the family's dinner table each day.

The little ones will also need at least two servings of fruit, with a serving size again of ½ cup or its equivalent in a piece of fresh fruit. Here, too, variety is of the essence. Anything you can do to make fruit more appealing during these formative years will make life easier for you and healthier for your children in the years to come. Make fruit available: in the refrigerator, keep it cleaned, cut, and ready to eat. Serve fruit platters during dinner and for dessert. Offer fruit as a snack when the child is hungry.

Breads and cereals offer preschool youngsters the best flexibility in terms of meeting caloric needs. The average child needs three to four servings a day. In this category, a serving is 1 slice of bread, ½ cup of pasta, or 1 ounce of cereal. This is the food group from which to increase calories if needed for growth and energy within the bounds of acceptable weight. An oat-bran cookie or granola bar makes a terrific snack that provides nutrients and fiber and builds a nice habit of choosing healthful foods.

In the ideal world, careful daily selection of foods from the basic food groups, especially with wide variety, satisfies all nutrient needs. In the real world, not all nutrients will be in the diet every day. Surveys of preschool children indicate that the nutrient most likely to be inadequately represented is iron. Some children consume fewer than the desired number of servings of fruits and vegetables, so their vitamin A and vitamin C statuses are less than adequate. There appears to be more than reasonable justification for providing children with a daily vitamin supplement that includes iron. It may very well be helpful, and there's little possibility of harm. I've given Ross and Jenny their morning chewable vitamin (with iron) along with their breakfast since they were toddlers.

Getting kids to eat the foods we want them to can be a real challenge. That's particularly true with the picky eater; I know that from first-hand experience with Ross. But there are some tricks that can make the process a lot easier for both of you.

Children like to succeed, and can easily be frustrated. Present them with an enormous platter of food, and they are discouraged at the start. Instead, provide small portions. Give lots of finger foods in bite-size pieces. Make food available throughout the day for when the kids are hungry, so they can get it themselves. Introduce new foods as "experiments" to try and potentially reject, rather than as mandated decisions on your part. Get children involved in the food process as early as possible, giving them a role in shopping, food preparation, and table setting.

Remember that kids are kids, not miniature adults. Most of them simply don't like very spicy, highly flavored foods. The exotic mango that might excite an adult's taste buds may very well turn off a youngster's because of its highly perfumed flavor. Few kids enjoy stews or soups with a heavy application of herbs and spices. Similarly, youngsters are less likely to want their foods very hot. Most prefer them at almost room temperature. Don't argue with your children. Let them eat food the way they like it. As they grow, they will change. Don't yell. Don't holler. Don't get angry.

Try very hard to remember when *you* were a kid! Why perpetuate the things you hated when you were little?

NUTRITION FOR THE ELEMENTARY-SCHOOL CHILD

Children entering kindergarten and on through the elementary-school years are likely to be fairly well nourished in the United States. That is to say, they're getting most of the nutrients needed for proper growth. That doesn't necessarily mean they are eating the right foods, however.

As might be expected, RDAs for children in this age group (see page 141) provide for higher levels of nutrients than those required for younger children; and caloric needs increase, too.

These are the years during which you as a parent need to exert some strong influence. Peers, environment, and advertising all pull kids in the wrong food directions. The habits picked up now until adolescence will make a huge difference in the rest of the child's life.

The same principles of providing foods from the four food groups still apply for children in this age group. The child needs three servings of milk or other dairy foods. A serving is an 8-ounce glass of skim or low-fat milk, 1 ounce of low-fat cheese, or 1 cup of nonfat or low-fat yogurt. Two servings of protein foods provide the needed amino acids. A serving for a child is 2 to 3 ounces of lean meat, fish, poultry, or meat substitutes such as dried beans or peas. Peanut butter can be used sparingly for an occasional sandwich, but remember that 2 tablespoons of peanut butter add about 17 grams of fat. No kid should be allowed to sit with a jar of peanut butter and eat it by the spoonful!

In the next two food groups—vegetables and fruits—at least two servings should be eaten daily. Encourage the liberal consumption of these foods, by all means. I've never heard of anyone, child or adult, who became overweight by eating too many fruits and vegetables!

Similarly, the elementary-school child should be eating at least four servings of foods from the breads and cereals group. For all practical purposes, if a youngster can sit down to a huge mound of pasta and eat it without gaining excessive weight, let him do it. If she wants 3 or 4 ounces of cereal at a time for breakfast, fine. The high-carbohydrate diet is definitely the wave of the future.

Forget the idea that carbohydrates make a person fat. Fat makes a person fat. Pasta with some marinara sauce is just fine; the same pasta with a greasy meat sauce or a butter sauce will add up the calories, however. Encourage a wide variety of breads, cereals, and grains at all meals and for snacks.

NUTRITION AND THE TEENAGER

If you start your family on a healthful, low-fat diet early on, the teenage years will be only somewhat difficult in terms of maintaining that diet. If you are only beginning at the teen years, then it will be very difficult. I wish I could make the blow less painful, but that's simply the way it is.

If you're the parent of a teenager, I don't have to tell you about peer influence. The opinions and habits of your child's friends mean a whole lot more than yours. No doubt about it; changing the teenage diet is tough. But it can be done. Let's start by talking about nutrient needs.

Once again, go back to the four food groups. Nutrient needs have changed little since elementary-school days, except that more calcium must be added to the diet. Girls beginning to menstruate will also need additional iron.

The calcium should be provided by increasing to four the number of servings from the milk group. Calcium sources can also include sardines and salmon with the bones, leafy green vegetables, and corn tortillas. And if girls simply will not or cannot consume enough calcium by way of the foods they eat, a supplement of this bone-building mineral helps prevent future development of osteoporosis. Research has shown that calcium intake early in life is essential for avoiding bone loss later on.

Girls in their teenage years are very conscious of their weight, and dairy foods are often sacrificed. You can show how nonfat dairy products supply the needed nutrients without excessive calories. Nonfat yogurt, in particular, appeals to teenagers' tastes.

The inadequacy of iron is not as easy to deal with, and foods will seldom if ever satisfy a young female's needs for iron. The main source of the mineral is red meat, and not only do many teens avoid red meat today but it's also a major source of fat and cholesterol. Therefore iron supplementation is practically essential for girls.

In any case, however, both boys and girls in their teens need two servings from the protein group each day. Again, lean meat, fish, poultry, and meat alternatives fit the bill. Boys in particular tend to view a double cheeseburger as one serving of meat. And advertising does nothing to discourage that disease-inducing practice.

A serving of meat, fish, or poultry should weigh 4 ounces when raw. For growing and often ravenously hungry teens, the trick is to supply volumes of food by way of the other food groups.

In a fast-food restaurant, suggest that they order a regular hamburger without cheese and supplement it with, say, a baked potato and several trips to the salad bar. At home, show how meat is just one part of the entire meal, with lots of breads, pasta, vegetables, and fruits filling out the bill of fare.

One authority, Dr. William Conner, of the University of Oregon Health Sciences Center, coined the phrase that meat should be used as "a condiment rather than an aliment." He points to the use of slivers of meat in Chinese and Mediterranean cookery. I'm not at all certain that we must go to such extremes. On the other hand, the old days of the "man-size" 1-pound (or more) steak should be long gone. After a while, even the most avid meat-eater will come to accept that 4 ounces of meat can be very satisfying.

As with younger children, the recommendations for eating at least two servings of fruits, two servings of vegetables, and four servings of breads and cereals apply; and I emphasize the words *at least* for the teenager. Remember that the 18-year-old male's appetite is considered to be larger than at any other time in life. The typical consumption of an 18-year-old male is used by USDA as its standard in studies done on food consumption.

To counter any objections, remind your growing teens that top-notch coaches and exercise physiologists have proved time and time again that the low-fat, high-carbohydrate diet is the route to winning at virtually every sport. Whether or not your son or daughter is a champion athlete, the winners' diet can build the best possible body.

Obviously, your best control is in your own home. There you can prepare the foods and snacks that will keep your children healthy and happy regardless of their age. The recipes in this book are sure to please kids, whether they're 6 or 16.

But what to do when they're away from home? The school lunch presents special problems. Developed literally to kill two birds with one stone, the school-lunch program supplies sufficient nutrients to children who might otherwise not get enough food at home, while at the same time it gets rid of some of the government's surplus commodities purchased to subsidize farmers. The major influence on the school-lunch program was the dairy industry. Needless to say, all the subsidized food programs in the country's schools prominently feature high-fat dairy foods.

And there's another problem. Years ago school lunches consisted of meat, potatoes, vegetables, fruits, and bread, served with a carton of milk. The plate waste was enormous. So those in power said in effect, "Let's feed the kids what they'll eat." Today's lunch menu reads like a fast-food restaurant: cheeseburgers, cheese tacos, cheese pizzas. The fat content of any given day's menu is astronomical.

The chances of you as a parent having any influence at your child's school are dismal at best. And, besides, you probably don't have the time or inclination to crusade for healthful, low-fat food items. Your best bet is to pack a lunch for your teen to bring to school.

In addition to the obvious benefits of superior food, the packed lunch eliminates time spent waiting in line and gives your youngster more time to eat and enjoy that lunch. By following some of the suggestions listed in Chapter 18, "Food Fit for a Kid," you'll supply lunches that will make the other kids drool. And that, in turn, will make your teen more likely to go along with the idea of brown-bagging it.

Similarly, kids should have the opportunity to take along some snacks for the day. Most teens, and even younger students, carry a day pack or backpack. Why not pack them some oat-bran cookies, granola bars, or fruit?

Next, make your home the place for kids to come together after school. I can well remember the homes all of us preferred to go to when I was a teen. In addition to the obvious welcome given by those parents, one of the biggest draws was available food. Why not make your home one of the "hangouts"? I can't speak with personal authority, since my kids are still in elementary school, but I guarantee that my childrens' friends love coming to our house to eat. They know they can always get a homemade cookie or a hot dog. But they don't know that the cookie is made with oat bran and the hot dog is made with turkey breast. They just know they taste good!

Finally, as I've mentioned before, I feel no guilt in spoiling my kids' appetites before they leave home to go to a party. Whether it's a birthday party at someone's house or a celebration at the local pizza parlor for the end of Little League season, I take the edge off those appetites by feeding some good foods before they leave.

Will our efforts to influence our kids' eating habits in the years to come be successful? Who knows? But no one can argue that it's a whole lot easier to form good habits early in life than to change bad habits later on.

Very recently I was shopping for a new mask, fins, and snorkel in a local dive shop. The salesman was a young guy of about 19 or 20. He was the picture of glowing young health. One thing led to another, and he mentioned that he'd been raised by parents who believed in the value of proper nutrition. Candy, potato chips, and greasy fried foods were nonexistent in his home. Instead he ate the kinds of foods I've been describing here. Today he feels nothing but fondness and appreciation toward his parents for their efforts.

He continues to eat those good foods, and now encourages his friends to do the same. He's very proud, and justifiably so, of his strength and health, and he has no doubt about the role good nutrition has played in his life. I wish you could meet him yourself; you'd see a vital young man who epitomizes the potential for all youngsters today. His parents may leave him a lot of money in their will, or perhaps not a cent. I don't know. But I do know they have given him the best gift of all: the legacy of life.

11

Nothin's As Lovin' As
Oat Bran from the Oven

Until recently, medical authorities have only been able to say "don't eat this, don't eat that" to those of us attempting to lower blood cholesterol levels. Now we're learning that some foods should be added to the diet to decrease cholesterol levels to a far greater extent. Of those foods, the star performer is the cereal oat bran.

Oat bran contains a water-soluble fiber with the special property of helping the body rid itself of excess cholesterol. Here's the way it happens: The liver produces cholesterol, which travels in the blood. Some of the cholesterol gets turned into bile salts and bile acids, which are released into the intestines. In its attempt to be efficient, the body recycles some of the bile, returning it to the liver for breakdown to cholesterol. The more bile that gets eliminated by the intestines, the more the liver has to make. That means that more cholesterol must be drawn from the blood. Little by little, the serum cholesterol level falls.

Ideally, then, you want to increase production and elimination of bile through the intestines. Enter our star: oat bran. Unlike other fiber, oat bran binds itself to the bile in the intestines, causing the bile—and with it, the cholesterol—to be passed through in the feces.

We've all been hearing a great deal about fiber and its health benefits. Most of the news and recommendations center on the potential of increased dietary fiber to lower the risk of some kinds of cancer. That appears to be true for insoluble fiber, including wheat fiber—the kind we usually see in breakfast cereals.

Insoluble fiber helps move food through the intestines faster.

Doctors refer to this as increased transit time. It is currently believed that if food and feces move through the body faster, cancer-
causing agents remain in the body for a shorter period, curtailing
the amount of damage they can do. While the definitive study has
yet to be done to prove this theory beyond any scientific doubt,
there appears to be very good reason to increase dietary fiber in the
form of cereals, whole-grain breads, and fruits and vegetables.

In addition to these insoluble fibers, we also have soluble
fibers. These fibers attract water in the intestine, forming a gel
which binds the bile and causes it to be eliminated. Such fiber
includes oat bran, pectin from apples and other fruits, and fiber
from dried beans and peas.

While it may be true that an apple a day keeps the doctor away,
there just isn't enough pectin in an apple to be very efficient in
lowering cholesterol levels. There are, of course, many other reasons for eating apples, and the pectin they contribute helps as part
of the total diet.

Dried beans and peas contribute a great deal of soluble fiber.
But the problem is that most kids just can't eat beans day in and day
out in sufficient quantities to effectively lower cholesterol levels.

That brings us to oat bran. This cereal can be found in most
supermarkets and health food stores. Quaker Oats produces most
of it, sold either as Quaker Oat Bran or Mother's Oat Bran. But
other companies process it as well, often at reduced prices. In any
case, oat bran looks like any other hot cereal grain, and, in fact,
that's the principal way most people eat it. Preparation is the same
as for Cream of Wheat or Maypo.

There are, however, a vast number of other ways you can work
oat bran into the diet on a daily basis. We'll talk about those ways
throughout this book. Oat bran can be used instead of flour or
cracker crumbs to coat other foods. It is a perfect binder in meat
loaves and casseroles. And it's just great to bake with.

By the time you finish reading this chapter, you'll agree with
my play on the words from a familiar television advertisement:
"nothin's as lovin' as oat bran from the oven." The recipes offer
delicious and exciting ways for you and your kids to eat oat bran
every day. Soon you'll be saying, "Eat your cookies—they're good
for you!"

But first, let's take a closer look at this marvelous food and how
scientists discovered its cholesterol-lowering properties.

THE OAT BRAN DISCOVERY

To produce oat bran, food processors first make rolled oats from the raw oat grain. They blast the grain with steam and roll it through steel rollers to create flakes. Subsequent processing results in the separation of the bran fraction, just as wheat bran is separated from whole-grain wheat when it is made into white flour. Oat bran has been sold only recently, as the result of a demand arising from a number of clinical observations of its health benefits.

In 1963, scientists in the Netherlands first noticed the cholesterol-lowering effect of rolled oats in rats. Following up on that observation, researchers at Rutgers University determined that the effective portion of the oats was the oat bran fraction. We can conclude from those studies that while oats can lower cholesterol, you have to eat a lot more of them than oat bran, to get equal health benefits.

But the most convincing data came indirectly. Dr. James Anderson, working at the University of Kentucky in Lexington, was looking for foods that helped diabetic patients keep their blood-sugar levels under control. Some foods, especially the simple sugars including sucrose, cause blood sugar to skyrocket. Others are metabolized more slowly, enabling diabetics to maintain a rather constant level of blood sugar throughout the day, avoiding the erratic up and down cycles that can lead to diabetic complications and difficulty in treating the disease. It turned out that oat bran was an excellent food for those diabetic patients. But when Dr. Anderson looked more closely at their blood tests, he found that their cholesterol levels dropped considerably, too.

To get a better idea of how oat bran works, and what amounts bring on the desired cholesterol lowering, Dr. Anderson designed and conducted a number of studies using men with elevated blood cholesterol levels. In one study, patients received 100 grams of oat bran in their daily diet. (That's equal to about 1 cup of uncooked oat bran.) The patients ate oat-bran muffins each day. Their cholesterol levels fell by 13 percent after just a few weeks.

In another, very carefully controlled study, men were given oat bran as part of a cholesterol- and fat-reduced diet. Eating 100 grams of oat bran a day on such a diet brought cholesterol levels down about 23 percent, from an average of 280 mg/dl. But, rather surprisingly, even when the men ate only 50 grams daily, they maintained their lowered cholesterol levels.

Other investigations have produced similar results, with expected cholesterol level drops between 10 and 20 percent. But one of the best aspects of this is that while the total cholesterol levels fall, the protective level of HDL remains unchanged. Only the harmful LDL fraction comes tumbling down. That's important, of course, but even more so when you consider that extreme low-fat diets and drugs designed to lower cholesterol often reduce HDL as well as LDL. By maintaining HDL while dropping LDL, a much improved ratio can be achieved. Many authorities believe that this ratio is particularly indicative of heart disease risk.

Several other foods contain water-soluble fiber, the active cholesterol-lowering substance found in oat bran. One excellent source is rice bran, now available in many health food stores as Vita-Fiber, made by Pacific Rice Products of Berkeley, California. There may also be other brands in your area.

Rice bran cannot be used interchangeably with oat bran. It can be added to other recipes, either by actually adding to the total flour or by substituting for an amount of flour. It can also be sprinkled on foods such as yogurt and cereal. In and of itself, however, rice bran is not eaten plain. It's also not as versatile as oat bran, since it has a distinct flavor rather than being bland as oat bran is.

Rice bran has a very high percentage of water-soluble fiber. In fact, 94 percent of its fiber is water-soluble. As a result, a small amount packs a lot of fiber. Two tablespoons of rice bran equal the water-soluble fiber found in ½ cup of oat bran.

You can incorporate rice bran in recipes for baked goods, or add it to meat loaves and so forth. It's another great way to get cholesterol-lowering fiber into your family's diet.

PUTTING OAT BRAN IN THE DIET

When I first learned of the studies with oat bran, I began eating the cereal in the form of muffins. Three muffins each morning provided the beneficial level of 50 grams of oat bran. I started eating those muffins in 1984, and I still enjoy them practically every day. My success story in lowering my cholesterol level from 284 to 169 mg/dl was told in the book *The 8-Week Cholesterol Cure*.

Needless to say, when I found that my son, Ross, had an elevated cholesterol level of 181 at the age of 7, I wanted to do something about it. At his age, that number put him in the 90th percentile; only 10 percent of kids in his age group have a higher level. I knew from reading the literature extensively that his cholesterol elevation would persist and increase if left unchecked, and that Ross's risk of coronary heart disease would grow as he entered adulthood.

Unfortunately, Ross isn't very fond of my muffins. Oh, he eats one now and then, but when it comes right down to it, most children's tastes are different from adults'. I find the muffins tasty and delicious, while Ross thinks they're bland. Older children do, in fact, enjoy the muffins, especially the ones I've included in this chapter. I'm certain that Ross will start to eat and enjoy his muffins later on. But in the meantime I needed ways to encourage him to eat oat bran.

Happily, Ross is a breakfast cereal eater. Just as I never tire of my muffins, Ross enjoys his daily bowl of cereal. One day I'll flavor it with honey, another day with maple syrup, and still another with a fruit-flavored syrup such as boysenberry or blueberry. For more variety, I mix oat bran with oatmeal.

It takes just a few minutes to get the water boiling and the cereal made. To make it, simply follow the recipe on the box, but with one little tip I came up with to make the process faster. The directions call for bringing water to a boil over high heat, stirring in the oat bran *slowly* to avoid lumping, then stirring constantly and returning the mixture to a boil, cooking it over reduced heat for one to two minutes. That business of *slowly* adding the cereal really slows down the operation.

So here's my tip: dump the measured amount of oat bran right into the boiling water, then stir it, not with a spoon but with a wire whisk. With just two or three swishes of a whisk, you've got creamy cereal set to go to the breakfast table. Even on the busiest of school days, there's just no excuse not to have delicious, hot cereal to start the day off right.

For those with a microwave oven, use the appropriate microwave-safe bowl to combine 1 cup of water and ⅓ cup oat bran. Cook on the HIGH setting for two minutes, stir, then cook for another minute—three minutes total. That's all.

Is your household chaotic in the morning? Then plan the breakfast the evening before. Put out the bowls, measure the water and oat bran, and decide what topping you'll serve the next day. Then in just a few minutes you can give your kid—and your whole family—a steaming, nutritious breakfast with very little hassle.

You'll notice that my recipes for making hot cereal eliminate the salt that's suggested on the box of oat bran. I've found that there's really no reason to add the extra sodium. The cereal tastes just fine without it.

On weekends or holidays you might want to make some oat-bran pancakes and oat-bran waffles (see Chapter 18). They're a delicious alternative to cereal and muffins, and a great change of pace.

In addition to breakfast foods, cookies have become a healthful staple in our home. When I first began experimenting with ways to get more oat bran into Ross's diet, the neighborhood children soon learned that Saturday was baking day. They swarmed around the oven, waiting for the timer to go off. The cookies I came up with are, in all truth, simply delicious. The kids all love them, and they don't care that the cookies and granola bars I prepare are good for them. My children's friends get the added benefit of lowered cholesterol levels without even knowing it.

The fact is that, while the fat intake of adults can be traced to fancy sauces and buttery croissants (among other foods), much of a child's fat intake comes from baked goods including cookies, pies, cakes, and granola bars. Ways to get the fat out of a kid's diet are detailed throughout this book. But when it comes to snack foods, nothing compares to baked goods made with oat bran.

Here are some facts and figures to consider. One of the inevitable ingredients listed on every bag or box of commercial cookies is hydrogenated oil, often the most saturated oils such as palm oil, palm kernel oil, and coconut oil. Frequently if not always, you'll read that the cookies are made with whole eggs or egg yolks. Of course the actual, devastating numbers are never spelled out for you as you move through the supermarket aisles.

According to *Food Values of Portions Commonly Used* by Pennington and Church, the dietitian's bible of such figures, two Pepperidge Farm Lemon Nut Crunch Cookies have 17.9 grams of fat. One chocolate-chip cookie from refrigerated dough contains 2.3 grams. One molasses cookie packs 2.9 grams. A commercial oatmeal cookie has 3.2 grams, while homemade cookies average 2.6 grams each.

Granola bars, advertised as a healthful snack, have very large amounts of fat. The Carnation Chocolate Chip Breakfast Bar gives you 11 grams. The General Mills product isn't much better, coming in at 7.6 grams of fat. Just read the labels of the brands in the supermarket, and you'll see where a lot of fat in the diet comes from.

The same applies to commercial cakes and pies. Two Hostess Chocolate Cup Cakes, a typical serving, contain 8.8 grams of fat. Two Hostess Ho-Hos (which should be called No-Nos!) have an astounding 11.8 grams. Just one piece of homemade yellow cake socks you with 12.4 grams. And many kids wash such goodies down with whole milk, at 8 grams of fat per 8-ounce glass.

But all is not lost. Your children and mine can grow up enjoying cookies, cakes, pies, and granola bars without the fat and cholesterol. And those treats can actually be good for them when made with oat bran, as in the recipes in this chapter.

When it comes to good health for your children today and protection from heart disease in the future, it's true that nothin's as lovin' as oat bran from the oven!

A FEW BAKING HINTS

Don't be afraid to start baking with oat bran, even if you've never baked before in your life. I had never done anything more than warm a dinner roll in the oven before I started my kitchen experiments with oat bran. I began by critically examining recipes in standard cookbooks and gradually modifying those recipes until they were just right in terms of both taste and healthfulness.

The major breakthrough came when I found that corn syrup makes a marvelous alternative to oils and shortenings. In the beginning, I used vegetable oil instead of butter and margarine, then cut the amount called for in half. That simple rule of thumb still works. If you have a special recipe of any kind, whether for baked goods or otherwise, just cut the fat by 50 percent. In most recipes, you'll never really notice the difference. (Certain baked goods simply must be forgotten, as their recipes call for large quantities of fat or certain kinds of fat in order to come out properly.)

But that wasn't good enough to produce baked goods for Ross that could be eaten frequently. After all, the cookies and granola bars were snacks or desserts in addition to his basic foods at meals.

I didn't want him to have *any* additional fat, even if it wasn't saturated as it is in commercial goods.

I found that very ripe bananas—literally to the point when they're black on the outside and runny on the inside—can substitute for shortening in many recipes. You'll find bananas used in the recipes for cakes and brownies in this chapter.

But there is one major problem with this approach. Often the banana taste overwhelms the other ingredients. For some baked goods, this is fine. But one might tire of the same taste when it pervades all goods.

I started to think in terms of what oil *looks* like. It's thick, clear, and viscous. Those properties provide characteristics which are needed in baking. I even thought about mineral oil, but obviously that wouldn't be very practical since while it isn't absorbed into the body, it's a potent laxative.

Then, quite accidentally, I picked up a bottle of light corn syrup (e.g., Karo). It looks just like very thick oil, with very little flavor other than some sweetness. Light corn syrup is nothing more than corn syrup and high-fructose corn syrup (which is more refined and sweeter). First I tried substituting corn syrup for oil on a half-and-half basis, gradually increasing the ratio until I could use light corn syrup in place of oil completely. All the recipes at the end of this chapter call for light corn syrup, with *no oil at all.*

What about cholesterol? Commercial baked goods are made with whole eggs or egg yolks, whether fresh, dried, or frozen. The cholesterol content is considerable. But in most home baking, and in most other recipes, two egg whites can be used in place of one whole egg. If a recipe specifically calls for egg yolks, use egg substitutes. My recipes in this chapter use egg whites exclusively.

What to do with the yolks? If you or your neighbor have a dog, egg yolks make a very delicious, protein-packed part of their diet. You may enjoy an egg shampoo—the original protein treatment as used many years ago. Or, if you have no other use for the yolks, don't feel too guilty about simply putting them down the drain. Better they should end up there than in your kids' arteries.

Next, think about the nuts in many baked goods. While the type of fat in nuts is primarily polyunsaturated, or monounsaturated in cashews, the amount of fat is considerable. However, let's look at the numbers, in terms of baking nuts into recipes.

Following is a breakdown of the fat content per ounce for five of the most commonly eaten nuts. The numbers are similar for other types of nuts:

Pecans—20 grams
Walnuts—16.2 grams
Almonds—15.1 grams
Cashews—12.9 grams
Peanuts—14.0 grams

While we're talking about nuts, it's worth noting that peanut butter contains about 7.2 grams of fat per tablespoon. Two tablespoons equal 1 ounce. Some products might be a bit higher in fat and others a bit lower; read the labels to see specific numbers on different brands.

I mention this because 3½ ounces of nuts turn out to be just slightly more than 1 full cup when measured as whole nuts. Again, this will vary a bit depending on nut size. As you chop the nuts, the weight remains the same, but they fill a smaller volume of space. Finally, when ground as peanut butter, the density is vastly increased. One cup of peanut butter contains about 130 grams of fat.

All this leads us to recipes using chopped nuts. If you use a full cup of nuts, you are working with 45 to 70 grams of fat for the total recipe. My recipes call for ¼ cup of chopped nuts. Even when chopped finely, the most you are dealing with is about 35 grams. Now divide that among three to five dozen cookies. For example, let's say you make three dozen cookies with nuts totaling 35 grams of fat; each cookie will contain about 1 gram. While that's not bad in comparison to commercial cookies, it does add up.

Next we come to chocolate. Most people don't realize that chocolate contains fat added in the manufacturing process. Pure cocoa (the powder) does not contain fat. Look at the ingredient listings of various chocolate products. You'll see whole milk, cream, butter, and hydrogenated fats listed. But you can use cocoa powder without guilt.

Want chocolate syrup? Mix cocoa with corn syrup (see Chapter 18). It'll look the same, act the same in recipes, and taste delicious. Added to the recipes for brownies, cakes, and cookies in this chapter, cocoa gives you and your kids the chocolate flavor everyone loves.

Many people have the mistaken notion that carob contains less fat than cocoa. Actually, neither contains any fat. But candies made with carob, sold frequently in health food stores, contain large amounts of hydrogenated fats.

Next we come to chocolate chips. Whether using the genuine article or the carob imitations, chips do provide a significant amount of fat. Depending on the particular brand, chips contain 8 to 9 grams of fat per ounce. Just ¼ cup of chips has approximately 14 grams of fat. For standard-size chips, this means your recipe uses about 130 chips, or about 4 chips per cookie when making three dozen cookies. I prefer to buy the smaller Nestlé Little Bits, since they give far more chips to the cookie, better distributing the chocolate throughout the recipe. The total fat contribution to each cookie, using these figures, is less than 0.4 gram.

I hasten to point out that if you combine the chips with chopped nuts, you get the fat of both. In our home, most cookies have neither chips nor nuts on a regular basis. When I sprinkle some chips into a cookie or granola recipe, it's a real treat.

When making cakes and muffins, I've found that evaporated skim milk works a lot better than fresh skim milk. In no instance do I use either whole or low-fat milk. Their fat contents are just too high.

Now that we've talked about the ingredients, let's turn to baking equipment. Whether you have a gas or electric oven, temperatures vary. That's why it's a good idea to use an oven thermometer. It's a small investment that can prevent burned or underdone baked goods.

You'll need one or two cookie sheets, a muffin tin, and one or two baking pans measuring 9 × 9 and 9 × 13 inches. When measuring those nuts and chocolate chips you might use once in a while, it's best to use a good-quality kitchen food scale. While most recipes, including mine, give these ingredients in volume (cup) measurements, you should know what they actually weigh. That way you'll know exactly how much fat a recipe contains. After a while, of course, you'll get a good idea of fat content, and you can rely entirely on the volume measurements.

Most kitchens already have a variety of measuring cups and spoons. I find it's very convenient to have more than one of each, so I don't have to keep cleaning between ingredients.

In other words, you don't need very much to get started in oat-bran cooking. But I will mention at least one optional piece of equipment you might already have.

While experimenting with oat bran, I found that it can achieve the consistency of flour when run through my food processor with the large metal blade. On baking mornings I put the oat bran into the processor while I get the other ingredients ready. Then I add the sugar and baking powder, and I'm set to go with a flourlike product. This adds a different consistency to the baked goods, making muffins a bit more cakelike. Certainly this procedure is not necessary for any of the recipes that follow, but it's something you, too, may wish to experiment with.

Good baking, and good eating for you and your kids! Get your kids involved in the process. They'll enjoy baking, and it'll give you a chance to spend some quality time together.

A LITTLE NOTE ABOUT SUGAR

You'll note that the recipes which follow use brown sugar, granulated sugar, or both. Some food "purists" may question this. I have three arguments in favor of using sugar:

First, baking requires sugar for structure. Besides the oat bran itself, there's not much else, volume-wise, in cookies.

Second, when it comes to snacks, I'd much rather that my children consume sugar than fat. These recipes provide that alternative. Since there is no added fat, there will be fewer calories than in commercial goods. And, of course, the deleted fat and cholesterol can't elevate my children's blood cholesterol levels. Also, the oat bran actually lowers those cholesterol levels.

Third, the body cannot tell the difference between sucrose, or table sugar, and fructose, or sugar found in fruit. Both will eventually be converted to glucose to travel through the bloodstream. We are fooling ourselves to believe that turbinado sugar, other unprocessed sugars, or other sweeteners have any advantage over plain old granulated sugar.

On the other hand, when there are occasions in which we can eliminate some sugar from the diet we do so. One example is soda pop and other soft drinks. We just don't have sugar-sweetened beverages in the house. There's no reason for the calories—I'd rather expend them on oat-bran products which do the body a lot of good, or at least on foods and drinks that provide valuable nutrients.

• • • • • • • • • • • • • • • **Oatmeal Cookies**

¾ cup light corn syrup
¼ cup water
1 teaspoon vanilla
   extract
2 egg whites
1 cup brown sugar
½ cup granulated sugar
2 cups rolled oats
2 cups oat bran
1 cup all-purpose flour
½ teaspoon baking soda
   Options: raisins,
   currants, chopped
   nuts, dates

*What could sound more
wholesome than oatmeal cookies
and a glass of milk? Well, with this
recipe and a glass of skim milk,
your children can enjoy this all-
American treat in good health.*

Preheat oven to 350°F. Mix all the
moist ingredients and sugars in a
large bowl, then gradually blend in
dry ingredients. Drop spoonfuls
onto a cookie pan lightly sprayed
with Baker's Joy. Bake for 15 to 17
minutes, (see Note) or until edges
are browned. *Makes about two
dozen large, three dozen medium,
or up to five dozen small cookies.*

NOTE: The larger the cookie, the
longer the baking time.

• • • • • • • • • • • • • • • **Chocolate Rum Cookies**

½ cup light corn syrup
2 tablespoons cocoa or
   carob powder
2 teaspoons rum extract
   or
2 tablespoons dark rum
4 egg whites
⅓ cup granulated sugar
⅓ cup brown sugar
2 cups oat bran
¾ cup self-rising flour
2 teaspoons baking
   powder
¼ cup chopped nuts
   (optional)

*Cutting back on Hershey bars
doesn't mean your kids have to be
deprived of the wonderful taste of
chocolate. This recipe delivers all
the flavor with none of the fat.
Remember that cocoa is fat-free; so
is carob, which can be used for
children with allergies to cocoa
and chocolate.*

Preheat oven to 350°F. Mix the
corn syrup with the cocoa or carob
powder in a large bowl and blend
completely. Blend the chocolate
mixture with the remaining moist
ingredients and sugars. Add the

dry ingredients. Drop with a spoon onto a cookie sheet sprayed lightly with Baker's Joy. Bake for about 15 minutes, or until the edges are browned; the larger the cookie, the longer the baking time. *Makes 3 dozen medium-size cookies.*

NOTE ON LEAVENING: You will notice that many of these recipes call for self-rising flour *and* baking powder. The baking powder is needed for extra leavening of the oat bran. The self-rising flour, of course, contains some soda, and the combination of the two, I find, works out very well.

● ● ● ● ● ● ● ● ● ● ● ● ● ● ● ● **Chocolate Chip Cookies**

½ cup light corn syrup
2 teaspoons vanilla
   extract
4 egg whites
⅓ cup granulated sugar
⅓ cup brown sugar
2 cups oat bran
¾ cup self-rising flour
2 teaspoons baking
   powder
¼ cup chocolate-chip
   morsels
¼ cup chopped nuts

Mention the word cookie, *and for most people and most kids, chocolate chips come to mind. But if you look at the ingredient list on a bag of cookies in the supermarket, you won't want them in your home. This recipe lets you serve these treats often, bringing the fat content down to a minimum even with the chocolate chips and chopped nuts.*

Preheat oven to 350°F. In a large bowl, mix the corn syrup, vanilla, egg whites, and sugars until creamy. Add the dry ingredients in the order listed. Drop with a spoon onto a cookie sheet sprayed lightly with Baker's Joy. Bake for about 15 minutes, or until edges are

(continued)

Chocolate Chip Cookies, Continued

browned; the larger the cookie, the longer the baking time. *Makes 3 dozen medium-size cookies.*

• • • • • • • • • • • • • • • • **Lemon Drop Cookies**

2 cups oat bran
¾ cup self-rising flour
2 teaspoons baking powder
½ cup light corn syrup
2 teaspoons lemon extract
4 egg whites
2 tablespoons lemon juice
1 lemon peel, grated (see Note)
⅔ cup granulated sugar

This recipe offers a nice change of pace. Adults as well as children enjoy the tang of cookies flavored with citrus. The recipe works equally well with orange, tangerine, or lime. No one will believe you've made these treats with no fat at all.

Preheat oven to 350°F. Mix the dry ingredients in a bowl. In a large bowl, mix the corn syrup, lemon extract, egg whites, and lemon juice and peel with the sugar until creamy. Add the dry ingredients. Drop by spoonfuls onto a cookie sheet sprayed lightly with Baker's Joy. Bake for about 15 minutes, or until the edges are browned; the larger the cookie, the longer the baking time. *Makes 3 dozen medium-size cookies.*

NOTE: Your kids may prefer less lemon peel if they don't normally like tart foods. Mine enjoy the tang, and so do I.

• • • • • • • • • • • • • • • • • **Peanut Butter Cookies**

½ cup light corn syrup
1 cup chunk-style
    peanut butter
4 egg whites
½ cup brown sugar
½ cup granulated sugar
2 cups oat bran
1 cup self-rising flour
1 teaspoon baking
    powder

Like many kids, Ross loves peanut butter cookies. Unfortunately, the fat content of this type of cookie soars above all others. I developed this recipe as a compromise for him to eat just once in a while. The peanut butter contributes 1¼ grams of fat per cookie; fortunately most of the fat is monounsaturated—only 20 percent is saturated.

In a large bowl, blend the corn syrup with the peanut butter and egg whites until creamy. Gradually add the sugars, then mix in the dry ingredients. This is a heavy batter, and you may wish to use your hands to mix it. Chill the batter in the refrigerator for at least 2 hours or overnight. Batter can also be kept in the refrigerator for a week or more.

Preheat oven to 350°F. Remove the batter one handful at a time from refrigerator to keep the rest cool, and form into walnut-size balls. Place on a cookie sheet and press down with a flour-coated fork to form the cookie and give it the traditional criss-cross pattern. Bake for 12 to 15 minutes, or until browned at the edges. *Makes 2 dozen cookies.*

• • • • • • • • • • • • • • • **Granola Bars**

½ cup light corn syrup
4 egg whites
2 tablespoons honey or
   molasses
2 teaspoons vanilla
   extract
1 cup brown sugar
¼ cup granulated sugar
3 cups oat bran
2 cups rolled oats
1 cup all-purpose flour
2½ cups Rice Krispies
1 teaspoon ground
   cinnamon
1 teaspoon baking
   powder
½ cup raisins or chopped
   dates
¼ cup chopped nuts
   Option: chocolate
   chips

Commercial granola bars, regardless of manufacturer, are way too high in fat. With this recipe your kids can have the granola bars they crave without the fat. They're super for after-school snacks.

Preheat oven to 350°F. In a large bowl, mix the corn syrup, egg whites, honey, and vanilla with the sugars, then gradually blend in the dry ingredients in the order listed. Spread the mixture to about a 1-inch depth in two 9 × 13-inch baking pans sprayed with Baker's Joy. Bake 20 minutes. (Or microwave in microwave-safe baking dishes for 9 minutes on MEDIUM setting.)

Allow to set for at least 30 minutes before cutting into bars. Bars will firm up as they cool, so be sure not to overbake. *Makes 16 granola bars.*

NOTE: Chopped nuts will add fat, as discussed earlier in this chapter. Chocolate chips add 9 grams of fat per ounce.

• • • • • • • • • • • • • • • **Apple–Cinnamon Muffins**

2¼ cups oat bran
1¼ teaspoons ground
   cinnamon
1 tablespoon baking
   powder

The younger the child, the more flavoring is needed to get him or her to enjoy a muffin for breakfast or for an after-school snack. This one fills the air with an aroma

½ cup evaporated skim
   milk
¾ cup frozen apple-juice
   concentrate
2 egg whites
2 tablespoons light corn
   syrup
1 medium apple, cored
   and chopped but
   not peeled
¼ cup chopped walnuts

*that sends everyone's taste buds
galloping.*

Preheat oven to 425°F. Mix the dry
ingredients in a bowl. In a large
bowl, mix the evaporated milk,
juice concentrate, egg whites, and
corn syrup. Blend in the dry
ingredients. Add the chopped
apple and walnuts. Line a muffin
tin with paper muffin cups and fill
with batter. Oat bran rises very
little, so you can fill the cups fuller
than if using wheat flour. Bake for
17 minutes. *Makes 12 muffins.*

• • • • • • • • • • • • • • • **Blueberry Muffins**

1¼ cups evaporated skim
   milk
2 egg whites
3 tablespoons light corn
   syrup
½ cup granulated sugar
¾ cup blueberries
2¼ cups oat bran
1 tablespoon baking
   powder

*Here's another kid-pleasing muffin
that the whole family will enjoy.
You can use either fresh
blueberries in season or frozen
berries during the winter months.
You'll be surprised how easy it is to
bake these treats. And think of all
the cholesterol-lowering oat bran
in each one.*

Preheat oven to 350°F. Mix the
evaporated milk, egg whites, corn
syrup, and sugar. In a large bowl,
combine the oat bran and baking
powder, then stir in the
blueberries. (This coats the berries
and prevents them from staining
the muffins with juice.) Add the
moist mixture and blend. Line a
muffin tin with paper muffin cups
and fill cups with batter. Bake for
17 minutes. *Makes 12 muffins.*

• • • • • • • • • • • • • • • **Fudge Brownies**

3 tablespoons cocoa
1 tablespoon instant
    coffee
1 tablespoon water
2 very ripe bananas
2 cups granulated sugar
6 egg whites
1 teaspoon vanilla
    extract
1 cup oat bran
¼ cup chopped walnuts

To fully appreciate this recipe, compare it to any other brownie recipe in a standard cookbook. This one is totally free of fat and cholesterol. Of course the calorie content remains high because of the sugar, but you can enjoy these brownies for dessert right along with your kids.

Preheat oven to 350°F. Place the cocoa, coffee, water, and bananas in a blender or large bowl and mix until liquefied. Add the sugar, egg whites, and vanilla. Stir in the oat bran and nuts. Pour into a 9-inch pan sprayed lightly with Baker's Joy. Bake for 45 minutes. Cool and cut into individual squares. *Makes 9 three-inch brownies.*

NOTE: You may substitute raisins for the nuts to cut the fat even more or increase the nuts to ½ cup for a special treat.

• • • • • • • • • • • • • • • **Pineapple Upside-Down Cake**

2 egg whites
2 tablespoons light corn
    syrup
2 (8-ounce) cans crushed
    unsweetened
    pineapple
2¼ cups oat bran
¼ cup brown sugar
1 tablespoon baking
    powder

Here's a great way to get fruit and oat bran into your kids' diet at the same time they're enjoying dessert. It's remarkably easy to prepare, and the whole family will love it.

Preheat oven to 425°F. Puree the egg whites, corn syrup, and 1 can of crushed pineapple along with its juice in a blender. Combine the

1 (8-ounce) can
  pineapple rings
6 maraschino cherries
½ cup evaporated skim
  milk

dry ingredients in a bowl and add puree. Drain the remaining can of crushed pineapple and add the fruit to the mixture. Drain the can of pineapple rings and place the rings on the bottom of a 9 × 13-inch baking pan lightly sprayed with Baker's Joy. Place 1 cherry in each ring. Pour in batter and bake for about 20 minutes. Test for doneness with a toothpick; pick should come out moist but not wet or tacky. Allow to cool, then invert cake onto a platter and serve. *Makes 12 three-inch squares.*

• • • • • • • • • • • • • • • **Devil's Food Cake**

¾ cup light corn syrup
1 ¼ cups nonfat or low-fat
  buttermilk
4 egg whites
1 teaspoon vanilla
  extract
¼ teaspoon red food
  coloring (optional)
1 cup oat bran
¾ cup all-purpose flour
1 cup granulated sugar
¼ cup brown sugar
1 tablespoon baking
  powder
2 tablespoons cocoa

You'd have the devil to pay to find a cake mix or bakery cake made without egg yolks or shortening. We enjoy this recipe with Jell-O Sugar-free Chocolate Pudding instead of frosting. It's good enough for a celebration.

Preheat oven to 350°F. Put all the ingredients into a large mixer bowl and mix at low to medium speed with a mixer until blended. Pour into baking pans lightly sprayed with Baker's Joy; use one 9 × 13-inch pan, two 9-inch square pans, or two 8-inch round pans, depending on whether you want a sheet cake or a layer cake. Bake 30 to 40 minutes and test for doneness with a toothpick. *Serves 8.*

Basic Yellow Cake

½ cup light corn syrup
1 cup evaporated skim
 milk
1½ teaspoons vanilla
 extract
4 egg whites
1¼ cups oat bran
1 cup all-purpose flour
1¼ cups granulated sugar
1½ tablespoons baking
 powder

This recipe can be the basis for a number of variations. Frost it with lemon pudding, use a fruit filling between the layers, even make cupcakes, if you prefer. This cake is ideal for birthday parties.

Preheat oven to 350°F. Put all the ingredients in a large mixer bowl and mix at low to medium speed with a mixer, then beat at high speed until creamy. Pour into two 8-inch round cake pans lightly sprayed with Baker's Joy. Bake for 30 to 35 minutes and test for doneness with a toothpick. Let cool and frost or fill. *Serves 8.*

Breakfast Pancakes

1 cup oat bran
1 cup all-purpose flour
1 tablespoon granulated
 sugar
1 tablespoon baking
 powder
¼ cup light corn syrup
2 cups nonfat or low-fat
 buttermilk
4 egg whites

Ross and I both love pancakes, but no longer eat them in restaurants because they're made with eggs. Now we enjoy them to our hearts' content at home on Sunday mornings, with pure maple syrup and a big glass of freshly squeezed orange juice. It's a delicious way to get more oat bran into our diets.

Heat griddle to very hot (375°F on an electric griddle). Combine the dry ingredients. Blend the corn syrup, buttermilk, and egg whites in a large bowl, then gradually add the dry ingredients and mix until smooth. Spray griddle with Pam. Pour batter onto griddle with small ladle. Cook until lightly browned on both sides. *Makes 24 small pancakes.*

NOTE:
See page 256 for waffles.

12
The Oil of Methuselah

Study the cooking habits of most cultures today and throughout history, and you'll find the use of cooking oil. In one form or another, oils are an indispensable ingredient in both modern kitchens and around primitive tribal campfires. But the choice of oils has never been greater than it is today. And in light of current medical advice, our purchasing decisions have never been more important.

To further complicate our purchase of oil as we walk down supermarket aisles laden with dozens of types and brands, television advertising can be misleading. Buy this brand because it has no cholesterol. Buy that brand because it has less saturated fat.

Let's clear up one point quickly and forever: there is no cholesterol in *any* vegetable oil, nor in any peanut butter. Remember that cholesterol comes solely from animal sources. Therefore any ads proclaiming the superiority of a product based on its lack of cholesterol are making much ado about nothing. *All* such products share the same distinction. So choices must be based on different criteria.

So much for the cholesterol issue. But what about saturated fat? How is it different from polyunsaturated fat? And what is monounsaturated fat?

The chemistry behind these terms is relatively simple. All fats are large organic molecules made up of carbon atoms which can attract hydrogen atoms. If a carbon molecule has all the hydrogen atoms it can hold, it is said to be saturated. If there are spaces left unfilled, the fat is unsaturated. If only one hydrogen atom can be added, the fat is monounsaturated. If there are many unfilled spaces, the fat is polyunsaturated.

Saturated fats usually are hard at room temperature. Examples are butter, beef tallow, bacon grease, and lard. Unsaturated fats are liquid at room temperature.

Literally *all* fats and oils are composed of all three types of fat: saturated, monounsaturated, and polyunsaturated. But the profiles differ considerably.

Animal fats tend to be primarily saturated fats. An exception to this rule, as we'll see later in this chapter, is the fat from marine animals found in cold waters. Three vegetable oils, conversely, have saturated fats as their principal components: coconut, palm, and palm kernel oils.

In vegetable oils, there is a spectrum of saturated-to-polyunsaturated ratios. While all the commonly used oils have excellent percentages of polyunsaturated fat and low levels of saturated fat, the best profiles are found in safflower and sunflower oils. These two have the lowest amount of saturated fats.

Two other oils depart from the typical ratios in oils, however. Olive oil and peanut oil both contain high levels of monounsaturated fats. More about the importance of that a bit later.

You may see reference to PUFA on some ingredients labels. That stands for "polyunsaturated fatty acid," the standard chemical designation. SFA is a similar abbreviation for "saturated fatty acid."

Researchers have found that saturated fats tend to elevate cholesterol levels in the blood. In fact, they elevate them even more than cholesterol itself. Conversely, studies have shown that replacing saturated fats with polyunsaturated fats lowers cholesterol. The recommendations, therefore, have been to reduce the amount of saturated fat in the diet and increase the amount of polyunsaturated fat, while keeping the total amount of fat in the diet limited to 30 percent of the total calories eaten. I have tried to simplify the confusing aspects of calorie percentages and to put all this on a more practical and personal level in Chapter 4, by breaking down an individual's daily intake on the basis of grams of fat which can be counted easily throughout the day.

Within the total fat consumed, authorities advise us to divide the quantity equally among saturated, monounsaturated, and polyunsaturated fats. At first glance this may seem confusing and contradictory.

First, one might ask, why include saturated fats at all if they elevate cholesterol levels? Actually, we don't really need to eat *any* foods that are composed primarily of saturated fats. Most of us prefer those foods, however, and it would be impractical to try to eliminate all of them from our diet. Remember, too, that you'll find *some* saturated fats in all fats and oils. It's just that most of the saturated fats in the typical Western diet come from animal sources. That's why you'll hear over and over that you should begin to cut back on your consumption of meat, whole milk, cheese, and other high-fat animal foods.

The second reason for not advocating a diet of polyunsaturated fats exclusively or almost exclusively is that no one really knows whether this would be healthful. If this seems confusing, remember that health authorities must be cautious and conservative when making recommendations for total populations. There is no evidence as to the effects of relying principally upon polyunsaturated fats because no population in history has ever done it. With polyunsaturated fats, however, we do know that a certain amount is not only not harmful but actually healthful. But this doesn't mean that they should be the only source of fat in the diet.

We *do* know what happens when saturated fats become the principal fat in the diet. People's cholesterol levels soar and heart disease rates rise accordingly. It can be no coincidence that people living in China, Japan, and other Asian countries, where the saturated-fat intake is low, have a low rate of heart disease; yet when individuals from those cultures migrate to the West and adopt the high-fat Western diet, the heart disease rate goes right up.

For many years, scientists puzzled over a population group that just didn't fit the pattern. Eskimos eat about a pound of meat each day, but their heart-disease rate is practically zero. How can that be? Some research gave us the answers that now seem very simple in retrospect.

Remember that saturated fat tends to be hard, even at room temperature. Think about a stick of butter when you remove it from the refrigerator; you can't even spread it. If whales, seals, and arctic fish—staples of the Eskimo diet—had a lot of saturated fat in their bodies, they'd be rigid as boards in the cold waters of the north. In fact, much if not most of that fat is polyunsaturated, a special type in the omega-3 category called eicosapentanoic acid, or EPA for short. Scientists have learned that the colder the water, the more of this EPA there is.

To make things even more interesting, we have learned that food containing EPA helps keep cholesterol levels down. Investigators in Germany gave two 8-ounce cans of mackerel (which has a high EPA content) to healthy adult volunteers each day, in addition to their other foods. Another group was given herring, a fish with a lower EPA content. Fourteen days later, the mackerel-eaters showed a 7 percent fall in cholesterol levels. And their triglycerides came down a full 47 percent. These benefits were not shared by the herring-eaters.

Certainly that's a lot of fish, though, and no one could expect a child to eat that much. I don't know many adults who could, either. But other studies demonstrate that much lower amounts of EPA fats can produce wonderful benefits.

For example, the death rate from heart disease was more than 50 percent lower among men who ate at least 30 grams of fish daily, when compared with men who didn't eat any fish at all. Thirty grams is only slightly more than 1 ounce. That means, the researchers wrote in the *New England Journal of Medicine,* that having a fish dish only once or twice a week could be expected to contribute significant benefits.

How might these special oils in fish achieve those results? A very probable answer came from a scientist at Oregon Health Sciences University in Portland. Dr. Kent Benner had done some research with rabbits to study the effects of EPA on lipid metabolism. Dr. Benner found that EPA is used by the body to produce phospholipids which, in turn, become part of the membranes of all our body's cells. Oleic acid, found in other animal foods, on the other hand, is used to make triglycerides. The latter, if you recall, are a storage form of lipids which transports fats into tissues, thus accelerating the process of atherosclerosis. (Dr. Benner explains that animal research in this area is necessary because radio isotopes are used to track metabolism. In addition, livers must be biopsied at the conclusion of the study period.)

Another reason the Eskimos may be relatively free of heart disease is that eating fish oil makes their blood platelets less sticky. The slippery platelets do not cling together and contribute to the process of atherosclerosis and blood clotting.

How can you and I and our kids get more of this EPA into our diets? Simply by eating more fish, especially fish from cold waters.

Salmon and mackerel are the best. Of course, we don't have access to whale and seal meat, as do the Eskimos, but we can always have a salmon-salad sandwich, steaming salmon patties, or a poached salmon filet.

Up until now, nutritionists have told us to avoid fatty fishes such as salmon. Now we know that the EPA they contain makes these fish the most desirable!

But what about the capsules of EPA being sold in health food stores? At this point, authorities do not recommend them. There may be other components in the fish that make the oil work better than the isolated oil. In addition, it would take a lot of capsules to equal the portion of EPA you would get in a serving of fish. Research studies using the capsules call for 20 to 30 grams daily. There is but 1 gram of EPA per capsule, and the cost of 90 capsules is about $18. To me, that's far too expensive for something that may or may not have benefit. Moreover, one would have to substitute the fish oil capsules for foods currently found in the diet. Otherwise the result would be an excess of total fat which could actually elevate cholesterol levels. Perhaps in the future the cost will come down and actual benefits will be shown; in the meantime, I'll stick with salmon. You may prefer mackerel, either fresh or canned.

Unfortunately, many fish with lots of EPA are not typically used for food. Schools of menhaden, for example, are harvested to extract quantities of up to 100,000 tons of oil each year. The oil is exported to Europe, where it is made into margarine. Little if any is consumed in the United States.

Like margarine manufactured in this country, the menhaden oil product in Europe is hydrogenated to achieve hardness and prevent spoilage. Manufacturers add hydrogen atoms to previously unfilled spaces along the carbon chain; the result is saturated fat.

In shopping for fats and oils to feed your family, you'll want to avoid those which have been hydrogenated. Choose soft margarines over hard, stick margarines. Avoid using butter except, perhaps, for special occasions. In our family, butter has been totally forgotten.

Look also on food labels for the words "partially hydrogenated." You know now that foods with such labels are made with saturated fats.

Also, don't be confused or misled by advertisements for certain products that boast "no cholesterol" when they are, in fact, made from highly saturated fat. Imitation ice creams, artificial whipped

toppings, and nondairy coffee creamers are made with hydrogenated oils, coconut oil, palm oil, and/or palm kernel oil. All of
these are actually *more* saturated than butterfat!

In Chapter 18 we'll discuss in greater detail which products to
look for and purchase for your family. But now let's return to our
discussion of dietary oils. Methuselah, who is referred to in the title
of this chapter, is the man in the Bible reported to have lived for
hundreds of years. The oil used in that Biblical region, then as
now, is olive oil.

For a long while, medical researchers wondered about people
living in the Mediterranean region. They ate a diet as high in fat as
any North American, yet experienced far less heart disease. People
in these countries cook primarily with olive oil. Did that make the
difference?

Dr. Scott Grundy at the University of Texas, in cooperation with
Dr. Fred Mattson at the University of California in San Diego, set up
a study to test the idea. In his tests, twenty patients consumed
liquid diets in which the principal fatty acid was either saturated,
monounsaturated (the predominant kind found in olive oil), or
polyunsaturated. The fats totaled 40 percent of their total calories
for each day, and the diet was eaten for four weeks.

Drs. Grundy and Mattson found that monounsaturates and polyunsaturates had almost the same effectiveness in reducing the
levels of total cholesterol in the blood. Only the diet with primarily
monounsaturated fats, however, did not lower the levels of the
protective HDL in the blood. (Polyunsaturates have been known to
have this effect, as do diets very low in total fat content.)

And, while authorities have been reluctant to advise eating predominantly polyunsaturates owing to the lack of long-term experience, that certainly isn't a problem with recommending olive oil.
It's been the cooking oil of cultures around the world for thousands of years and has the longest track record of any edible oil,
with proven safety. Another advantage, Dr. Grundy points out, is
that olive oil has a far longer shelf life than other vegetable oils. If
you don't like the heaviness of typical olive oil, try Bertolli Extra
Light olive oil. You can use it in place of corn oil without any
perceptible change in taste.

An alternative to olive oil might be peanut oil, which also has
predominantly monounsaturated fat in its composition. Olive oil
has 17.1 percent saturated fat and peanut oil has 17.4 percent.
Olive oil is higher in monounsaturated fat at 72.3 percent, com-

pared to peanut oil's 48.1 percent. Conversely, peanut oil has 31.5 percent polyunsaturates, while olive oil has 10.6 percent. Products made from canola oil, a type of rapeseed oil, are currently lowest in saturated fats and also contain significant amounts of monounsaturated fat.

Bear in mind that two of the cuisines of the world associated with populations characterized by low rates of coronary heart disease are from the Mediterranean region and the Orient. Most Americans enjoy the foods of these cultures. It shouldn't be difficult to increase consumption of foods such as spaghetti and tomato sauce made with olive oil or Chinese foods stir-fried with peanut oil. My kids love both, and yours probably do also.

It's interesting—and *very* important—that adding olive oil to the diet may be even more effective than *simply* lowering total fat intake. In a second study, Dr. Grundy compared three diets: one with 40 percent of total calories as saturated fat, one with 40 percent of total calories as monounsaturated fat, and the third with 20 percent of total calories as fat of all three types. The diet with monounsaturated fats was as effective in lowering total cholesterol levels as was the one reducing total fat to 20 percent. And again, the protective HDL level was not reduced, as it was with the low-fat diet.

Think how effective you can be in reducing your family's total fat intake *and* including this oil of Methuselah!

So what might the recommendations be?

It is close to impossible to duplicate the diet of monounsaturated fat alone, so it's still best to consume both polyunsaturated and monounsaturated fats. Perhaps you might want to boost the level of monounsaturated fats at the expense of saturated fats.

The body does require a small amount of polyunsaturated fat, which serves as a source of prostaglandins in the body. These affect organs and functions throughout the body. But grains in the diet can provide the small amount needed.

As we learn more and more about fats and oils and their impact on total health, it seems that earlier concepts of slashing fat intake to the lowest possible levels are not necessarily the way to go. Especially in children, a certain amount of fat assures normal growth and development. Cutting fat back to levels previously advocated by Nathan Pritikin and others may have deleterious effects on growth. While we want to protect our kids from future heart disease, we also want them to develop to their full potential.

So what do Ross and Jenny eat in the Kowalski household? We use peanut oil in the Chinese wok cooking all of us enjoy so much. Olive oil goes into Italian cookery and salad dressings. For general kitchen use, we rely either on safflower or sunflower oil. The four give us a nice balance of the fatty acids we need, without the saturates we want to avoid.

In all our recipes, my wife and I have found that cutting the called-for quantity of fat or oil in half does the job nicely. We don't miss the extra fat or calories one bit. In fact, most of the United States has experienced a surge of interest in "lite" or light foods. In introducing its new extra-light olive oil, Bertolli, Inc., proclaimed it the first new olive oil in 2,000 years. This new product appeals to those who want to include olive oil in their diets but don't like the heavier taste of other olive oils. Lighter in taste and consistency, it is produced from later pressings of olives. Calorie content remains the same.

Try the oil of Methuselah—and other cholesterol-lowering oils and foods—and your children can perhaps become the Methuselahs of tomorrow.

13

The Vegetarian Solution?

Most of the excess fat and cholesterol in the average diet comes from animal foods. So it might be logical to consider totally eliminating those foods and adopting a vegetarian lifestyle. But is it right for you? There are some pros and cons to think about.

More and more people are turning to vegetarianism for a variety of reasons. Some do it out of health concerns. In addition to worry about heart disease, vegetarians cite problems with pesticide and antibiotic contamination of animal foods. They also point out that high intake of animal protein places additional burdens on the kidneys to excrete nitrogenous waste products. Certainly many of these health-related considerations may justify vegetarianism.

Of course there are religious and moral justifications as well. Some people view the killing of animals for food as unconscionable. I once knew a young vegetarian who even refused to eat honey because it "exploited" bees. Many refuse to wear leather belts or shoes.

Certain religious groups embrace vegetarianism as a precept of their beliefs. Abstaining from animal flesh is a way of life for millions of persons around the world. The major sect advocating vegetarianism in the United States is the Seventh-Day Adventists. The church's members have been the object of many studies, one of which we'll look at a bit later in this chapter.

The term "vegetarian" refers to anyone who routinely avoids any meat, be it beef, poultry, or fish. But within that broad category there are a number of types of vegetarians. The vegan, pronounced *VEE-jan*, eats literally nothing of animal origin; the vegan's foods come exclusively from plant sources. The lacto-ovo-vegetarian eats dairy foods and eggs in addition to plant foods. Lacto-vegetarians consume milk and other dairy foods, while ovo-vegetarians include eggs in their diet.

At the extreme, macrobiotic vegetarians eat only cereal products. This practice began with a religious cult which suggested that practitioners go through several stages, gradually eliminating other foods until they reach a state of spiritual purity marked by the consumption of only grains. Followed to the letter, this dietary regime has claimed the lives of a number of individuals who gradually became malnourished and literally starved to death.

Some vegetarians, called "frugivores" or "fruitarians," include in their diet only fruit or foods derived from fruit. They choose olive oil over corn oil, for example, since olives are fruits and corn is a vegetable.

Seventh-Day Adventists (SDAs) practice a lifestyle that prohibits smoking, discourages alcohol consumption, and encourages a lacto-ovo-vegetarian diet. Several studies have revealed that SDAs have a much lower serum cholesterol level than do nonmembers of the church. One such study closely examined SDA children.

Researchers worked with students in an Illinois SDA boarding high school. The 200 pupils attending the school ate the majority of their food from the school cafeteria, which served only lacto-ovo-vegetarian fare. Occasionally the students went out to restaurants or were allowed to order pizza delivery about once a month. Total dietary intake was carefully studied.

On average, the SDA students' diet derived 34 percent of its total calories from fat, with 11 percent as saturated fat. Their food supplied slightly less than 200 milligrams of cholesterol, mostly from eggs. Actually, this represents the level of fat and cholesterol intake advocated by many health authorities. While no meat products were eaten, the diets could not be considered low in fat. In fact, similar percentages could very easily be obtained while including meat in the diet. It would be a matter of trading off meat for the cheese and butter consumed by SDAs.

But regardless of the manner in which the diet was determined, the results were striking. Students exhibited a remarkably low total serum cholesterol. The highest level was 166 mg/dl, and the lowest was 109. Levels of protective HDL cholesterol averaged the comfortable level of about 49. This average total cholesterol of 138 put the SDA students in the 15th percentile, meaning that 85 percent of the children in the nation had higher cholesterol levels.

Cholesterol levels this low mean that the SDA children can be expected to mature into adults with similarly reduced counts and, importantly, with significantly reduced risk of coronary heart disease. This study correlates well with others and with surveys which have shown again and again that SDA members practicing a lacto-ovo-vegetarian lifestyle have much lower rates of death from heart disease than other segments of the population.

Such low cholesterol levels have only been reported in other vegetarian groups. One study of vegans, who totally abstained from any foods of animal origin, showed total cholesterol levels of an average of 123. Another study of young adults following the vegan lifestyle revealed cholesterol counts averaging 125.

Return for a moment to the boarding school example. A similar study in a boarding school serving the typical American diet was conducted. There, average serum cholesterol levels were 170 for students in the same age group. That represents a 32 milligram difference. But that difference can determine whether or not a student will mature into an adult with coronary heart disease.

Such studies with vegetarians clearly demonstrate the advantage of limiting fat and cholesterol in the diet by reducing or completely eliminating animal foods. But it's important to notice that the SDA students ate foods which were just as high in cholesterol and saturated fats as hot dogs and hamburgers. Cheese, eggs, and butter contribute large amounts of fat and cholesterol.

So what appears to be the answer to this seeming paradox? It all comes down to numbers. SDA students consumed a diet with less than 200 milligrams of cholesterol and about 34 percent of their total calories coming from fat. It really doesn't matter how those numbers are reduced. The important thing seems to be the reduction. So, in a more typical American diet, the SDAs' cheese can one day be replaced by beef and another day by chicken. The numbers will remain the same. And the resulting serum cholesterol levels can be expected to remain low.

We also know that totally abstaining from animal foods will further reduce cholesterol levels in the blood. This is an excellent example of the direct correlation between the diet and serum cholesterol level.

NUTRITION STATUS OF VEGETARIANS

The two most commonly asked questions about vegetarianism are whether someone can be well nourished on such a diet and whether children can be expected to grow normally. The answer to both questions is yes.

In a statement issued in 1974, the Food and Nutrition Board of the National Academy of Sciences reported that all vegetarians, including vegans, can be well nourished, providing they select foods which will supply needed nutrients, including balanced essential amino acids; adequate amounts of vitamins A, B_{12}, D, and riboflavin; and calcium and iron. Obviously, the more restricted the diet, the more difficult it is to supply those nutrients. Vegans have a harder time than lacto-ovo-vegetarians. Protein and sufficient calories often are a problem for the former.

And how well do vegetarian children grow? Many people believe that vegetarian youngsters are malnourished. In truth, the only children shown to be poorly nourished are those from families practicing macrobiotics or those whose parents were in unusual circumstances. For the most part, vegetarian children develop quite normally.

Studies conducted at Tufts University showed that older vegetarian children were leaner and shorter than average. But closer examination revealed that the smaller children were from macrobiotic families. It is true that children placed on a vegetarian diet before the age of 2 do grow more slowly. But after 2 years, vegetarian boys actually grew faster than average, and vegetarian girls developed at a normal rate. There is, however, greater variation in growth rates among vegetarian children, reflecting a diversity of diets and how well those meals are planned and served.

Those embracing or at least experimenting with a vegetarian lifestyle should pay particular attention to the nutrients mentioned earlier. Let's consider how to get enough.

AMINO ACIDS

While it's certainly true that we need far less protein than previously thought (see Chapter 10), sufficient protein must be supplied for growth and development. When a person eats food from animal sources, the body breaks that protein down to its component amino acids, which are then reassembled as building blocks for muscle and other tissues. No single plant food supplies all the amino acids necessary for growth as do animal foods. But eating a wide variety of vegetable foods provides all the amino acids needed. Grains offer certain amino acids, while legumes provide others. One of the major problems with the macrobiotic diet is its severe reliance on grains alone, excluding other foods which would complement them.

It has long been recognized that Latin American cultures as well as many others receive a perfectly acceptable amino acid complement by eating beans and rice as staples of their diet. We now know they need not even be eaten together at the same meal. Other combinations are virtually unlimited, including split pea soup with a slice of rye bread, baked beans and wheat rolls, or garbanzo bean dip with pita bread.

For persons newly emigrated to the United States, such combinations are a natural part of life. Mexicans enjoy tortillas with re-fried beans. East Indians eat lentils and rice. Italians relish pasta e fagioli, a soup of macaroni with beans. For more "homogenized" Americans, particular attention would have to be paid to preparing such combinations.

VITAMINS

Certain vitamins are typically lacking in vegetarian diets, so special efforts must be made to increase those levels.

Vitamin A exists as such only in animal foods such as milk and liver. But the precursor of this vitamin, beta-carotene, very adequately supplies all the vitamin A the body needs by converting to vitamin A once it enters the body. Plant sources of beta-carotene include carrots, sweet potatoes, yams, and many green vegetables.

Riboflavin abounds in milk and other dairy foods. But for strict vegetarians, fortified cereals, avocado, broccoli, turnip greens, squash, and many other vegetables supply all they need when eaten in sufficient quantities.

Vitamin D may be missing from the diets of strict vegetarians living in cold climates. The action of the sun on the skin provides all the vitamin D needed for persons in sunny areas. Milk comes fortified with this vitamin. Vegetarians may obtain vitamin D from fortified soy milk or from a vitamin supplement.

Vitamin B$_{12}$ is abundant in meat, fish, poultry, and dairy products. But the only natural plant source is algae. However, fortified cereals frequently supply this essential vitamin. Again, vegetarians are encouraged to seek additional vitamin B$_{12}$ in vitamin supplement form.

MINERALS

The two minerals frequently inadequately represented in vegetarian diets—as well as in the diets of many others eating animal foods—are calcium and iron. Growing children need calcium to build bones and teeth and iron to form red blood cells.

It may be that vegetarians actually need less calcium than others, since calcium absorption may be reduced by protein, phosphorus, and fats found in animal foods. But to ensure a sufficient supply for the growing body, the diet of strict vegetarians should include almonds, fortified tofu or soy milk, various kinds of greens, and enriched corn products such as tortillas.

Without meat in the diet, iron may be difficult to supply in adequate quantities. Fortified grain products, dried beans and lentils, and whole wheat products such as bulgur provide some iron. But it's best to add iron in the form of supplementation. This is particularly important for girls entering puberty.

CALORIES

While many Americans try to reduce calories in their diets, strict vegetarians may have to work at getting enough. The reason is quite simple. Fat supplies 9 calories per gram, while carbohydrates supply only 4 per gram. Since most of the fat in our diets comes from animal sources, vegetarians may have to eat far more food to get the same number of calories. At first it may sound amusing to think of being calorie deficient, but in underdeveloped countries the protein- and calorie-deficiency disease known as marasmus claims the lives of thousands of children each year.

Snacks become a very important part of the diet for vegetarians. People frequently remark that friends who are vegetarian seem to be eating all the time. Well-chosen snacks can provide the nutrients and calories needed to complete a nutritionally balanced diet. An apple or a handful of raisins or nuts should replace candy and pretzels.

For a nonvegetarian, nutrients can come from all four food groups. For strict vegetarians, choices must be made from the fruit and vegetable group, the grain group, and what might be called the meat alternative group. For the strict vegetarian, this includes dried beans, peas, nuts, and seeds. Vitamin and mineral supplementation certainly is prudent.

For lacto-ovo-vegetarians, food choices become much simpler. They have four food groups from which to choose. For such individuals, the meat alternative group consists of dried beans, peas, nuts, and seeds, but also includes additional foods from the milk group as well as eggs. It is relatively easy to plan and eat a well-balanced diet assuring all needed nutrients, when following a lacto-ovo-vegetarian diet.

For some people, this may be a possible approach to consider. The lessons of the Seventh-Day Adventists are striking. But remember that while the total amount of fat and cholesterol is limited in members of that church and in other lacto-ovo-vegetarians, the foods they eat still contain a heavy load of those culprits. Just because someone avoids meat doesn't mean he or she can eat unlimited amounts of milk, cheese, ice cream, butter, and eggs. Even SDA authorities urge moderation.

With that in mind, we come back to the original question of whether vegetarianism is the answer to controlling cholesterol levels in your children and others in your family. Certainly the strict vegetarian approach completely eliminates the problem. But this solution brings with it problems of balanced nutrition as well as the additional work of more thoughtful food preparation.

In an article I once read detailing the writer's transition to strict vegetarianism, she described with great relish the dishes that convinced her that animal foods were not necessary for delicious cuisine. Then came the recipes; they consisted of dozens of ingredients to be mixed, chopped, beaten, separated, folded, baked, blended, and cooked for more than just a few minutes.

While that might be possible for an old-fashioned family in which the mother stays home and cooks and cleans all day, it seems more than a bit unreasonable for a modern family. One of the major reasons the American diet has so much fat and cholesterol is our reliance on fast foods and convenience foods. It is unlikely that someone accustomed to thawing a frozen dinner in the microwave after a day's work will suddenly find the time or inclination to spend hours shopping and cooking every week.

If you have the wherewithal to prepare vegetarian delights every day, bake whole-grain breads, and plan between-meals nourishing snacks, fine. Perhaps you will want to give vegetarianism a try. If so, there are many excellent books on the market to get you started. Two of the best are *Diet for a Small Planet* and *Laurel's Kitchen*.

Unless you have specific reasons not to do so, it is best to include dairy foods in the vegetarian diet. This lacto-vegetarian approach makes it much easier to supply your family with all the nutrients for growth and development. Skim milk, nonfat and low-fat yogurt, and foods including milk provide calcium, protein, vitamins, and other minerals for a small number of calories, with virtually no fat or cholesterol.

The next step up the ladder might be to consider becoming a part-time vegetarian. Why not serve vegetarian dishes once in a while? After all, the idea of eating a wide variety of foods should include some of the same foods in the vegetarian's meat alternative group. I've included in this book a number of recipes for you to experiment with (see Chapter 18).

But for most of us, various kinds of meats will still remain a regular part of our diets. With that in mind, Dr. William Conner, of the University of Oregon Health Sciences Center, has suggested that meat become "a condiment rather than an aliment." By that he means adding just enough meat to a dish to provide flavor. The meat must not dominate the meal, he and his nutritionist wife Sonja believe.

Many cultures around the world have practiced this concept for years. Mediterranean dishes feature pasta and vegetables in sauces that may include just a little bit of meat. Oriental meals call for finely shredded, small quantities of meat, fish, or poultry. The same goes for East Indian dishes.

It may take a bit of time and doing, but you can get your family to enjoy less and less meat. Don't try to change habits overnight. It took years to develop tastes, and it may take years to change them. Gradually decrease the amount of meat you prepare for each meal.

Most very small children don't even like meat. They have to be cajoled and threatened into eating all that's put on their plates. You probably talked them into eating that meat; now talk them out of it.

One way to start is by having the child first eat the other foods on the plate before attacking the meat. The appetite is sharpest at the start of the meal. If a child eats the meat first, as is often the case, he or she won't be as hungry to eat the potatoes, bread, and vegetables. Turn the normal procedure around.

Whether you want to consider vegetarianism on a part-time or a full-time basis, there's still no need to have meat at all three meals, day in and day out. Typically, Americans eat a breakfast of bacon and eggs, a lunch of a cheeseburger washed down with a thick milkshake, and a dinner of steak or chops. That's atherosclerotic fare any way you look at it.

Start cutting back gradually. Eventually it will be quite natural to have meat—and by that I mean also fish and poultry—only once daily. Even at that, it's a good idea to have one or more completely meatless days each week.

That's really not as hard to do as it may at first sound. Actually, lots of the foods that children really like don't include meats. A meatless day might start in the morning with cereal, milk, juice, and a piece of fruit. Lunch might center on a peanut butter sandwich with some crunchy carrot sticks and a glass of milk. The afternoon snack should be made with oat bran, such as granola bars or cookies. Then the evening meal might be spaghetti with a tasty marinara sauce, bread, a salad, some vegetable, and perhaps pudding for dessert. Those are all foods most kids love to have, over and over again.

Look through magazines for variations on pasta recipes. Consider fruit platters for luncheons, maybe with some nonfat yogurt. How about a meatless pizza? Or create a salad bar at home. There are lots of meatless meal suggestions in Chapter 18. They're all kid-approved delights.

14

Shopping with the Kids

Improving your family's health by way of the foods you serve doesn't mean a radical change in the way you shop for foods. You don't, for example, have to seek exotic ingredients in specialty shops or health food stores. But, like anything new, healthful food shopping means learning a few new tricks. By using what you learn from this chapter and the education you'll receive in the market, you'll be able to dramatically reduce fat and cholesterol intake without a lot of fuss and hassle.

For the next two or three times you plan to shop, try to schedule an extra twenty minutes per trip. You'll need that extra time to make some comparisons between various foods and different brands. Once you've established the foods that best fit your family's needs and tastes, you'll be able to select those preferred foods right off the bat, without any extra time.

You can start making some of those comparisons right in your home by looking at the table in Chapter 20, which lists the amounts of fat, cholesterol, calories, and sodium in many kinds of the foods you currently enjoy. There are, of course, literally tens of thousands of food products on the market, and new ones are added each year. But the table gives you a good idea as to categories of foods that should be restricted and those that are truly healthful.

As discussed earlier in the book, the easiest way to determine the amount of fat in your family's diet is to count the grams of fat in the foods they eat. The government has made that particularly easy by mandating explicit labeling on all processed foods and those foods which make any kind of nutrition claim. That means any foods which claim to be low-fat, reduced-calorie, lite, or the like must have descriptive labels telling consumers just what the items contain. Pick up a can of soup, a carton of milk, or a package of cereal and you'll see the nutrition label. There are two important parts of that label.

At the top of the label you'll find nutrition information per serving. The label states how many servings are in the package, and how large each serving is. Next listed are the number of calories and the amount of protein, fat, and carbohydrates present in each serving. The amounts of these nutrients are expressed in grams. You'll also notice other nutrients listed, and the amounts of protein, vitamin A, vitamin C, thiamine, riboflavin, niacin, calcium, and iron expressed as a percentage of the U.S. recommended daily allowance. If the food contains less than 2 percent of any of those nutrients, an asterisk (*) is used to show that fact.

Some manufacturers voluntarily list the amounts of sodium and cholesterol in their foods; most, however, do not. To learn about the amount of cholesterol in portions of commonly eaten foods, consult the table in Chapter 20.

At the bottom of the nutrition label, you'll find a listing of ingredients in the food, arranged in descending order by volume. In other words, if there's more water than anything else, water will be the first item in the list. If, say, salt or coloring is listed last, it means that every other ingredient is present in greater volume.

Pay close attention to both parts of the label; both provide the information you need to make a wise purchasing decision.

Here's an example. Let's say you find a breakfast cereal with 2 grams of fat per 1-ounce serving. First, you realize that your kids eat more than 1 ounce for breakfast, so you must multiply that number accordingly. Then you glance at the bottom of the panel and notice that one of the ingredients is coconut oil. Since coconut oil contains more saturated fat than even butter or lard, you may decide that even those few grams of fat are too much.

Let me digress for just a moment to recap some information on fats that you might see listed on these food labels. As we have discussed, the more saturated a fat is, the more artery clogging it is for you and your children. Most saturated fats come from animal sources. That's why we all want to cut back on fatty meats, whole milk, butter, ice cream, and so forth. But three fats from the vegetable kingdom are just as saturated. Those are coconut oil, palm oil, and palm kernel oil. Avoid them in the same way you'd avoid lard.

As you begin to read food labels, you'll notice a frequently used phrase: "Contains one or more of the following partially hydroge-nated oils. . . ." Whether the oil is corn oil, soybean oil, or another, the manufacturer has hydrogenated it by chemically adding hydrogen atoms. The reason is that hydrogenated fats—those which are more saturated with hydrogen atoms—have a longer shelf life. Such oils are less likely to spoil than natural oils.

Should you select a food that has such phrasing on its label? Well, if you have a choice of another product that lists unprocessed oil instead, that is the product to choose. But if it's a matter of selecting between a food made with lard or coconut oil or one made with a partially hydrogenated soybean oil, go for the latter every time. While you never know for sure, most of the time the partial hydrogenation is just enough to retard spoilage, and the resulting oil is less atherogenic than other possibilities.

You might ask why a manufacturer states that the product con-tains "one or more of the following . . ." rather than saying it contains one or the other. It's a matter of economics. The price of oils changes rapidly, and one batch of the product may contain one oil and another batch two months later might contain another. So the government has permitted the current phrasing.

Reading those food labels will certainly provide you with more than an occasional surprise—some good and some not so good. Let's look briefly at two examples. Then we'll examine specific foods in greater detail in the coming pages.

You've decided to have a Mexican dinner tonight? Pick up a can of refried beans. Surely, you think, there won't be a problem, since beans are vegetables and there's little if any fat in such foods. Then you look at the label and read that lard has been used in the preparation. This unhappy surprise shouldn't spoil your dinner plans, however. Pick up a can of beans labeled "vegetarian" and notice that it's been made with soybean oil instead.

Now here's a good surprise. You've learned that turkey is a terrific alternative to beef, so when you're shopping for lunch meat, you pick up a package of turkey bologna, salami, or the like. Then you read the label to find that turkey *thigh* meat was used to make the sausage, and, as a result, the fat content is way up. The Louis Rich turkey bologna, for example, has 5 grams of fat per slice. Now multiply that by two or three slices in a typical sandwich. That particular manufacturer, one of the major producers of turkey prod-ucts, proudly states the product is "82% fat-free." In *much* smaller type you see "18% fat." They count on you *not* to read the fine print on the nutrition label, where you learn the details of the product.

But wait, you say, how can that be a *good* surprise? Well, look a bit further in the luncheon meat department. There's a package of sliced luncheon ham. Ham is high in fat, right? Again, read the label. Lo and behold, the package informs you that Danola ham is "98% fat-free." And the nutrition label spells that good news out in detail. A slice of ham contains less than 1 gram of fat. In fact, a full 3½-ounce portion has only 2 grams of fat. That's very little fat for a lot of meat. While Danola, at 2 percent fat, is one of the lowest fat products available, most ham you'll find in the market is no more than 6 percent fat. Don't be overly concerned about the sodium, either. Other changes you'll be making in the family's diet will more than enable you to enjoy ham despite its sodium content. Most sodium in our diet comes from the salt shaker on the table and from fast foods and processed foods—the same foods you'll be avoiding in order to cut down on fat. So there you have it: in this instance, the pork product is actually better for you than the turkey product. Have you been avoiding ham because of the supposed fat? How about other foods? Start reading those labels!

Now let me turn you into a metric-Imperial conversion genius in one easy step. In the last paragraph I mentioned that the 3½-ounce portion of ham contained only 2 grams of fat. How did I know that? It's really simple.

Three and one-half ounces is the Imperial (or U.S. standard measure) equivalent of 100 grams. While most of us don't think of eating 100 grams of meat, we do think of eating a 3½-ounce serving. Just remember that the two are the same. Now think of this: When you see that a food is listed as "98% fat-free," there must be 2 percent of fat remaining. Two percent of 100 grams is 2 grams. Even those of us who struggled with arithmetic in school will be able to handle that calculation.

If a product is 90 percent fat-free, that means it has 10 grams of fat per 3½ ounces. Isn't that easy? It's even a good way to help your kids learn math.

And, speaking of the children, once you get used to reading those nutrition labels at the market, bring your children with you. Make them part of the entire process. That's the best way to give them an awareness of the role of food in their lives.

Food is always a matter of choice. There are tens of thousands of choices to be made every time you step into the store. Obviously you can't buy all those foods, so right off the bat you have to make selections. Cutting back on fats should be simply one more consideration when making your choices, just as cost is another consideration.

Let the kids become part of the decision-making process. They'll enjoy being able to decide what fruits and vegetables are purchased and eaten. Let them talk with the produce manager about some of the more exotic types. When you arrive back home, let them clean and prepare some of the produce so they can have it ready to eat when hungry.

Even very small children can learn to read nutrition labels. Show them how to determine the amount of fat in a serving. Then let them decide on some foods.

Kids particularly will enjoy picking out desserts and snacks for themselves. In the frozen foods section, let them choose a frozen confection rather than the traditional ice cream. Again, the nutrition label is the guide. My children get really excited about some of their "finds"—foods that sound delicious, yet have few if any grams of fat.

Food selections based on nutrition labeling can make a terrific show-and-tell project. Work with your children in preparing a school presentation with some of the foods you have purchased in the supermarket. They'll enjoy the idea of showing their classmates how to enjoy delicious foods that are also good for them.

As you spend a bit more time with your children, deciding on and preparing foods, think of it all as a hobby rather than as a chore. Give it a chance. After a while, like me, you'll get tremendous satisfaction in knowing that you've been able to please your family with foods that ensure a healthy life. New foods which are designed with health-conscious people like us in mind keep coming onto the market. As time goes by there will be more and more. Like a stamp collector coming across a new stamp, view each of these discoveries of new, exciting foods as "finds."

Working your way through the supermarket, go for the widest variety possible. That way you'll not only ensure the nutrients your family needs, but you'll also keep up the enthusiasm for those foods. In addition to the foods you automatically put on the shopping list, pick up a new item to be taste-tested at home. Make shopping a positive experience.

Practically everything about good nutrition today can be put into practice simply by selecting a wide variety of foods from the basic food groups. I go into greater detail on nutrition in Chapter 10, but wise food selection is really the bottom line. As you prepare for your trip to the market, keep those basic food groups in mind.

MILK AND OTHER DAIRY FOODS

Milk is one of the best examples of how you can cut down on the fat in your diet gradually and without "culture shock" for your family. An 8-ounce glass of whole milk contains 8 grams of largely saturated fat. Substitute nonfat skim milk and you get all the same nutrients with just a trace of fat and virtually no cholesterol. But to go directly from whole milk to skim might get you a chorus of "yuck!" from the family. Do it step by step.

First make the switch to low-fat milk, also labeled as 2 percent milk. That cuts the fat down to 4 grams per glass. After a month or so, it's time to take the next step to 1 percent milk. If that's not available in your community, you can mix equal portions of 2 percent milk and skim milk to achieve the 1 percent level. And after another month or so graduate to drinking only skim milk. By that time no one in your family will have any complaints.

You can also find nonfat flavored milks, including chocolate milk. If your market doesn't stock them, ask the manager to please do so.

A number of recipes call for buttermilk. Pancakes made with this cultured product are particularly good. Buttermilk is available either as nonfat or lowfat. Of course it's better to use the former, but in recipes the latter won't add that much fat.

You can also make your own version of nonfat chocolate milk by mixing skim milk with a chocolate syrup made with corn syrup and cocoa (recipe on page 272).

Do you keep powdered milk in the cupboard or pantry for emergencies when you run out of milk or when you use such a product for various recipes? Then start buying nonfat dry milk.

Similarly, look for evaporated skim milk in the canned milk section of the store. This is a *wonderful* product, and you'll want to keep a good supply on hand. Since it's evaporated, the milk has a rich, thick texture similar to cream but without any fat. You can use it as a coffee creamer instead of heavy cream or half-and-half. And it's far better than using nondairy creamers, which are invariably made with highly saturated oils. Virtually any recipe you treasure which calls for cream can be made wonderfully by substituting evaporated skim milk.

When it comes to choosing yogurt, again opt for the nonfat products. I'll be the first to admit that when nonfat yogurts first came on the market, they didn't taste very good at all. But since then food technology has come a long way, and today the products are simply delicious. Two of our favorites are Yoplait 150 and Alta Dena nonfat yogurt. Both have a smooth, creamy texture with none of the harsh tartness that kids seldom like. My kids love these yogurts, and I'll bet yours will, too. There are a number of brands on the market in all parts of the country; experiment to find which ones your family likes best.

You'll also want to pick up a container of plain nonfat yogurt to use in a variety of recipes. Mixed half and half with cottage cheese, it makes a delicious substitute for sour cream; see Chapter 18 for details. The Mock Sour Cream (page 248) can be used with chopped chives on baked potatoes and as a base for vegetable dips and salad dressings.

The cottage cheese we prefer is the 1-percent low-fat variety. Weight Watchers makes one that is distributed nationwide, and I'm sure there are many others equally good.

Selecting cheese is not as simple. Practically all cheese is extremely high in saturated fat, cholesterol, and sodium. A glance at the food charts at the back of this book gives you the grim details. I've listed the food composition for a 1-ounce serving, but remember that most kids eat lots more than 1 ounce at a time, if given half a chance.

Borden has the best product on the market at the time of this writing. (But remember that things are changing fast and that manufacturers are getting wise to the increasing demand for more healthful foods.) Instead of the typical 7 to 9 grams of fat in regular cheese, the Borden's Lite-Line contains only 2 grams for the same size portion. It comes in a number of flavors, including American, cheddar, Monterey Jack, Swiss, and jalapeño.

There also are a number of so-called filled cheeses. These are made by replacing butterfat with vegetable oil. Unfortunately, most of the oil has been partially hydrogenated. In the process, however, almost all the cholesterol gets eliminated, and the fat is far less saturated than butterfat. Two filled cheeses we use in the

Kowalski kitchen are shredded cheddar and shredded mozzarella flavors. We use these for making our tacos and pizzas, for example.

Ultimately, however, the best bet is to gradually get your children's tastes away from cheese. In restaurants it's impossible to get anything but the high-fat varieties, and that becomes frustrating. Interestingly, many children do not even like cheese during their young years, and have to acquire the taste. It would be better not to enjoy this particular dairy food. Kids can get all the calcium their growing bodies need by drinking lots of skim milk and eating yogurt for snacks and with meals. When you do serve cheese, use it sparingly.

The last item typically found in listings of dairy foods is usually ice cream. However, this food contains few nutrients for its high density of calories and fat, so I don't even consider it part of the milk group. Be especially careful to avoid the newer, high-fat varieties such as Häagen Dazs, which have a walloping 24 grams of fat per 1-cup serving. There are lots of frozen-treat alternatives for snacks and desserts, and we'll discuss them soon.

PROTEIN FOODS

Traditionally, this category of foods has been called the meat group. But as we'll see, meat is just one of the many foods that supply the protein and other nutrients that characterize this food group. From this protein group, you want to choose a wide variety of meat, fish, seafood, egg products, poultry, and meat alternatives such as tofu and dried beans and peas.

Let's start with that all-American beef. Should you eliminate red meat entirely? Not at all. Simply make your selections a bit more wisely. Take a look at the table in the back of the book, and you'll see that some cuts of beef contain lots more fat than others. So you want to pick the leanest cuts. If it's time for a steak, it's better to buy tenderloin rather than rib-eye or porterhouse. When making a stew, cut all the visible fat off your chuck steak before chunking it.

When you have a taste for a juicy hamburger grilled over the charcoals, take an extra bit of effort to purchase a piece of round steak, perhaps a london broil, and have the butcher first cut off all the visible fat, then grind it. You'll have all the rich flavor without much fat at all. In fact, you can enjoy lean hamburgers frequently in your family without any guilt at all.

As people begin to select foods lower in fat and cholesterol, beef producers will undoubtedly offer more lean beef. At least one company has already made such a product available. The Dakota Lean Meats company sells cuts of beef which test out at as little as 1.2 percent fat. You can get New York strip, rib-eye, and sirloin steaks, roasts, and hamburger—all with a fraction of the fat normally found in similar cuts.

The first time I served the steaks for dinner and told Ross and Jenny that finally there was red meat they could have frequently that had as little fat as turkey breast, they were really excited. And when they tasted the meat they were even happier. It's very tasty and tender.

Predictably, the cost of the beef is more, about one-third higher than you'd find in the supermarket, but all the meat is completely deboned and fat is completely trimmed off so there's no waste. And you can shop from home. Write for more information to Dakota Lean Meats at 136 W. Tripp Avenue, Winner, South Dakota, 57580. Or you can order by phone at (800) 843-1300, ext. "Lean" (5326).

Veal certainly is a leaner red meat to begin with, and you can make it even better by selecting the leanest cuts of this young beef. As with beef, have your butcher cut off all the fat from veal stew meat and then grind it. Lean veal is absolutely delicious when used in any recipes calling for ground beef. To cut the fat content even further, mix ground veal equally with ground turkey breast.

Pork is a more difficult proposition. Most pork cuts are very fatty, but there are exceptions. Canadian bacon and low-fat ham are excellent choices for breakfast meats, replacing very fatty bacon and sausage. Look for the 2-percent ham for making sandwiches.

Another red meat, lamb, ranks high in fat content, more so than beef. A 3½-ounce serving of loin chop, counting the lean and fat, contains 22.5 grams of fat; a similar size of rib chop comes in at 37.2 grams. Of course you can trim some of the visible fat. For lamb, your best bet is a roast leg, with 14.5 grams of fat; again, you can trim some of the visible fat to bring that total down a bit.

Meat from wild game is naturally low in fat. A 3½-ounce serving of venison has only 2.2 grams of fat. The same size portion of rabbit contains 5 grams. If you're ever tempted to taste an alligator, count on 4.2 grams. There are, however, some exceptions to the low-fat rule of thumb. Roast raccoon has 14.5 grams of fat in the 3½-ounce portion, opossum contains 10.2 grams.

If there's no hunter in your family, but you'd like to experiment a bit with exotic meats, now you can do so. Ranchers in New Zealand are now raising venison on their pastures. To find out where you might find the products in your area, call New Zealand Gourmet at (213) 417-4099. We've tried it in our family, and it's really quite good, with none of the "gamey" taste you might expect from wild game.

There's no question that certain meats should be phased out of your family's eating patterns altogether. Corned beef, pastrami, hot dogs, salami, bacon, and commercial sausages all contain extremely high amounts of fat and aren't in anyone's best interests.

But, happily, there are some ways of enjoying the flavors of these foods without the fat problems. For a long time, Ross and I had done without hot dogs and sausages. And we both continued to miss them. So I came up with an idea.

If you look in the supermarket cooler, you'll find that hot dogs are loaded with fat. Even the products made with chicken and turkey are high, because the thigh meat and fatty portions are used in production since they're the cheapest.

"What if there could be a hot dog made with good old turkey breast meat?" I thought. So I "let my fingers do the walking" and checked the yellow pages of my telephone directory under "meats wholesale/retail." I asked various places whether they made their own sausages, and whether they'd be willing to do a special order. After just a couple of calls I found a sausage shop that agreed to make batches of both hot dogs and bratwursts from pure turkey breast. I had to buy a minimum of 20 pounds, but that was no problem since I have a freezer, and I knew a number of other families who wanted to share the purchase.

Let me tell you that these are some of the most delicious hot dogs and brats you've ever tasted in your life! My friend Pete makes them with his own European recipes, and you just can't tell the difference from the standard, high-fat offerings. To make them even better, these sausages cost no more than those sold in supermarkets.

It's worked out beautifully for us, and I'm sure it'll suit your needs as well. Get out the yellow pages and start making a few calls! Your boys and girls will love them, and you'll feel good in serving fast foods that are loaded with nothing but good nutrition.

Now I'll share my methods of enjoying such no-no's as pepperoni, salami, bologna, and jerky. There's a company in Phoenix, Arizona, that packages all the curing agents and spices needed for making sausages right in your own kitchen. There's nothing to it. You just mix 2 pounds of freshly ground turkey breast with the contents of the package, form into rolls or flatten into jerky, and pop it all into the oven. It's absolutely delicious! If you want to try these for your family, just write to this address for ordering information:

Seagull Family Products
P. O. Box 26051
Phoenix, AZ 85068

What about this ground turkey breast that I use? If you look at the ground turkey packaged in the market, you'll see it's ground turkey thigh. So I ask the butcher to skin and bone a breast then grind it. At the same time I order some turkey cutlets, cut in the same way as veal. I can use them in a wide variety of recipes; they're juicy and tender. And, of course, now and then we enjoy an old-fashioned roast turkey with all the trimmings. No reason to wait for Thanksgiving for this treat!

Chicken is also a wonderful, low-fat protein food. Be sure to select the breasts. The amount of fat in the tissue increases, starting lowest with the breast, then the wings, then the drumsticks, followed by the thighs and finally the back. Remove the skin, of course. And in our house we never have the thighs or backs. Chicken is extremely versatile, and practically every family has its favorite recipes.

Quite a few restaurants now feature chicken breast sandwiches grilled over coals. My recipe is on page 268, and calls for some boneless, skinless chicken breasts, sliced into cutlets. Another rapidly growing restaurant item is Mexican-style chicken marinated in fruit juices and spices, then grilled over coals. You can prepare this easily at home as well. Simply marinate chicken breasts in a mixture of one cup pineapple/papaya juice, one minced garlic clove, one teaspoon of salt, and two tablespoons of minced fresh cilantro for one hour before broiling. Serve with vegetarian refried beans and tortillas.

Next let's add some fish and seafood to the shopping list. If you haven't heard recently about the health benefits of eating fish, you must have just returned from outer space. Researchers have shown that the fat found in cold-water fish is actually polyunsaturated, rather than saturated as it is in land animals. Moreover, the fat is rich in the omega-3 fatty acids, which can protect against heart disease when consumed regularly, as the Eskimos do. Seeing a way to make a fast dollar, some drug companies have started selling fish-oil capsules. What they don't tell you is that to equal the amount of oil consumed by the Eskimos, you'd have to swallow anywhere between twenty-five and fifty capsules. Moreover, you'd be adding extra fat to the diet. Taking those capsules can actually raise the cholesterol levels. Virtually every medical authority who has commented on this issue has given the same advice: it's better to eat the fish than to take the capsules.

Table 15 is a breakdown of the omega-3 content of a variety of fish. But by all means, don't restrict your family only to those high in this nutrient. Enjoy a wide variety of all kinds of fish and seafood.

Largely depending on the family, some kids like fish and others don't. If children are raised on fish from early childhood, they will automatically eat it. But even if your boy or girl doesn't relish a fish filet grilled over the coals, he or she can enjoy a tuna sandwich or casserole. Make that sandwich with a reduced-calorie mayonnaise, with less than half the fat of regular mayonnaise. Try making a salmon salad sandwich now and then for a change.

You might also want to experiment with some of the new imitation-seafood (Sealeg) products. Such items as King Krab and Sea Claws are made with whitefish and pollock and are flavored and formed to resemble shellfish. While a bit high in sodium, these are nutritious foods that can be used in a number of recipes.

And while we're on the subject of shellfish, I must tell you that the old information about the high cholesterol content of shellfish is now completely out the window. In the past, equipment and techniques used to measure cholesterol in foods weren't as sophisticated and sensitive as they are today. As a result, the numbers

Table 15. OMEGA-3 FATTY ACID CONTENT OF 3½-OUNCE SERVINGS OF FISH (GRAMS)

Sardines (Nor.)	5.1	Bluefish	1.2
Sockeye salmon	2.7	Mackerel (Pac.)	1.1
Mackerel (Atl.)	2.5	Striped bass	0.8
King salmon	1.9	Yellowfin tuna	0.6
Herring	1.7	Pollock	0.5
Lake trout	1.4	Brook trout	0.4
Albacore tuna	1.3	Yellow perch	0.3
Halibut	1.3	Catfish	0.2

quoted actually included a group of related substances, the neutral sterols, which are completely harmless. By all means, enjoy all the shellfish your family can eat—and that you can afford. These foods are not only reasonable in cholesterol content, they're particularly low in fat.

Some shellfish, in fact, represent ideal animal sources of protein, with very low fat *and* low cholesterol contents. Take a look at clams and scallops in the table at the back of the book. Now conjure up the savory flavors of chowders simmering on a cool autumn evening. Even kids love those soups.

Because of their high protein content, eggs are also included in this food group. But the egg yolk is a major source of cholesterol, with about 250 milligrams per yolk. So the Kowalskis rely on egg whites and egg substitutes. For any recipe calling for one egg, substitute two whites. If the recipe demands yolks, use egg substitutes instead. As I've said before, I particularly enjoy using Egg Beaters, since that product is made without any additional oil. Read the labels before you make a purchase. Next weekend, make some French toast or omelets with Egg Beaters. Your family will never know the difference.

We now do a lot of baking in our house, and we hate to waste the yolks. But all we want are the whites. So now we buy dried egg whites by mail order. One pound is the equivalent of twelve dozen fresh egg whites. This is the form used by all cake manufacturers in their angel food cake mixes. To use egg white solids, mix two teaspoons of egg whites with two tablespoons of water. Or simply mix two teaspoons of the dried egg whites right into the recipe. It's not available in stores, so write to Henningsen Foods, 2 Corporate Park Drive, White Plains, New York, 10604.

Now let's move on to the nonmeat members of the "meat" group. Because of their high protein content, peanuts, peanut butter, dried beans and peas, and nuts and seeds are included in this category. Some are better choices than others.

Peanut butter—an all-time kids' favorite—contains no cholesterol (remember: cholesterol only comes from animal sources), but it's on the high side for fat. Each tablespoon contains about 7 to 8 grams. While its fat is primarily monounsaturated, and thus better for children than the saturated fat found in salami or bologna, that's still a lot of fat. There's no need to cut peanut butter out entirely, but serving it once a week is enough.

All nuts are high in fat. Look at the charts in Chapter 20; at least half of all the calories in nuts comes from fat. By all means, when snacking, substitute pretzels when you can.

The best meat alternatives are dried beans and peas. Like oat bran, these legumes are rich in water-soluble fiber, which binds onto the bile acids in the gut and ultimately reduces cholesterol stores in the body. Bring out all your mother's and grandmother's recipes for lentil soups, split-pea porridge, and the like. The list in this food group also includes navy beans, red beans, pinto beans, black beans, garbanzo beans (also known as chick-peas), and kidney beans. These foods can be enjoyed in a number of ways: three-bean salads, dips, soups, stews, baked beans, casseroles, refried beans, and on and on. I know that these are not usually high on kids' lists of favorite foods, but as time goes on you might be able to talk your youngsters into trying them. And if they see *you* eating them often, the habits will soon start to rub off. Remember that part of this program is to instill in your children healthful eating habits for life.

The final food in this group may sound way out to you because you may associate it with vegetarians or food faddists. But tofu is a wonderful food, low in fat and high in protein. It's also known as bean curd, since it's made from soybeans. Because of its essentially bland taste, tofu can be prepared in a variety of ways that help it take on the flavor and even the texture of other foods, making it a perfect filler in casseroles, sauces, salad dressings—even baked goods. Try a few tofu recipes; you and your family just might enjoy them.

Now, just before I leave the protein group of foods, I'd like to mention that getting enough protein in the diet isn't a problem for Americans or those in other Western countries. In fact, we typically eat far more protein than we really need. There is absolutely no reason to fear that cutting back on red meat, for example, will result in too little protein in your family's diet. In addition to the foods just discussed, all dairy products contain a large percentage of protein. And protein is also present to a lesser extent in other foods as well, such as cereals and vegetables.

FRUITS AND VEGETABLES

This is the group of foods you should encourage your family—all the members of your family—to eat far more of. Practically every recent nutrition survey done in the United States, Canada, and elsewhere indicates that we could all use more of these foods. In addition to their supplies of vitamins A and C, they give us the fiber we all need. And, when you think about it, fruits and vegetables really are the most beautiful of all foods. Picture a cornucopia spilling over with multicolored fruits and vegetables. And I've never seen a still-life painting of raw lamb chops, have you?

There's only one item in this group that has to be limited. Avocados are quite high in monounsaturated fats and should be restricted. On the other hand, I don't know too many kids who are fond of avocados. So you and your children can go wild in the produce section.

There are a few tricks you can use to increase fruit and vegetable consumption. These seem so simple that at first you might dismiss them out of hand. But give them a try, and you'll see that you'll be buying more and more in the produce section.

The first trick calls for feeding children when they're hungry, and then giving them the foods you want them to eat. When youngsters aren't very hungry, it takes something special to get them to eat. But when they say, "Hey Mom, I'm *starving!*" you can get them to eat almost anything. That's the time to offer a peach, an apple, some raw vegetables with yogurt dip. If the response is, "But I want a cheeseburger; can't I have some money to go get one?", simply stick to your guns. You're hungry, so eat this good food. After just a while, the kids will get used to the idea and they'll go right along with it. Especially when they come to realize that those fruits and vegetables make terrific snacks.

The next trick is having fruits and vegetables always accessible. There's little point in buying them and hiding them in the recesses of the refrigerator, where they have to be fished out, cleaned, and prepared before eating. How about having some plastic containers filled with cut vegetables and yogurt dip anytime the kids want some? Or displaying an attractive fruit bowl on the table or in the family room? A bowl of pineapple chunks with some toothpicks sticking in them won't last long sitting on a refrigerator shelf. Nor will bowls of berries, cherries, and orange slices.

It may not always be possible to prepare fresh produce, and in that case don't hesitate to use some canned fruits and vegetables as well. Pick fruits canned in their own juices rather than in heavy syrup. How about a gelatin mold with some fruit cocktail? Or with chopped vegetables such as carrots and cabbage? Stock your pantry shelves so you'll have those foods on hand when you need them.

Encourage your children to drink fruit juice rather than soda. You might even consider buying a juicer and letting the kids make their own juices and combinations of juices. My Jenny really loves to do that.

Dried fruits also make nice snacks, especially in sack lunches for school or field trips. The only caution is to instruct kids to rinse their mouths out with water after eating those fruits, since they tend to cling to the teeth.

The only other red flags in the fruit and vegetable group are found in the canned goods section of your market. Both baked beans and refried beans can contain a lot of animal fats. Baked beans often come with pork fat, and refried beans are often made with lard. Buy the vegetarian versions instead. Keep in mind that it's always better to use fresh or frozen vegetables, which retain more nutrients and have less sodium, but if it's a choice between canned vegetables or no vegetables, by all means, eat the canned.

While you're still in the aisle with canned goods, pick up some cans of pizza sauce and spaghetti sauce. Look at the labels to make sure they don't contain animal fats. A splash of pizza sauce on an English muffin with a few toppings makes a great snack or lunch with little effort. In fact, your kids can do the work. And no child I've ever known gets tired of spaghetti.

BREADS AND CEREALS

Pasta and noodles, breads and rolls, grains, and cereals all constitute this high-carbohydrate food group. Worldwide, this is the group of foods that "grow" children. Everywhere you look, health authorities are recommending that we all eat more high-fiber, high-carbohydrate foods. The health benefits stretch across the board.

Your shopping list should be filled with foods from this group. But once again, you have to read labels. Examine two different packages of hot dog or hamburger buns, and you'll see that one brand is made with corn or soybean oil and another lists coconut, palm, or palm kernel oil, or "partially hydrogenated" oil. You know which one to buy.

After a while you'll know which brands have the best ingredients, and you won't have to check the labels anymore. But at the beginning look closely at baked goods because that's where a lot of the hidden fats are.

Commercial cookies are a disaster. One of the top brands, Pepperidge Farm, is a major offender, with many grams of fat to offer the unsuspecting consumer. Make your selections carefully. Or, better still, make some of the easy cookies in this book instead.

Crackers are also dangerous. Most have too much fat, the wrong kinds of fat, or both. We've cut way back on our cracker consumption. I can only hope that commercial bakers will take heed of the increasing demand for more healthful products.

But other foods in this group are not so difficult to purchase. There is a wide variety of breads to choose from. Of course you'd like your kids to eat nothing but the whole-grain breads you yourself may prefer. But reality is something else. Just turn back the clock in your mind and remember that you probably didn't like those breads when you were a kid either, and that you wanted the crusts trimmed off. But today we have it a lot easier as parents. Take the granddaddy of them all: Wonder Bread. Just a year ago, I wouldn't permit it in the house because it had all kinds of shortenings and contained practically no fiber. Now my kids can enjoy Wonder Lite, made with no hydrogenated oils and with added fiber; I can breathe a sigh of relief.

Another soft bread your children can enjoy is Roman Meal. It makes great sandwiches and toast, without added hydrogenated shortenings.

Try bringing home some pita bread. Pita pocket sandwiches are a favorite with kids, and the sandwich fillings don't spill out all over the floor.

Bagels are really fun food—without the "bad stuff." Eat them as they come, or try this very special treat: Slice the bagels to form circles about ⅛ inch thick. Put them on a cookie sheet and bake for 7 to 10 minutes in a 325°F oven until crunchy. Play around with the timing until you find the degree of crispness you prefer. I've never known *anyone* who didn't enjoy Dawn's bagel chips. You can also find commercially produced bagel chips, but they just don't taste as good as the homemade ones.

Another way your family can enjoy chips without guilt is to cut corn tortillas into quarters and bake them for about 10 minutes in a 400°F oven until crispy. If you prefer, as we do, spray the wedges with a light dusting of Pam and sprinkle on a few grains of salt.

You can also make your own potato chips. Slice peeled or unpeeled potatoes as thin as possible. (Use a cheese plane or a potato peeler; an electric meat slicer also does a wonderful job.)

Then spread the slices on a cookie sheet and bake in a 350°F oven until crisp, about 15 to 20 minutes. Again, you can spray the chips with a bit of Pam and sprinkle on a tiny bit of salt.

Forget about the commercial chips, including those sold in health food stores. They're all made with far too much oil. These homemade bagel, tortilla, and potato chips more than satisfy your family's cravings for crunchy snacks. Serve them plain or with salsa dips.

Tortillas are a staple of the diet in Mexican culture. From ancient times, Indians ground corn into meal with stone implements. Because corn is prepared with slaked lime, corn tortillas are also an excellent source of calcium. You'll want to keep a supply of corn chips on hand for snacking, of course, but you'll also find corn tortillas useful for a number of recipes such as enchiladas, tacos, and tostados.

Flour tortillas are best for making burritos. But read the labels before buying, some flour tortillas are made with lard. Choose brands prepared with soybean oil.

While tortillas predominate in Mexican cooking, rice is the staple for Asians. Experiment to find the kind of rice your family enjoys most, but all types are excellent sources of nutrients with no troublesome fat.

As players of Trivial Pursuit know, although people most often associate pasta with Italian cookery, the long noodles called spaghetti were actually invented in China and brought to Europe by Marco Polo. Today there are more than 600 different types of pasta, and as any aficionado will tell you, each tastes a bit different even though all are made with the same basic ingredients.

Variety in pasta, especially for kids, can make all the difference in the world. One day serve spaghetti, another day fusilli, or wagon wheels, or shells, or any other fun shape. Even the packaged spaghetti and noodle dinners can be healthful, if you prepare them with skim milk instead of whole milk.

There's only one caution while filling your shopping cart with pasta. Egg noodles are, not surprisingly, made with eggs. For recipes calling for such noodles, substitute fettuccine. I actually find the flavor better. Read the labels of pasta products to be sure they're not made with eggs.

Now what about cereals? At the top of your list, of course, you'll want to put oat bran. This hot cereal is a versatile cholesterol fighter you'll want to include in your family's diet every day, in one form or another. You'll also want to try some rice bran as a change of pace. It, too, is rich in soluble fiber, which helps lower those cholesterol levels.

Since oat bran has gotten a lot of publicity owing to its healthful attributes, a number of cereal products have come onto the market in a jump-on-the-bandwagon effect. Are those cereals including oat bran just as good as straight oat bran? Read the label and quite often you'll see oat bran listed as the second, third, or even fourth ingredient. You'd have to eat a lot of the cereal to get as much oat bran as you're looking for. Table 16 is a breakdown of the fiber content of various cereals. As you can see from those figures, you'd have to eat twice as much oatmeal or flakes to get the same amount of cholesterol-lowering soluble fiber as found in oat bran itself.

Most kids enjoy having different kinds of cereals. By all means don't force them to eat oat-bran cereal every morning. That'll defeat your purpose in the long run, when they completely rebel against it. Instead, try for variety. Make some oat-bran cookies and granola bars. Mix equal parts oat bran with oatmeal. Sprinkle some oat bran over other kinds of cereals, too. Work it into lunch and dinner recipes.

The old-time cereals are still the best: Cheerios, Rice Krispies, Wheat Chex, Corn Flakes, Grape-Nuts, Puffed Wheat, and many others. And some of the new high-fiber cereals are very nutritious as well: Fiber One, All-Bran, and the like. Eaten with fresh fruit and perhaps a sprinkling of oat bran, they're wonderful food.

What about those other cereals that are advertised so aggressively on television—Krunchy This and Krispy That? Look at the labels to see just what you're getting. It won't be pleasant reading. Most of the cereals aimed at kids are about half sugar. That's a spooky thought. For every cup of actual cereal the kids eat, they're gobbling half a cup of sugar. To make it even worse, most of those new cereals are loaded with hydrogenated fats: coconut oil, palm oil, and palm kernel oil, as well as hydrogenated vegetable oils. Some have up to 4 grams of fat per 1-ounce serving, and most kids

Table 16. FIBER CONTENT OF OAT-BRAN CEREALS

Fiber*	Oatmeal	Oat Bran	Oat Bran Crunch	Oat Bran Flakes
Total	12.1	18.6	na	na
Soluble	4.9	7.2	7.2	3.8

* Grams per 3½-ounce serving (uncooked)
na = not available

eat 2, 3, or even 4 ounces at a crack. But kids like the colors, the advertising, the taste, and the prizes offered at the bottom of the box. What to do?

I've taken three approaches in my home that should be just as successful in yours. I mix equal amounts of a traditional cereal with one of the sugary (but low-fat) cereals. (Ross likes to mix Rice Krispies with Frosted Flakes.) That's really not too bad when you consider that kids add some sugar to the bowl of Rice Krispies anyway. And certainly most little ones can use the calories without worrying about weight gain. That's especially true for Ross and Jenny, who eat far less fat than the other kids on the block.

Another idea that works for us is to allow certain new cereals into the house with the agreement that they not be eaten at breakfast. First we look at the label to make sure the fat content is low. Then the kids have the sugary cereals, complete with clown shapes or colored marshmallow bits, for evening snacks. If that sounds horrible at first, think of this: those cereals are only half sugar, while candy is primarily sugar. It's not a bad trade-off.

Here's my final solution. For years kids have lusted after that prize at the bottom of the box, or the one earned by saving proofs of purchase. We all have memories of such prizes and gizmos from childhood. So here's what I do for Ross and Jenny. I invent prizes to be awarded for eating boxes of oat bran. That might be Garbage Pail Kids' collectors' cards, whistles, or Gummy Bears. It works beautifully.

As a last stop in this food section we'll take a look at pizza crusts. Pick up almost any package of frozen dough or packaged mixes and you'll see that they contain hydrogenated oil in significant amounts. Instead of buying such products, why not try a homemade crust? You'll find that the recipe on page 244 is really easy to follow. As an alternative, you can buy a prepared crust from the deli section of the supermarket, wherever take-home pizzas are sold. Ask what type of shortening they use; most are made with a bit of olive oil or vegetable oil.

COMBINATION FOODS

Most of us buy foods that don't fall neatly into one category or another. There are frozen dinners, soups, pasta meals, and canned goods that contain combinations of foods. Should you buy those? The label on each product gives you the answer to that question.

The best frozen dinners, of course, are the ones you make yourself. Whenever possible, we double the recipes that take a bit more preparation, so there's some left over to freeze. If the recipe serves four, we make it for eight and freeze the rest for another day when we don't have time to cook. Then right into the microwave it goes, and in no time we have dinner ready. Quite a few recipes in Chapter 18 are particularly well suited for freezing.

In some instances we actually package individual servings of a meal. For example, when we make enchiladas, we put two or three on a segmented plastic plate along with some refried beans and rice. Then if the kids need a meal when we're going out for the evening or when I'm out of town on business, these Kowalski Frozen Dinners come to the rescue.

Happily, a number of companies now recognize the growing demand for more healthful frozen foods. Weight Watchers produces an excellent line of meals with fat levels quite low. Look in the frozen foods case and take a glance at the nutrition labels for the grams of fat.

How about soups? Some canned soups have almost no fat, while others have too much. There's not much you can do with cream-style soups, but those with a broth base can be chilled in the refrigerator to make the fat rise to the surface and solidify, then you can remove it before heating.

While they certainly don't qualify as gourmet food, canned foods that kids often enjoy can offer sufficient nutrition with a reasonable level of fat. Labels reveal that corned beef hash is absolutely out of the question, while Franco-American Spaghetti is just fine. There's more sodium than we'd prefer in these products, but if such foods are used just once in a while, when time is short, the sodium shouldn't be too much of a problem.

A very popular quick meal is *ramen* noodles, which are also very low in cost. Fast-food noodles are an Oriental tradition. In Tokyo, people buy cups of steaming noodles on streetcorners, just as we buy hot dogs from vendors in our own cities. But take a look at the nutrition label on a packet of *ramen* noodles, and you'll find that between the noodles themselves and the packet of flavoring to be added, the fat content is about 16 grams—way too high.

Since my kids and I really enjoy these noodles, here's what I did. I went back to the basics to prepare noodles the way they do in Japan. Instead of buying packets of *ramen,* I now purchase Oriental *soba* noodles, which have no fat in them at all. Then I boil them in chicken broth for about 3 minutes, and they're ready to eat. You can also add some powdered broth granules to plain water, and then boil the noodles. The brand I prefer because of its very low fat content is Romanoff MBT, available in chicken, beef, and vegetable flavors.

DESSERTS AND SNACK FOODS

After all is said and done, there are some foods all of us like to eat just because they taste good. There's really nothing wrong with that as long as no damage is done. Most of the desserts and snacks kids like contain a lot of sugar. As long as your children aren't greatly overweight and they rinse the sugar out of their mouths to prevent cavities, sugar in itself isn't harmful. Certainly it is not associated with heart disease. And it should be noted that while children with diabetes may not be able to tolerate sugar, the sugar itself does not cause diabetes. In an ideal world, only highly nutritious, low-fat, and low-sugar foods would be eaten. In the real world of my house and probably yours, snacks and dessert are a part of life. But you can make some wise choices here, too.

First, let's get down to business and rid ourselves of some foods that are just too high in fat under any circumstances: doughnuts, fried pastries, cookies, and pies. Certain candies also are made with hydrogenated fats, and chocolate is very high in fat.

But that leaves lots and lots of foods kids can enjoy. Instead of ice cream, suggest some frozen confections such as popsicles and fruit bars. Then there's sorbet, sherbet, and frozen yogurt. All are on the approved list.

Homemade oat-bran cookies and granola bars are delicious in all their varieties. Stock up also on pudding mixes, tapioca, and Jell-O. The puddings, when made with skim milk, add extra nutrition as well as a taste treat. And Jell-O is an all-time kids' favorite, in all its variations.

Bake an angel food cake from one of the mixes. The Betty Crocker brand, for example, contains no fat or cholesterol. It's made with egg whites and no shortening. This is also an easy cake to make from scratch.

Do you have a fireplace? What could be more family fun than toasting some marshmallows on a cold winter evening? Do you have a gas range? Surprise the kids by letting them toast a few marshmallows over the flames. It works very well.

The hot-air corn popper is a wonderful invention for making nonfat popcorn. To make the popcorn taste even better, do it the way we do in the Kowalski household. Pop the corn directly into a 20-pound grocery bag and spray the kernels with just enough Weight Watchers Popcorn Spray to allow a few granules of salt to stick. Or shake the bag of popcorn with a sprinkling of Butter Buds or Molly McButter.

Skip the canned chocolate syrups from the store and make your own with corn syrup and cocoa (see page 272). Or, if you prefer, use carob powder, which does not contain the caffeine-like stimulant theobromine as does cocoa.

OILS, SPICES, AND CONDIMENTS

Here's another category of foods which are added to the diet exclusively for taste. They provide no particular nutritional advantages —just pure pleasure.

While most kids don't start to enjoy a variety of spices and herbs until they're well into their teens, they do relish some seasonings. My kids both like garlic a lot, and almost all kids like tomato ketchup. Keep adding such flavorings to foods and eventually your youngsters will start enjoying them.

Oil is so important that I've included an entire chapter on it—Chapter 12, "The Oil of Methuselah." And whenever you can, use Pam or one of the other vegetable-oil cooking sprays to cut down on total fat while cooking. The butter-flavor sprays are terrific on steamed vegetables and for making garlic bread with just a smidgen of fat.

Margarine is better than butter, tub margarine is better than stick margarine, and squeezable margarine is better than tub. Mayonnaise is better than any margarine. And Weight Watchers mayo is best of all. It all comes down to which contains less saturated fat.

To eliminate fat altogether while enjoying the flavor of butter, try Butter Buds. This is a wonderful product. (Other brands of imitation butter are now available, including Molly McButter. Try them to see which you prefer.) Sprinkle Butter Buds directly over vegetables, mix with some evaporated skim milk to mash potatoes, or use in any number of recipes to replace butter entirely. This one's a winner!

How about salad dressings? Only recently have oil-free dressings been put on the market. My two favorites are El Molino Herbal

Secrets Italian and Mrs. Pickford's Herb Magic Gypsy. You can also make dressings yourself; see Chapter 18. Or try a few substitutions when mixing a packet dressing (see page 252).

Remember that no matter what foods you select in the supermarket, the bottom line remains their fat content. By reading both the labels on the foods and the charts in the back of this book, you'll be well on your way to keeping your family healthy for years to come.

MAKING SENSE OF CLAIMS

Nutrition labels are straightforward, but some of the claims made by manufacturers are not. Just what do those claims mean? Here's how to interpret supermarket jargon.

Diet or *Dietetic* are terms mandated by the U.S. Food and Drug Administration (FDA) to describe foods which contain no more than 40 calories per serving, or that have at least 33 percent fewer calories than the regular product.

Enriched or *Fortified* foods have added vitamins, minerals, or protein beyond what the natural food contains.

Good, Choice, and *Prime* refer to grades of beef based on their fat content. The more fat or "marbling," the higher the grade. For health-conscious shoppers, then, "good" is the best.

High in Polyunsaturates is a nebulous phrase which does not specify a ratio of polyunsaturated to saturated fats. Generally speaking, products labeled as such contain vegetable oils other than coconut, palm, or palm kernel.

Imitation means not only a substitute for the "real" food but also implies nutritional inferiority. If the word *substitute* is used, nutrient content will be as good as that in the naturally occurring food it replaces.

Lean meat and poultry must contain no more than 10 percent fat by weight, according to new U.S. Department of Agriculture regulations. *Extra Lean* means no more than 5 percent fat. *Leaner* means the product has at least 25 percent less fat than the regular product. In all cases, the actual fat content will be listed.

Light or *Lite* have almost no specific meaning. As frightening as this may sound, those words can mean that the product weighs less, or simply that it has a lighter color. Don't be lulled into thinking you're buying less fat or fewer calories. Read the nutrition labels to see exactly what the fat content is.

Low-Calorie means that the food contains either no more than 40 calories per serving or fewer calories than the regular product. The label will be more exact.

Low-Fat can mean different things on different products. On milk and other dairy products it means no more than 2 percent fat and no less than .5 percent fat. On meat, it means no more than 10 percent fat.

Natural may or may not mean anything at all. It has no significance on baked goods and is simply an advertising word. On meats and poultry, it means no artificial coloring or additive has been used. Let the buyer beware.

Naturally Flavored means that the flavor is from the designated product itself, and does not refer to any artificial colors, preservatives, or other additives.

Naturally Sweetened has no specific meaning. Sucrose is a "natural" sweetener because it comes from a vegetable source rather than a chemical factory. Manufacturers will often use the term to refer to other naturally occurring sweeteners.

New is an advertising term that can be used within six months of the introduction of a product. It has no nutritional implications.

No Preservatives means exactly what it says. But that's not necessarily good. Many of the preservatives used in food technology today are completely and totally safe. In many instances I'd rather consume some preservatives than risk bacterial contamination resulting from spoilage.

Organic has no legal meaning whatever, and manufacturers can use the term to their heart's content. Suffice it to say that *all* food is organic because all food is composed of naturally occurring organic compounds consisting of carbon, hydrogen, and oxygen. The term is hype.

Reduced-Calorie means that the food must have at least one-third fewer calories than the regular product. A comparison must be shown on the label.

Low-Salt vs. *Low-Sodium* provides an insight into the minds of advertisers. Salt is not the only source of sodium in the diet. Thus a product such as soy sauce could be low in salt yet still high in sodium. Read the descriptive label on the back.

Sugar-Free or *Sugarless* both mean that sucrose is not used. But the product can contain any number of other sugars.

The terms referring to cholesterol that have been regulated by the government are finally specific. In the past they were rather misleading. Today you have some assurance of just what you're getting in foods.

No Cholesterol means just that. The food contains no cholesterol at all. But it could be loaded with fat. Ads for peanut butter and vegetable oils exemplify this.

Cholesterol-Free means the product has less than 2 milligrams of cholesterol per serving.

Low-Cholesterol means the food contains less than 20 milligrams of cholesterol per serving.

Cholesterol-Reduced implies that the food contains 75 percent less cholesterol than a comparable product.

Ultimately, by cutting down on saturated fat you'll automatically reduce your family's cholesterol intake. Remember that the only place you find cholesterol is in animal foods. After just a few glances at the table in the back of this book, you'll be familiar with the major contributors of cholesterol in foods you normally eat.

And by following some of the suggestions in this chapter, you'll be bringing home much more healthful foods.

15

Ross's Chapter: A Boy's Views

You've been reading my opinions on food, diet, cholesterol, and heart disease. As a parent, I have the duty and obligation to set directions for my children. But what do kids think about all this?

My son has been following the low-fat, low-cholesterol program described in this book for quite some time now; his own cholesterol level has responded very nicely. So how does Ross feel about the changes in his life and diet?

I want to share his own words with you, completely free of editing. As a second grader, Ross received writing assignments from school of a paragraph per week. His teacher assigned the topics. So, to maintain a familiar format, I wrote a number of topics for Ross to address. Each topic was put at the top of a lined, 8½ × 11-inch sheet, and he could choose whatever topic he wanted for that particular day. My only editing has been to correct some spelling errors and to place the paragraphs in order rather than as they were randomly written.

Without further ado, then, here are Ross's feelings and opinions about foods, diet, and health.

MY DAD'S HEART ATTACK AND OPERATION

My Dad had a heart attack. He almost died. But they did an operation. He has scars. His Dad died. My Dad has too much cholesterol.

WHY MY DAD IS HEALTHY NOW

My Dad is healthy now. He eats only good food. He never cheats. He does a lot of exercise. He is not fat.

BLOOD TESTS—WHY ARE THEY GOOD AND WHY ARE THEY BAD?

Blood tests are good because you know about your cholesterol. My Dad and I have a doughnut for breakfast after the test. Blood tests are bad because they hurt. I get scared. But my Dad is with me.

WHY I KNOW ABOUT CHOLESTEROL

I'm glad I know about cholesterol so I don't have a heart attack or an operation. I hate scars.

WHY I'M LUCKY

I'm lucky because I am healthy and my Dad is healthy. We live in a nice house and we go on vacations. I like to ski. I play with my friends Garrett and Michael and Edler. I like school, but this year my teacher is mean. She makes us work too much.

TALKING TO MY MOM AND DAD

I can talk to my Mom and Dad when I have questions. They are nice. They tell me about things.

HOW AND WHEN I LIKE TO TALK

I like to talk after school. I don't like to talk at dark time. Some times I like to talk and some times I don't. I like to talk about animals. Some times I talk about my diet so my Dad knows the food I like and don't like.

WHY OTHER KIDS HAVE SPECIAL DIETS

Some other kids have special diets. They do not have cholesterol all of them. Some kids are too fat and should not eat so much food. Some kids are allergic to food. My uncle Brian is allergic to bread. Michael is my friend who is too fat.

WHY SHOULDN'T KIDS BE FAT?

Kids shouldn't be fat because it's not healthy. If you're fat you die faster too. And you move slower. Fat kids aren't good at moving games like baseball.

There are some ways to lose weight. Do a lot of exercise and eat more fruit and vegetables.

WHY SHOULD KIDS EXERCISE?

I like to exercise because it's fun. There are other reasons to exercise too. I exercise because it's healthy. I like to exercise so I don't get fat. I exercise so I get strong. I exercise so I look good. I feel good when I exercise. You get fat by sitting around the house.

WHERE I HEAR ABOUT HEALTHY FOODS

I hear about healthy foods from my Dad. We learn about foods in school too. My teacher says to drink skim milk and eat lots of fruit and vegetables. They talk about food on TV, too.

WHY DO I STAY ON MY DIET?

I stay on my diet so I can be healthy and not have a heart attack. I won't get fat on my diet. The food is good and makes me strong.

FOODS I MISS MOST. FOODS I DON'T MISS

On my diet there are foods I miss and don't miss. One of the foods I miss is hot dogs and hamburgers. Another food I miss is ribs. I love cheese but I can't have it. Another food I like but is bad for me is chocolate. One of my favorite foods is real cookies.

FOODS I LIKE TO EAT THAT ARE GOOD FOR ME

One of my favorite foods that are good for me is pizza that my Dad and I make. Another good food that I like is spaghetti. My favorite food that is good for me is Chinese food. Another food that is good for me is chicken. Another food that I like is veal cutlets.

SPECIAL TREATS THAT I LIKE TO EAT ONCE IN A WHILE

There are special treats I like to eat once in a while. One treat is Del Taco. When I go to Del Taco I have a taco salad and a taco. Another treat I like is McDonald's. When I go to McDonald's I have a hamburger, Coke, and French fries.

DESSERTS THAT ARE GOOD FOR ME

Not all desserts are bad for you and not all desserts are good for you. One of my favorite desserts is mountain coffee ice cream.* I like popsicles, too. One of my favorite desserts is raspberries. I like rainbow sherbet, too.

WAYS I LIKE TO EAT OAT BRAN

There are many ways I like to eat oat bran. Oat bran is a kind of cereal. I like to eat oat bran in pancakes, granola bars, and hot cereal. After school I have a cookie and a glass of milk. One of my favorite breakfasts is waffles with oat bran. I like oat bran because it's good and it's good for me.

FOODS I CAN COOK MYSELF

There are some foods I can cook myself. I can cook scrambled eggs with Egg Beaters. I like to eat eggs with English muffins I make in the toaster. I can make a peanut butter sandwich. Sometimes I help my Dad make granola bars and cookies. I can make spaghetti if my Mom or Dad helps. I wish I could cook more foods.

FOODS I LIKE ON PICNICS

I like to have foods at picnics at the beach or in a park. I like to bring cold pizza. I like to have peanut butter sandwiches at picnics. Some times we have grapes. I like peaches, too, when they are ripe. I like milk to drink best. Sometimes I drink punch.

* The ice cream Ross refers to is a special low-fat product from Baskin-Robbins which has, unfortunately, been dropped from their product line.

IS IT BETTER TO EAT SCHOOL LUNCH OR HAVE A TREAT NOW AND THEN?

I like to eat lunch at school but it is not always good. My Dad says it has too much fat. So I bring my lunch. Now I can have a McDonald's hamburger instead of lunch. McDonald's is always good.* School lunch is not always good.

SHOPPING FOR FOODS

I go shopping for foods with my Mom or my Dad once in a while. I can pick foods that I like that they forget. But I don't like to take a lot of time.

WOULD I LIKE TO BE A VEGETARIAN?

I would not like to be a vegetarian because then I could not eat meat. I could not have hamburgers. I could not eat chicken. I like vegetables, but not all the time.

I admit that there are some things I wish Ross said and things I wish he didn't say. It's obvious that the boy misses hamburgers and other fast foods, and that he would like to eat the school lunch instead of bringing it from home. But notice that he does get to eat some of those foods as treats.

I wish he said—and felt—that it's just terrific that we don't eat foods with lots of fat, and that he doesn't miss them at all. But Ross was only 7 when he wrote this. I'm confident that as time goes on he'll grow more and more accustomed to the foods we eat and those we avoid. I'm especially certain that he'll start to enjoy more varied kinds of food. For example, he has started to enjoy Chinese food, as he wrote; last year he wouldn't touch it, but now it's a treat.

And, because he was only 7 years old, he didn't do a complete listing of all the foods that he does truly enjoy. I've spelled those foods out in Chapter 18, "Food Fit for a Kid."

As Ross said, there are times he likes to talk and times he doesn't. That can be frustrating. But don't force the issue with your kids. Let the talk come freely, at a time that's both comfortable and convenient.

The most important thing is that Ross doesn't feel cheated in life. He doesn't feel like some kind of weirdo. He's a normal, healthy, and happy kid and I hope to keep him that way.

* Since Ross doesn't eat the hamburgers at school, which he admits aren't very good, he does get to have a burger at McDonald's every once in a while as a treat.

16
Jenny's Chapter: The Sister's Story

When one person's eating habits change, it affects the entire family. In our case, Ross and I both must carefully limit the amount of fat and cholesterol in our diets to prevent future heart disease. What do other family members think about this?

There's no question that the contents of the kitchen cupboards, pantry, and refrigerator have changed quite a bit. We no longer have any chips around the house. Ice cream is gone from the freezer, replaced by sherbets, sorbets, frozen yogurt, and popsicles. What little candy slips in is now mostly the sorbitol-based, sucrose-free type instead of chocolates and other candies made with hydrogenated oil.

At meal times we make our own pizzas rather than eat commercial types. Our hot dogs and sausages are specially prepared from turkey breast. Burgers on the barbecue most frequently are also made with ground turkey breast. On down the line, there have been quite a few modifications. Details of those dietary innovations are spelled out elsewhere in this book.

How does Jenny, Ross's 5-year-old sister, react to all of this? I had and still have some insights, but I thought I'd sit down and actually talk with her about it. I explained that this would be Jenny's chapter, and that because she couldn't write very well yet, we'd use the tape recorder to get down all her ideas.

Jenny knew that Ross was working on a chapter for the book, and she was actually a bit jealous about that. She was disappointed that, owing to her lowly kindergarten status, she couldn't actually pencil down her words. But she really liked the idea that she'd be talking to lots of people who wanted to know what it was like to be the sister of a kid who was on a diet like Ross's.

What we share here, then, is a transcription of the conversation Jenny and I had.

DAD: Are you on a diet?

JENNY: No.

DAD: You're not on a diet?

JENNY: No.

DAD: Do you eat potato chips?

JENNY: No.

DAD: Do you eat lots of McDonald's?

JENNY: No.

DAD: Do you eat lots of pizza in restaurants?

JENNY: No.

DAD: So you're not on a diet.

JENNY: No. Is Ross on a diet?

DAD: Ross is on a diet. Because he doesn't eat a lot of ice cream, and pizza, and potato chips.

JENNY: Is that why he's on a diet?

DAD: Those are the things Ross doesn't eat on his diet, yes.

JENNY: Should other kids and big people?

DAD: Everybody should eat less of those foods.

JENNY: Daddy, I just want to go on Ross's diet or your diet.

DAD: Are you mad that Ross is on a diet?

JENNY: No.

DAD: Are you happy about the food we eat in this house?

JENNY: Yes.

DAD: What do you like to eat?

JENNY: Peaches, pears, and stuff like that.

DAD: How about for dinner?

JENNY: Soup, chicken, noodles, pizza.

DAD: What else?

JENNY: Chinese food.

DAD: Do you like the food at Angelina's [a friend] house?

JENNY: I get to eat food that's bad for you guys there.

DAD: And you get to eat other food sometimes—you get to "cheat" sometimes when you're not with Ross, right?

JENNY: [Giggle] Don't tell Ross.

DAD: I won't.

JENNY: Besides, I eat better food than Ross.

DAD: What do you mean?

JENNY: I eat more fruit, like bananas, and applesauce, and plums, and peaches, and soup, and apples, and more milk now. And, Daddy, could you make pear juice sometime?

DAD: Sure. And we have strawberry juice in the refrigerator now.

JENNY: Oh, goodie. But, Dad, I don't eat as good food as you do.

DAD: Sure you do. You eat very good food. It's actually easier for you, isn't it?

JENNY: I like all that stuff. Angelina doesn't have so much good food in her house. She likes to eat here.

DAD: What happens if *you* don't eat good food?

JENNY: I'd get fat. Like Grandma.

DAD: Do you wish Grandma wasn't fat?

JENNY: Uh huh, 'cause it can make you sick.

DAD: When you first came to California, Jenny, you were a little bit chubby. And when Mommy was your age, she was a little bit chubby. . . .

JENNY: But now I eat good foods, so now I'm not chubby, right?

DAD: Right.

JENNY: Not even a little bit chubby.

DAD: You're just right.

JENNY: I always want to eat good foods. But I'm not on a diet.

So there you have it. Jenny's not on a diet in her mind. And actually, of course, she's not, since there is no medical need. But she does eat the "good foods" in our house and she doesn't eat the "bad foods" that aren't in our house. After a couple of years of eating this way, she just doesn't know the difference.

It's like a kid being raised as a vegetarian. Someone told me once that their kids consider McDonald's and Burger King to be places to go to the playground, not to eat.

Jenny does know, however, that she eats good food. She's proud of the fact that she eats and enjoys lots of fruits. And she's proud that she isn't even a little bit chubby. She knows that food and overweight are linked. Notice, please, that we're not talking about having too much food. Rather, we talk about eating the right foods—or good foods, as the kids call them.

I have no worries that my Jenny will grow up with a fixation on weight that could lead to the eating disorders seen so often in teenage girls. Bulimia and anorexia nervosa result from poor self-image and obsession with thinness as well as with a feeling that too much food—and finally any food—makes one fat. Jenny's self-image is developing in a nice, healthy way. And in the meantime she's learning the eating patterns that will assure her a nice figure as she grows older. She won't have to go on a diet because her diet is part of her life.

One of Jenny's comments was that she drinks more milk now. That was a bit of a problem with her. She seldom wanted a glass, and much preferred apple juice. Osteoporosis is a problem on my wife's side of the family, afflicting both her mother and her grandmother. While calcium is only a part of the total prevention of this bone-degenerating disease, certainly we know that it's best to develop as strong a bone structure as possible early in life. Drinking the recommended amounts of milk and eating other calcium-rich dairy foods can be steps toward eliminating the osteoporosis problem in Jenny's future. And, of course, all those dairy foods are nonfat or low-fat varieties.

Jenny is an excellent example of how ridiculous it is to feed children anything but nonfat yogurt. She absolutely loves nonfat types. She can't tell the difference when a product with fat is given to her; so why not eliminate those unnecessary grams of fat and excess calories?

There's no question that Jenny enjoys pleasing her father, just as other little girls do. And she knows that eating good foods makes her Daddy happy. I don't see any reason this should be interpreted as anything but a very positive attitude about food. Today she tries to please me, and tomorrow she'll continue eating good foods to please herself.

You read that Jenny enjoys eating away from home once in a while. She eats at friends' homes and at fast-food restaurants occasionally, just as other children do. To Jenny, this is enough. And actually, she eats such foods no more often than Ross. I don't worry about what either of them eats when away from home since it's balanced by what they eat at home. In addition, both automatically choose the foods that are best for them whenever possible.

I don't believe that Jenny is much different from other little sisters placed in the same situation. And the earlier a child starts on the program, the easier it is. For Jenny it's much more of a way of life than it is for Ross.

Certainly there's no trauma involved. I have a very happy, healthy little girl whom I love a great deal. And I enjoy all the love she gives right back. Even though Jenny doesn't have a cholesterol problem, she'll be a major beneficiary in the legacy of life that this eating program can assure.

17

The Research Continues

Early in the book I talked about research that convinced me I had to do something about putting my own children on the path to a future free of heart disease. That research continues, even as I write this final chapter and even as you read it.

Both pediatricians and cardiologists recognize that prevention is the best medicine, and that the roots of heart disease are found in childhood. Project after project is being initiated both to screen for high cholesterol levels in youngsters and to intervene in order to change lifestyles.

Some of those efforts are small, truly grassroots community efforts. Others are vast in size and scope and have the cooperation of federal agencies. All, however, have as their driving motivation the sincere belief that all of us can work together to eliminate a major risk factor in heart disease.

Perhaps some of the projects are happening right in your own community. In Orange County, just south of Los Angeles, an inter-agency effort has been made to screen schoolchildren and to educate both students and parents about the need for changing dietary habits. The project was spearheaded by an all-volunteer group called Hereditary Hearts, which was begun by two men who have family histories of heart disease. They contacted the University of California at Irvine, the American Heart Association, and some corporations for support.

Harbour Diagnostics, a private business in Huntington Beach, contributed money to purchase disposables to test 460 fourth-grade students in the Westminster School District. The Eastman

Kodak Company contributed a blood analyzer and also supplied a technician, who processed blood samples at the screening clinics.

Under the supervision of Sandra Landry, R.N., of the Westminster School District, health services personnel got parental consent; collected blood samples by finger pricks; trained classroom teachers; organized the screening clinics; obtained family histories, blood pressure readings, and body weights; and compiled all the data. Those data were then analyzed by personnel from the Preventive Cardiology Division at UCI under the direction of Dennis Davidson, M.D. UCI also offered free follow-up for students with high cholesterol levels. And the American Heart Association contributed educational materials for all the fourth-grade classes in the school district.

Parents of all students were informed of the test results in writing, in either Spanish or English. If levels of cholesterol were 190 or more, parents were advised to consult family physicians or pediatricians. Dr. Paul Qaqundah, president of the local chapter of the American Academy of Pediatrics, worked to communicate progress of the efforts to area pediatricians.

This project demonstrated both the value and effectiveness of such screening. Of the 460 students screened, 64 were found to have cholesterol levels above 190. Many had values above average, which could and should be lowered by proper dietary changes. Those 64 students represent 14 percent of the total student population in their schools. And those numbers correlate directly with other studies which have shown similar percentages of youngsters whose futures almost certainly will include heart disease unless something is done to prevent it. The average cholesterol level in the Westminster School District was 166, compared to about 160 nationwide. Thus a very large percentage of those fourth-graders need dietary changes. Interestingly, the high numbers were not restricted to certain ethnic groups. Even the researchers themselves expected lower readings in the many Vietnamese students. But apparently the American way of eating which leads to high cholesterol levels is quickly learned and adopted by our young immigrants.

Larry Grannis, one of the co-founders of Hereditary Hearts, is a tireless worker. His goal is eventually to test all 30,000 school-age children in Orange County! All he can think of is the large number of youngsters in that population in whom a time bomb is quietly ticking away. He wants to defuse that bomb as soon as possible.

Perhaps you might be interested in getting involved with a similar project in your own community. The place to start might be the local office of the American Heart Association. Find out what's currently going on, and what could be done to help the youngsters in your area.

Much of the research being done in communities stems from the universities. One such program began at the Institute for Health Promotion and Disease Prevention Research at the University of Southern California in Pasadena. Their Project Smart, funded by the National Institutes of Health, focused on the prevention of cigarette smoking and the promotion of healthful lifestyles in junior high school students.

In that project, researchers worked with three area junior high schools in the communities of Palos Verdes, La Habra, and El Segundo. There was a good balance of students representing all socioeconomic and ethnic groups. Cholesterol screening was done along with measurements of height and weight. Both parents and children received education regarding potential changes in lifestyle, including additional exercise and better food habits. In all three groups, after just a few weeks, there was a notable loss of weight and a distinct change in attitude about taking personal responsibility for health, both by students and parents.

At the end of the study, I was invited to address the groups at all three schools. It was very edifying to see the tremendous enthusiasm and very positive attitude toward reducing the risk of future heart disease.

In Texas, researchers directed their efforts right to one of the sources of fat in youngsters' diets: the school lunch program. In a study published in the April 1987 issue of the *Journal of School Health*, the school lunches provided 31.4 grams of total fat and 1,244.4 milligrams of sodium. Fat represented 38.8 percent of the total calories in the meal. Compare that with the recommendations of 30 percent of calories derived from fat as recommended in the U.S. dietary goals. And I'm not at all sure that even that 30 percent figure is low enough. The amount of sodium was 107.4 percent higher than the maximum recommended amount.

A program called Go For Health was implemented in the Texas schools. Its three components included school lunch, physical education, and classroom instruction. The idea was to reduce the average per lunch content of sodium to 600 mg or less, and total fat to 30 percent or less of total calories. The researchers also wanted to increase class time devoted to vigorous physical activity and to develop students' knowledge of and skills in healthful eating practices.

How well will they succeed? The research is going on for the next three years, concluding at the end of 1990. But I can certainly predict that even if all the goals are not reached to the maximum extent, those children will benefit a great deal. And one of the very nice aspects of this program is that all the children are in it together. Not just a few are singled out.

Remember the Bogalusa Study? That's the one in Louisiana, in which researchers found that cholesterol levels "track" throughout youth and on into young adulthood, and that the higher the cholesterol levels in youngsters, the greater the amount of atherosclerotic buildup even as teens. So it's fitting that research is now going on to try to do something to prevent heart disease in Louisiana children. The program is called Heart Smart. Specific objectives are directed at promoting regular exercise to increase cardiovascular fitness; decreasing consumption of dietary fat, sodium, and sugar to enhance nutritional health; attaining and maintaining optimal weight; learning to deal with stress; and preventing present or future cigarette smoking. There's also a parent-education component of the program, so that knowledge and skills can be carried from the classroom into the home.

The ongoing study, now underway in four New Orleans schools, is detailed in the March 1987 issue of the *Journal of School Health*. Interestingly, that journal contains more and more such reports of studies going on all over the country.

In New York, under the auspices of the American Health Foundation, the Know Your Body health-education program attempts to reduce children's risk for future disease through a multidimensional approach combining health screening, a Health Passport that provides feedback to students on their results, teacher training, and curriculum materials on behavior-oriented learning activities and special activities for high-risk students. The project is part of an international collaborative project with fourteen other nations. In New York, more than 3,600 children ages 12 to 15 underwent health screening including height, weight, and obesity determinations, blood pressure readings, cholesterol levels, recovery after exercise, and cigarette smoking history. Both upper- and lower-income students are represented. Heart disease knows no financial barriers.

But the largest study of all is a five-year project funded through the National Heart, Lung, and Blood Institute. This is a collaborative trial to assess feasibility, acceptability, efficacy, and safety of dietary intervention in children 8 to 10 years of age with elevated levels of cholesterol. Researchers picked that age group to permit examination of the issue of safety of recommended dietary interventions because it represents the years of most rapid growth and development beyond that of infancy.

The project is being coordinated by Linda Van Horn, Ph.D., of Northwestern University in Chicago. A total of six universities across the country will contribute data after following the identical protocol, the research design by which children will be screened and efforts will be made to lower cholesterol levels by dietary means.

There's absolutely no doubt in my mind, or in the opinions of the many cardiologists and pediatricians I've spoken with since beginning this book, that such research will continue and that we'll see an increasing array of data which demonstrate the effectiveness of changing the diets and lifestyles of our children. We *can* give our children a future free of heart disease. You are on the leading edge!

There's no reason to delay. Start today. Your children will thank you tomorrow. And for the many years to come.

One of the greatest villains of all time once made a coldly analytical statement about life and death. "One man's death is a tragedy," Joseph Stalin said, "while the deaths of a million men are a statistic."

To me, the death of *any* child is a tragedy. And it's no less a tragedy when death, in the form of heart disease, strikes at any time early in life. It's especially tragic because we now know largely how to prevent those future deaths—how to give our children a future free of heart disease.

As I complete this book, Ross is 9 years old and Jenny is 6. Both are healthy, happy youngsters. They're growing strong on the wonderfully healthful program I've described for you. I urge you to give your own children that same opportunity.

18
Food Fit for a Kid

A long, long time ago, in a galaxy far away, you and I were kids. Try to remember way back then. What kind of foods did you like? Did you look forward to quiche? Was *fettuccine Alfredo* one of your favorites? Did your taste buds dance at the thought of spinach soufflé?

Probably not. If you were anything like me, you liked much simpler foods. In fact, I was a picky eater who enjoyed only a few dishes. Any efforts to get fancy were met with resistance—to say the least.

Talk to your kids. Listen to what they say they like to eat. I'll bet they don't list more than eight types of food, and they really don't mind if those foods are repeated over and over again. If two weeks pass without a hamburger, it seems like forever to youthful taste buds.

Most parents resist giving in to this very natural tendency in their kids. They can't understand why their gourmet culinary efforts meet with little or no enthusiasm. The wiser parent, hoping to survive childhood, learns to go with the flow.

Eventually your child will come to enjoy some of the finer foods in life. But in the meantime, there's no point in fighting the natural preferences of youth. And, for the purposes of reducing cholesterol levels, you can use those preferences to your advantage.

In our family, Ross and Jenny have different tastes but share certain typical kids' favorites. What I've done is simply to modify recipes and find some alternatives. We have a list in the kitchen of all the "kid-tested-and-approved" foods, and they're prepared in regular rotation.

Think about the practicality of that. How many times have you asked your children what they want for dinner? Probably they don't come up with an immediate response, or if they do, it's for something that you don't have the ingredients for or that will take too long to prepare. By talking with your kids and taking notes on what their favorite foods are, and what foods they're willing to eat without too much protest, you can prepare meals that are not only good for them but which you can reasonably expect them to eat.

Maybe you're one of the really lucky parents in the world whose children will eat everything you put in front of them. Maybe your son and daughter even gobble up all the vegetables. If so, count your blessings.

But for the rest of us mortals, the list of kid-approved foods won't be very long. In this chapter I've shared with you the Kowalski kids' favorites. Each of the recipes and meal plans packs lots of nutrition with very little fat and cholesterol. And they're really kid-pleasers.

We have the kind of home where all the kids in the neighborhood tend to congregate. Friends of Ross or Jenny are frequent guests at dinner. And it's a real pleasure to watch those children clean their plates. Often they say they wish they got this or that food at their homes. That's not bragging; it's just our way of emphasizing that these foods will be welcomed by your youngsters also.

But before I give you the specifics of those recipes and meal plans, I'd like to discuss some of the principles that should go into meal planning. First, I don't believe that people can or should radically change their eating habits. It's just not necessary to do so, and trying to avoid all favorite foods is almost certain to destroy hopes of staying with a diet. Remember that you're trying to establish eating patterns that will stick with your kids for life.

Second, all those favorites can be modified to reduce fat and cholesterol content. That's not as difficult as it may at first seem because most of the fat and cholesterol in our foods come from just a few sources. I'll go into more detail shortly.

Third, serving sizes should be realistic. When determining the amount of meat to serve, for example, figure on 4 ounces raw for each person. Small children may need even less. Build the meal around that entree using a wide variety of other foods, rather than concentrating on the meat almost entirely.

Fourth, try to avoid fried foods. There's no way around the fact that frying adds a great deal of fat. Focus on baking, broiling, boiling, steaming roasting, and barbecuing instead.

Fifth, get to know your butcher. Explain that you're trying to cut back on fat for your family's health. If he or she isn't willing to do a few things to accommodate your needs, find another place to shop.

Now let's look at those principles in a bit more detail. How will you modify your favorite recipes and new ones you'll find in newspapers and magazines to be more healthful?

The most frequent modification involves eggs. Use two egg whites for each whole egg in most cooking and baking recipes. If the recipe specifically needs egg yolks, use an egg substitute. I prefer Egg Beaters because that product contains no added oil, as do most other brands. Egg Beaters are also terrific for making scrambled eggs and French toast.

The next category of substitution includes the dairy foods. Instead of cream, use canned evaporated skim milk. Pet makes an excellent product, but not all stores carry it; ask your supermarket manager to order a case for you. Whole milk should be replaced by skim milk. Ice cream should bow out in favor of ice milk, frozen yogurt, or sherbet.

For sour cream, use nonfat yogurt or try a mock version made with nonfat yogurt and low-fat cottage cheese blended with lemon juice (see page 248). This makes an excellent topping for potatoes and serves as a base for dips and other recipes.

Instead of butter, use vegetable oil for cooking and baking. Serve soft tub margarine at the table. Avoid stick margarines, which contain saturated fats produced by the hydrogenation process. Try some of the imitation margarines, which have either water or air beaten into them to increase the volume and cut fat and calories. Or, before serving, beat margarine with an electric mixer at high speed to work in some air, thus reducing the fat content per portion.

Discover the possibilities offered by a wonderful product called Butter Buds. It comes in a shaker and also in packets and is a powder which can be mixed with water, sprinkled straight over hot foods, or worked into recipes to provide the flavor of butter with none of the fat. You'll see Butter Buds in the recipes in this chapter.

Another product to consider is called Molly McButter. This comes in a little shaker container so you can sprinkle it directly onto fresh steaming vegetables and baked potatoes.

When frying, spray the pan with Pam or other vegetable oil spray. While the principal ingredient is hydrogenated oil, the amount actually used is small. A two-second blast puts less than a gram of fat on the pan. You'll be surprised at how little you really need to get the job done—say, when making pancakes or waffles.

When baking, try Baker's Joy. This is a spray product containing flour and oil. It works beautifully when making cookies, granola bars, and the other oat-bran recipes in Chapter 11.

Next comes cheese. Unfortunately, this is one of the most unhealthful foods on earth. Ironically, it's advertised as being one of the most healthful. But then the dairy industry has painted that picture. In truth, most cheese consists of about 50 percent fat, a lot of cholesterol, and a huge amount of sodium. The calories also contribute to weight problems.

Let's look at some examples of 1-ounce servings of common cheeses—and keep in mind that most people don't stop at 1 ounce. Cheddar cheese has 30 milligrams of cholesterol, 9.1 grams of fat, and 197 milligrams of sodium. Cream cheese socks you with 34 milligrams of cholesterol, 9.9 grams of fat, and 84 milligrams of sodium. The figures are similar for other cheeses. And remember that the fat we're talking about is saturated.

But all is not lost. Borden has developed Lite-Line cheeses in many flavors. They've cut the fat down to only 2 grams per ounce, with similarly reduced cholesterol content. One slice weighs less than 1 ounce, so the numbers can be even lower in the servings you prepare.

Next come the filled cheeses, so termed because the animal fat has been removed and replaced with vegetable oil. Lo-Chol is an imitation muenster that my kids and I particularly enjoy. Look for others in your supermarket.

For cooking, try shredded imitation cheeses such as Cheddamelt and Mozzamelt. There are many other brands of similar imitation cheeses on the market; read the labels to see that they are fat- and cholesterol-reduced products. Here, too, you cut way down on cholesterol and completely eliminate the saturated animal fat.

Watch out, however, for certain nondairy products that contain hydrogenated oils. Coffee creamers, whipped toppings, and imitation sour cream too often list hydrogenated oils and/or coconut oil as the principal fat. That's just as saturated, if not more so, than butterfat. It's very important to start reading labels carefully when shopping.

On to the meats you use in cooking. As practically all the major health organizations in the United States and other countries have advised, select more poultry and fish and less red meat. Red meats contain at least twice, and up to three times, as much fat as poultry and seafood. See Table 17 for specifics. When looking at recipes, you'll find that turkey can take the place of veal almost every time. For example, veal cutlets can become turkey cutlets. Ground beef can become turkey burgers. The possibilities are almost endless.

Chicken also provides great alternatives. Remember that the fat in poultry is in the skin and dark meat. Select chicken breasts and remove the skin before cooking.

Cutting back on salt means using a bit of creativity with alternative spices and herbs. While most kids don't like very spicy dishes, many enjoy the flavor of lemon. For a bit of variety, put lime slices on the table to squeeze over foods. Youngsters also enjoy garlic a lot.

Armed with those alternatives, you can adapt almost any recipe to a more healthful version. And when you do, keep the serving sizes down, too. The day should be long gone when boys grow up to be men who brag about eating a 2-pound steak at one sitting. McDonald's boasts about its quarter-pounder. That's 4 ounces of meat *before* cooking. Unfortunately, they add more fat by way of their toppings, cheese, and even the bun. But the fact remains that no one needs more than 4 ounces of meat per meal.

You may hear some complaints at first, but soon all in the family will come to accept that meat will not be the dominating feature of the meal. You can diminish those complaints by thinking of other foods to serve, such as corn on the cob, plenty of bread, baked potatoes, and other family favorites.

As said earlier, try to avoid fried foods whenever possible. Instead, bake, roast, boil, steam, or broil your foods. When you do have a recipe that calls for frying, use a nonstick pan and spray with Pam rather than add tablespoons of oil or butter. You can sauté foods in a little chicken broth rather than butter, as well.

Many recipes call for initial frying prior to subsequent cooking. In those cases, the food simply needs to be cooked, and frying is a fast, easy way to get the job done. Instead, parboil the foods to render them tender. Poaching chicken in either plain water or herb-flavored white wine actually gives a more tender piece of meat that beautifully complements the flavor of a sauce.

When you want ground meat, it's best to buy it fresh. Select a slice of lean beef round steak, ask the butcher to slice off the visible fat, and have him grind the meat. The butcher can do the same with veal, to obtain an even lower fat content. And for the lowest possible fat content in meat, have the butcher grind a turkey breast that's been skinned and boned.

While you're in the butcher shop or the meat section of the supermarket, order some turkey cutlets. Simply ask to have a turkey breast cut the same way as for veal.

The next suggestion calls for real cooperation from your butcher. Find a butcher who makes sausage on the premises. Then convince him or her to make a special batch to your specifications, using either ground turkey breast or ultralean veal. With the right seasonings and preparation, this is a delicious alternative to commercial high-fat sausages. You can have your butcher make bratwurst, hot dogs, breakfast sausage, or other types. Typically he'll ask for a minimum order of, say, 10 or 20 pounds.

If you have a large refrigerator-freezer, or a large family, that may be fine. But you might also consider splitting an order with other families interested in improving their health. You may even convince your butcher to offer these low-fat varieties to other customers on a normal basis. Mine has.

Until we started bringing such sausages into our home, we had a difficult time replacing such foods as hot dogs. Look at the labels of franks in the market, and you'll see that even chicken and turkey dogs have a high fat content. Some beef frankfurters contain as much as 20 grams of fat, and most people eat two at a time.

Many other turkey products have similarly high fat levels. The reason is that packagers use dark meat rather than the more expensive breasts, and they include the fat and skin in the manufacturing process. That often brings the fat content close to that in beef products.

The best way to go is with freshly ground turkey and veal. A friendly butcher can get you started on a great new way to lower your children's cholesterol counts.

While it may take a bit of effort to purchase such sausages, they provide tremendous convenience in the home. Probably one of the major reasons the typical American diet contains so much fat is that people like you and I need to save time. It's so much easier to pop a hot dog into the microwave oven than to make a more elaborate meal. Now you can have the benefits of convenience foods without the health hazards. And the cost is remarkably low.

Every kid likes hot dogs. But what are some other favorites? I assure you, your kids can eat like kids and still reduce the total fat and cholesterol in their diet.

What does a month's menus look like in a family that restricts fat and cholesterol? Not much different from that in a family that never heard the words. I've selected thirty dinner menus, enough for a month's planning, that are among my family's favorites. Each has been specially designed or modified to bring the fat and cholesterol contents down to very low levels. But not one scrap of flavor has been left out. My kids really enjoy these foods, and I'll bet yours will, too.

Here are the menu plans, with recipes to follow:

Roast turkey breast, sweet potatoes, broccoli, and cranberry sauce.

Mexican food: tacos, burritos, or tostados with refried beans and rice; chicken enchiladas.

Spaghetti and sauce with tossed green salad.

Cheese omelet with potatoes, served with sliced tomatoes, fruit and cucumber spears, and toast.

Chinese food: wok favorites with chicken, sprouts, snow peas, carrots, broccoli, and mushrooms.

Chicken pot pie with peas and carrots, mashed potatoes, and a salad.

Special pizza with green peppers, tomatoes, onions, mushrooms, ham, and, yes, cheese.

Macaroni and cheese, served with green beans and applesauce.

Ham with sweet potatoes and peas, and a delicious raisin sauce.

Chicken, barbecued indoors or on the outdoor grill, and served with sweet corn and broasted potatoes.

Turkey sausages with mashed potatoes, applesauce, and no-fat gravy.

Roast beef, baked potatoes and mock sour cream, and acorn squash.

Salad bar with many options.

Grilled cheese sandwiches and soup.

Teriyaki chicken with Oriental vegetables and rice.

Backwards breakfasts (breakfast for dinner).

Turkey burgers with sweet corn and broasted potatoes.
Salmon patties with mashed potatoes and peas.
Wagon wheel pasta with marinara sauce.
Meat loaf or meat balls with potatoes and vegetables.
Chili with macaroni—a meal in a bowl.
Turkey cutlets with mashed potatoes, gravy, and beets.
Hearty vegetable soup with bread.
Oven-fried chicken, low-fat French fries, and corn.
Vegetable pasta and pepper sauce.
Turkey sandwiches, mashed potatoes and gravy, and cranberry
    sauce.
Barbecued chicken sandwiches served with baked potatoes.
Tuna sandwiches with raw vegetable sticks and dip.
Fruit platter with yogurt.

ROAST TURKEY AND TRIMMINGS

If turkey means Thanksgiving, then it's Thanksgiving Day at the
Kowalski household many times each year. Not only do we have a
lot to be thankful for, and we are, but we eat a lot of turkey because
it's a wonderful, delicious, and low-fat meat. You can do the same,
but forget all the hassle and hours of preparation that marked
turkey dinners of the past.

The best part of the turkey is the breast; the other parts are
much higher in fat. So purchase a fresh or frozen whole turkey
breast. Roasting it in a kettle-type outdoor charcoal grill makes it
really simple. Use the indirect method of cooking, whereby you
place the coals along the sides and put the turkey breast on the grill
above a drip pan. Or try using one of the cooking bags available
now in all supermarkets. Follow the directions on the package,
pop the breast into the bag and then into the oven, and you have a
cooked turkey with no mess.

But what about the dressing? If you stuff a turkey with dressing,
when it roasts the fat drips directly into the dressing, literally soak-
ing it with fat. That's why I prefer to make the dressing on the side.
Although commercial dressing mixes contain some hydrogenated
fat, their total content is low. And I substitute Butter Buds for the
suggested margarine or butter.

On the other hand, you may be feeling energetic and festive,
and want to make a stuffing from scratch. Use your favorite family

recipe—omitting sausage and excessive fats—and wrap the dressing mixture in heavy-duty aluminum foil, or use another cooking bag. Here is the Kowalski family's dressing recipe, followed by the sweet potato recipe.

• • • • • • • • • • • • • • • Festive Family Dressing

1 tablespoon corn or
   olive oil
4 celery stalks, chopped
1 medium onion,
   chopped
1 pound ground turkey
   breast
1 tablespoon powdered
   sage
1 teaspoon thyme leaves
1 teaspoon ground
   pepper
1 teaspoon salt
1 (16-ounce) box
   stuffing bread cubes
½ cup chicken or turkey
   broth

Preheat oven to 350°F. In a large skillet or Dutch oven, heat the oil and sauté the celery and onion until transparent but not browned. Add the ground turkey and brown with the vegetables, breaking up the pieces of meat as it browns. Mix in the seasonings. Add bread cubes all at once, mixing rapidly. Drizzle the broth over the dressing and toss to keep bread cubes from becoming soaked. Place in a cooking bag or wrap in heavy-duty aluminum foil. Bake in oven for 45 minutes. *Serves 6.*

• • • • • • • • • • • • • • Baked Sweet Potatoes

Forget the yucky yams of yore, dripping with butter, sugar, and marshmallows. Start to enjoy the delicious flavor of this rich source of vitamins A and C and fiber. Just wash the potatoes, pierce with a fork, spray with a bit of butter-flavored Pam, wrap with aluminum foil, and pop into the oven along with the stuffing for 30 to 45 minutes, depending on the size of the potatoes and how much other food you have in the oven. Encourage your family to eat the potato skins as well as the flesh.

The turkey, stuffing, and potatoes, served with some cranberry sauce and maybe a piece of bread, make a complete meal. You don't really need more. Who wants to have that bloated feeling we remember from Thanksgivings past?

And you'll enjoy any turkey breast that is left over. It makes fabulous sandwiches, or add some slivers of cold turkey breast to salads.

On the other hand, you might want to invite some friends or neighbors to the house when you decide to do your turkey dinner. Just watch the happy expressions on their faces when they sit down to a succulent turkey dinner in the middle of July!

MEXICAN FOOD

Just as pizza made the American scene years ago and quickly became part of our culture, so Mexican foods are rapidly making inroads. When I moved to California in 1980, I thought it was only this part of the country that went taco-wild. But now everywhere we travel we see Mexican fast-food places as well as finer restaurants. The problem, however, is that Mexican foods are often if not always made with staple ingredients such as lard and cheese. But with a few substitutions in your home, Mexican food can become a welcome delight for you and the kids.

• • • • • • • • • • • • • • **Tacos**

Whether for dinner, lunch, or a snack, tacos can be healthful and nutritious if made properly. Start with corn tortillas. Spray them very lightly with Pam and fold to form a pocket in which you'll place the filling. Place them on a cookie sheet in a 400°F oven for 10 minutes.

Use any of the commercial taco seasoning mixes; none contains any fat. Mix with browned ground turkey breast in a large skillet according to the directions on the package.

Fill the tacos with the meat mixture, chopped lettuce and tomatoes, grated low-fat cheese, chopped black olives, a dollop of taco sauce, and maybe a teaspoonful or two of plain nonfat yogurt. Or, better yet, put all the ingredients on a serving platter and let the family build their own tacos.

• • • • • • • • • • • • • • • • **Burritos**

Burritos are made with flour tortillas, which can be folded and
filled to form Mexican sandwiches. But looking at the label,
you'll see that most flour tortillas are made with lard. Buy the
kind labeled "vegetarian," made with soybean oil.

Using any brand of burrito seasoning, follow the directions on
the seasoning packet, but substitute ground turkey breast for
beef. With all the seasonings, no one will know the difference.
Another possibility is to combine ground turkey breast and very
lean ground veal; it's good.

Once again, let the family put together their own burritos,
made with meat filling, some refried beans, grated low-fat or
imitation cheese, sliced black olives, and perhaps some minced
onion.

We keep a supply of vegetarian flour tortillas in the house
practically all the time. Ross and Jenny both like to make burritos
for snacks on weekends and after school. If we happen to have
some meat filling left over, that's fine. But if not, Ross simply
smears some refried beans on the tortilla, sprinkles on a bit of
cheese, folds it over, and pops it into the microwave oven. It's
instant good food.

• • • • • • • • • • • • • • • • **Tostados**

This is another terrific lunch or snack item that's very easy to
prepare. Just bake some corn tortillas flat in the oven for 10
minutes at 350°F. When they're crispy, smear some refried beans
on top and sprinkle with a bit of low-fat or imitation cheese.
Bake for another 5 minutes and enjoy.

• • • • • • • • • • • • • • • • **Chicken Enchiladas**

1 pound chicken breasts
1 package any brand
   enchilada sauce mix
   (1¾ ounce)
1 (6-ounce) can tomato
   paste
8 corn tortillas

*One day my kids and I stopped
into a restaurant that had, since
the last time we visited, converted
the menu to all-Mexican food.
"You said you can eat anywhere,
Dad. How are we going to eat
here?" Jenny asked. The menu*

½ cup shredded
    cheddar-flavor
    imitation cheese

was, of course, filled with items made with cheese and sour cream. I surprised both children by ordering chicken enchiladas (no cheese) with ranchero sauce, rice, and dinner salads with dressing on the side. The meal was delicious, and since we all enjoyed it so much we started making the same dish at home.

Peel off and discard the skin from the chicken breasts. Place the breasts in a pot with enough boiling water to cover and simmer them for 20 minutes. Drain and allow to cool; shred into small bits. Prepare the sauce by combining the mix with the tomato paste and 3 cups of water in a saucepan. Pour 1 cup of the sauce into a 12″ × 8″ × 2″ casserole dish. Dip each of the corn tortillas into the sauce, covering both sides. Divide the shredded chicken among the 8 tortillas, placing the meat in a line down the center third of each tortilla. Fold the filled tortillas and place seam down in the dish. Pour the remaining sauce over the enchiladas and sprinkle the cheese over the top. Bake for 20 minutes at 350°F. Serve with rice and salad. *Serves 4.*

• • • • • • • • • • • • • • **Corn Chips**

We've banished potato chips and their ilk from our house, but we still have a taste for crunchy snacks. So instead we buy corn tortillas, cut them into quarters, spray with just a bit of Pam, sprinkle with a tiny bit of salt or Mrs. Dash, and bake them for 10 minutes at 350°F.

• • • • • • • • • • • • • • • **Refried Beans and Rice**

No one knows exactly how or why it happened, but centuries ago certain cultural groups including the Hispanics began to combine beans and rice in their cooking. The result is a very healthful combination because the two foods contain complementary amino acids; together they provide as many amino acids as in any animal food.

Today refried beans and rice are traditionally served with Mexican foods of all kinds. They are delicious and nutritious. But you have to be careful about the beans you buy. Most brands are made with lard. Look for vegetarian refried beans, made with soybean oil.

SPAGHETTI AND _____ SAUCE

No, the name of the recipe isn't incorrect. While practically everyone loves spaghetti (or linguini or fidelini or spaghettini, or whatever), people's tastes in sauce differ. In my family of four, we wind up with three sauce preferences. Ross and Dawn prefer meat sauce. I like red clam sauce. And little Jenny likes the plain bottled Ragu sauce. We buy the traditional flavor, without beef or pepperoni. But pleasing us all isn't that difficult.

Start with two saucepans: one for the meat sauce, the other for the clam sauce. That's assuming, of course, that you don't all want to have the meat sauce.

• • • • • • • • • • • • • • • **Meat Sauce**

1 pound ground veal 2–3 garlic cloves, minced 1 (15-ounce) can Italian tomato sauce, plus ½ can water Salt to taste (optional)	Brown the veal in a heavy saucepan and drain off excess fat. Add garlic and cook until tender with the meat. Drain off remaining fat. Add the tomato sauce. (The Italian variety has some nice seasonings and you won't need any more—a nice time-saver.) Mix in water and simmer sauce for 10 to

15 minutes. Serve over pasta.
Serves 6.

• • • • • • • • • • • • • • • **Red Clam Sauce**

2–3 garlic cloves,
        minced
   1 (7½-ounce) can
        chopped clams,
        packed in water
   ½ (7½-ounce) can
        Italian tomato
        sauce

You can prepare this recipe
simultaneously. Just spray a skillet
with Pam and sauté the garlic until
tender. Drain the clams and
reserve the juice. Add the clams to
the garlic and cook until tender.
Add the clam juice and simmer
until reduced by one-half. Add the
tomato sauce and simmer for 5 to
10 minutes. Serve over pasta.
Serves 2.

• • • • • • • • • • • • • • • **Pasta**

For the best-tasting pasta, use the biggest pot you have in the
house, fill it half full with water, and bring the water to a rolling
boil. Add the pasta in 4 portions so the water doesn't cool down
to stop boiling. Linguini takes 8 minutes to reach the *al dente*
point of just a bit of chewiness. Thinner pasta takes
proportionately less time. Fidelini, for example, cooks in just 5
minutes. Drain in a colander, but do not rinse.

Both the meat and clam sauces freeze beautifully, and make
wonderful meals when time is at a premium. We like to eat our
pasta meals with a big salad of lots of different greens and
vegetables.

DINNER OMELETS

This menu almost falls into the category of Backwards Breakfast (see page 254), except that omelets are, in fact, a perfectly acceptable dinner option. Thanks to Egg Beaters, you can enjoy omelets whenever you want, and you'll probably want to put them on your monthly menus.

One carton of Egg Beaters is equivalent to four eggs. We like to mix in one fresh egg white. That's just enough for two kid-size omelets. Adults may need more.

To prepare, spray a nonstick pan with butter-flavor Pam and pour in the Egg Beater mixture. Set pan over medium heat and cook until the eggs start to set. Then add any other ingredients to one side of the omelet. Fold the other side over, and you have an omelet on the way. Flip the whole thing over to brown the other side and serve with specially fried potatoes.

There are almost no limits to the ingredients you can put in an omelet. Most kids enjoy simpler ones such as cheese; use the Borden's Lite-Line varieties. Or spread on some fruit preserves. If the youngsters are a little older or more adventurous, add some chopped green peppers, onions, and mushrooms. Or how about some low-fat ham? I find an omelet of smoked salmon an absolute delicacy, though with the price of lox being what it is, I have it infrequently. But the kids think I'm goofy to enjoy such a meal. They'll learn.

In Europe, and less frequently in the United States, restaurants serve omelets with French-fried potatoes. And sometimes they even put the potatoes into the omelet. In either case, potatoes seem to grace an omelet perfectly. Here's the kind we especially like. We like to keep some leftover, unpeeled baked potatoes in the vegetable crisper of the refrigerator; they come in handy for this recipe.

• • • • • • • • • • • • • • • • **Breakfast or Dinner Fried Potatoes**

Per person:

1 medium baked potato
2 tablespoons finely chopped green peppers

Cut the potatoes into small chunks, then mix with the green pepper and onion. Spray mixture with a light coating of Pam, then spread in a nonstick pan. Now here's

1 tablespoon finely
  chopped onion
Salt or Mrs. Dash

Dawn's secret for success: cook over a medium to low heat for about 30 minutes to get the potatoes crisp on the outside. Sprinkle with a bit of salt or other seasoning such as Mrs. Dash and serve with omelets. Boy, that's good eating! And watch those kids dig in!

NOTE: Serve the omelet and potatoes with side dishes of sliced fruits, tomato slices, and cucumber spears.

CHINESE FOOD

Do you ever get tired of hearing the kids complain that they don't like this or that ingredient in a dish you spent hours preparing? It drives parents nuts to watch the little dears pick out bits of "green stuff" or refuse to eat the meal at all. Stir-fry cookery is just the ticket for such families.

You can involve the kids in the food preparation. Have them decide what ingredients they'd like to use. Ross likes broccoli and snow peas. Jenny won't touch the snow peas but likes carrots. My wife and I want all the ingredients possible, including mushrooms, miniature corn, and other exotics. After selection come the peeling and chopping. Even the smallest child can peel a few carrots. So while the kids are preparing the vegetables, you can slice some chicken breast into slivers or slices, as you prefer.

While all the preparation is going on, get out the wok. We prefer using an electric wok, which maintains a constant heat and avoids the problem of open flames. (The Maxim is a terrific brand and a great investment that will last for years.)

Use peanut oil very sparingly. It takes just a little bit to coat the bottom of a wok. As an alternative, Dawn uses some chicken or vegetable broth to further reduce the fat content of the meal.

For a family of four, use about 1 pound of chicken breast meat. When the oil is heated, cook the meat at a rate of ¼ pound at a time so it cooks quickly. When the meat turns white, add the vegetables you're using for your kids' meal and stir-fry until just tender. Nobody really likes mushy veggies, and maybe that's why so many youngsters are turned off by vegetables cooked in traditional ways. Again, you can vary the ingredients to please each person at a time.

When the children are already digging into their portions, you can cook your own meal. Let the wok come back to full heat, add the chicken, and then add your vegetables. By spacing out our meals, Dawn and I get to eat alone together for a nice change.

Now a word about sauces. Anything goes. We like oyster sauce in our house. You may want to add a splash of soy sauce. Or maybe some sweet and sour sauce. Your supermarket has them all. You don't have to bother making sauces from scratch; the ones out of jars are just fine. Add them to taste when the vegetables have cooked until tender-crisp.

Serve the vegetables and meat with lots and lots of steamed rice. Here are two surefire ways to make rice that comes out properly each time. First, invest in a rice maker. For just a few dollars—they're really not at all expensive—you'll have an appliance that can be used for years and years and save lots of money on wrecked rice. As an alternative, use a pot with a tight cover that provides a good seal. Remember that if steam escapes from the pot, it's not going into the rice, where it belongs. Oriental steamed rice calls for 1 cup of rice to 1 cup of water. Cooking should be relatively slow, not rushed; again, that's how steam escapes. Time varies with the amount of rice; ultimately, it comes down to measuring doneness by all the water being absorbed into the rice. Try giving your family brown rice instead of white rice for added nutrition and variety. Many people actually prefer the chewy texture of brown rice.

To make this kind of cooking even more fun, try teaching the kids to use chopsticks. Also give them spoons and forks, so they don't become frustrated. Suggest practicing with the chopsticks other than at meal times as well, so they'll be ready before the next stir-fry evening.

While you're eating, talk about other ingredients that could be cooked in the wok. Would they go for a bit of fish? Shrimp? Some sealegs? How about different kinds of vegetables?

You'll notice I haven't provided a specific recipe for a stir-fry dinner. That's because the variations are limitless. Dawn can make stir-fry dinners each night for the next month and never repeat herself. It's remarkably easy.

Whenever we make stir-fried food, we prepare a bit more than needed so that some leftovers will be available for snacks or lunches. You can even heat up some leftover stir-fry to send off with the kids in one of those wide-mouth thermos jugs.

Stir-fry meals are a particular favorite for us because we have two of the world's pickiest eaters living with us. Ross and Jenny can have their plain chicken and simple vegetables with rice and be perfectly happy, while my wife and I can enjoy spicier and more exotic variations. For example, I love scallops stir-fried, and they're about the lowest in fat and cholesterol of all animal foods. Combined with some snow peas and waterchestnuts in a spicy garlic-chili sauce (again, straight out of the jar), this is fantastic eating. And, believe it or not, as time goes on the children will start to widen their taste horizons.

• • • • • • • • • • • • • • • • **Chicken Pot Pie**

4 chicken breasts
1 (10¾-ounce) can chicken broth
1 (10¾-ounce) can cream of chicken soup
¼ cup water
2 tablespoons cornstarch
½ teaspoon dried tarragon
1 (12-ounce) can peas and carrots, or equivalent frozen
1 pound phyllo (filo) dough (found in frozen foods section), thawed

Remember the days of doughy, tasteless TV-dinner pot pies? Not only did they taste bad, but they were also full of fat. Here's a terrific recipe Dawn developed that, while it takes some time to make, tastes wonderful. Make a few extra pies to freeze.

Skin the chicken breasts and simmer in a pot of water for 20 minutes or until fork-tender. Drain, cool, and cut or tear into bite-size pieces. Preheat oven to 350°F.

Place broth and cream of chicken soup in a pot and heat, stirring until smooth. Stir water into the cornstarch and add this mixture to the warm soup, stirring until thickened. Add the chicken and vegetables.

Separate layers of phyllo dough and spray one at a time, with a bit of butter-flavor Pam. Place in a

(*continued*)

Chicken Pot Pie, Continued

casserole dish. Place 12 sheets of dough on the bottom of the dish, fill with the chicken and vegetable mixture, and place 12 more sheets on top. Bake for 35 to 45 minutes. Serve with mashed potatoes and a salad. *Serves 4.*

PIZZA

Make up for those pizzas you don't want the kids to eat in restaurants by preparing your own at home. You can make the crust from scratch, or buy one of the prepared crusts in the deli of the supermarket. Pile on the toppings:

Pizza sauce, or Italian stewed tomatoes blended until smooth
Strips of low-fat ham or pieces of Canadian bacon
Sliced tomatoes
Sliced green peppers
Sliced onions
Sliced mushrooms
Imitation pizza cheese (use moderately)

• • • • • • • • • • • • • • • **Crust from Scratch**

1 package active dry yeast
1 cup warm water (105°–115°F)
½ teaspoon salt
½ teaspoon sugar
3 cups all-purpose flour
2 teaspoons olive oil

Dissolve the yeast in warm water. Add salt, sugar, and olive oil, then blend well. Stir in flour and knead with hands until dough is easy to handle and all the flour is used. Shape dough into a disc. Drizzle a bit of olive oil on the bottom of a pizza pan and place dough in pan, turning it to coat both sides with the oil. Cover with cloth and place in an area with no drafts (inside the oven with the oven turned off is a good place). Let rise until doubled in size, about 1 hour.
Preheat oven to 400°F. Punch

dough down and shape to fit pan. (Dawn makes dough up to 24 hours in advance and stores it in the refrigerator.) Cover with toppings and bake for 15 to 20 minutes, or until the cheese is bubbly and the edges of the crust are browned. *Makes a 12-inch pizza.*

MACARONI AND CHEESE DINNER

Look at any kid's list of favorite foods, and you'll probably find macaroni and cheese. But, you say, isn't this the kind of food we should avoid? Well, Dawn discovered an interesting thing when she was shopping. She read the instructions and nutrition listings on a package of Kraft Macaroni & Cheese Dinner. She found that the box ingredients contained only 2 grams of fat, but the dinner had 13 grams of fat when prepared as directed, with whole milk and lots of margarine. So here's her recipe, which tastes wonderful without the added fat.

• • • • • • • • • • • • • • • **Macaroni and Cheese**

1 (7¼-ounce) package Kraft Macaroni & Cheese Dinner
6 cups boiling water
⅓ cup skim milk
1 packet Butter Buds

Per the instructions on the package, add the macaroni to boiling water. (You needn't add the salt to the water.) Boil rapidly, stirring now and then, for about 8 minutes. Drain the water through a strainer and return the cooked macaroni to the pot. Add the milk, Butter buds, and package of cheese sauce. Mix and stir. The kids will never know the difference—you won't either! *Serves 4.*

Ross likes his macaroni and cheese served with fresh green beans. Jenny prefers hers with a little dish of applesauce.

HAM 'N' YAMS

Now why would any nutrition-minded author suggest ham for dinner? I'll let the numbers speak for themselves: ham no longer has to be the high-fat meat it used to be. In any supermarket you can find ham slices with a fat content as low as 2 percent. That means that for a 3½-ounce serving, there are only 2 grams of fat. That compares well with fish! Just read the label to see that you're buying the right brand.

The cooking is simple, and starts by making the delicious raisin sauce.

• • • • • • • • • • • • • • • • **Ham with Raisin Sauce**

½ cup raisins
1 tablespoon brown
    sugar
1 cup water
½ packet Butter Buds
4 slices smoked ham

In a small saucepan, mix all the ingredients and slowly bring to a simmer. Stirring now and then, continue to simmer the sauce until it's reduced by one-half its volume and the raisins have plumped.

Place the ham slices in the sauce and simmer until heated through. *Serves 4.*

• • • • • • • • • • • • • • • **Sweet 'n' Bubbly Yams**

2 cups chunked peeled
    yams
½ packet Butter Buds
2 tablespoons brown
    sugar

Boil the yams in water to cover for 15 to 20 minutes. Drain all but about 2 tablespoons of water. Sprinkle in Butter Buds and brown sugar, then mix. Cover and let rest for 2 minutes, then serve.

As a side dish, I find that sweet peas give a terrific color balance to the plate of ham and yams, and they taste wonderful with this meal. Add a slice of bread, and you're all set to eat. Preparation time will be no more than 20 minutes, so start with the yams and then prepare the other parts of the meal while the yams are boiling.

BARBECUED CHICKEN AND BROASTED POTATOES

This dinner began as a way to make particularly delicious ribs. But now we avoid that greasy food in favor of chicken. The result is the same: tender and succulent barbecue. I'll bet this method of preparation—boiling, then broiling—will be one of the biggest cooking surprises you've read thus far. It's the boiling that makes the meat so tender.

• • • • • • • • • • • • • • • • • **Barbecued Chicken**

2 pounds chicken
   breasts, drumsticks,
   and wings, skinned
3 bay leaves
2 large garlic cloves,
   quartered
8 black peppercorns

In a large pot, mix chicken and seasonings. Add water to cover and bring to a boil. Reduce heat and simmer for 20 minutes. Drain and cool. Make the barbecue sauce, then coat the chicken parts with the sauce and broil just long enough to brown the sauce and heat the chicken through. You can do this either outdoors over charcoal or indoors in the oven broiler. Serve with Broasted Potatoes. *Serves 4.*

• • • • • • • • • • • • • • • • **Barbecue Sauce**

1 cup tomato ketchup
1 tablespoon
   Worcestershire sauce
1 teaspoon distilled
   white vinegar
2 tablespoons brown
   sugar

Combine ingredients and blend until smooth. (The sauce can be stored like ketchup.)

•••••••••••••••• **Broasted Potatoes**

Partially cook 1 potato per person; either bake them in a microwave oven or parboil in water until tender but not too soft. Let
cool. (This can be done anytime in advance.) Slice the potatoes
lengthwise into eighths. Place on a cookie sheet and spray lightly
with Pam. Sprinkle with just a bit of salt or other seasoning such
as Mrs. Dash. Bake in a 400°F oven for 30 minutes. Potatoes will
be crispy on the outside and soft and tender on the inside—a
wonderful accompaniment to the barbecued chicken, but terrific
with other foods as well. We love these potatoes with hamburgers, chicken sandwiches, and turkey burgers.

ROAST BEEF AND BAKED POTATOES

There's no reason to completely eliminate red meat from the family menu. Simply choose leaner cuts such as a rump roast or chuck
shoulder roast. For these leaner cuts, increase the cooking time
and roast at a lower temperature. Roast in a 300°F oven for 20
minutes per pound for a 3-pound roast; use a meat thermometer to
judge when the meat is at desired doneness.

For leaner cuts of meat, thin slicing makes the meat more tender. Any beef left over should be sliced very thin, the way they do
in fast-food restaurants, and you can then use it for hot beef sandwiches with mashed potatoes and gravy.

Another excellent investment is an electric slicer. It will more
than pay for itself by allowing you to use inexpensive cuts of meat
for main meals and sandwiches.

What about those baked potatoes to go along with the roast?
How can you enjoy them without fat-laden sour cream? Try this
recipe for an imitation sour cream that's just terrific. You can also
use it as a base for dips and salad dressings.

•••••••••••••••• **Mock Sour Cream**

1 cup low-fat cottage
  cheese
½ cup plain nonfat yogurt

In a blender, whip cottage cheese
until smooth. Fold in yogurt and
other ingredients. You may also

1 teaspoon salt
   (optional)
1 teaspoon lemon juice
   Finely minced fresh
   chives (optional)

wish to add some chives, at least for the adults. *Makes about 1½ cups.*

SUPER SALAD BAR

Salad bars are cropping up even in fast-food restaurants, and kids like to create their own combinations. Why not make a salad bar at home? The key to success is putting out as many ingredients as possible. Dawn also likes to take the kids out to buy salads from one of the supermarkets that now sell salad by the pound. That way Ross and Jenny get to pick out what they want. And it gives them a feeling of doing something special to buy the salads and bring them home. Serve with a low-fat or nonfat dressing. Dig in and enjoy!

Lettuce: iceberg, bibb, romaine, leaf
Spinach
Chopped celery
Radishes
Raw mushrooms
Chopped green and red bell peppers
Grated or shaved carrots
Chopped zucchini
Garbanzo beans (chick-peas)
Pinto beans
Kidney beans
Green peas
Raisins
Chopped tomatoes
Chopped onions (use green onions or Bermuda onions)
Chopped or slivered jicama
Bean sprouts
Alfalfa sprouts
Shoestring beets
Croutons (Make your own from diced sourdough bread, coated with a little spray of butter-flavor Pam and baked for 10 minutes at 400°F.)

• • • • • • • • • • • • • • • • **Tofu Green-Goddess Dressing**

4 ounces fresh tofu
1 teaspoon Dijon-style
   mustard
½ teaspoon salt
1 tablespoon lemon juice
1 tablespoon cider
   vinegar
2 tablespoons chopped
   fresh parsley
1 tablespoon finely
   minced fresh chives
1 tablespoon olive oil

Blend all ingredients in a jar and store in refrigerator for up to 1 week. *Makes 7 ounces.*

• • • • • • • • • • • • • • • **Jenny's Thousand Island Dressing**

¼ cup Weight Watchers
   Reduced-calorie
   Mayonnaise
½ cup plain nonfat yogurt
½ teaspoon salt
2 tablespoons tomato
   ketchup
2 tablespoons pickle
   relish

Blend all ingredients in a jar and store for up to 3 weeks in refrigerator. A truly low-fat creamy dressing! *Makes about 1 cup.*

• • • • • • • • • • • • • • • **Ross's Favorite Ranch Dressing**

1 cup Weight Watchers
   Reduced-calorie
   Mayonnaise
½ cup plain nonfat yogurt
½ cup skim milk
1 (4-ounce) package
   Ranch Dressing mix

Here's an example of using a commercial product and modifying the directions. Instead of buttermilk, use the yogurt and skim milk. Cut the fat in half by using the reduced-calorie mayonnaise rather than regular. And Ross loves it. *Makes about 2 cups.*

• • • • • • • • • • • • • • • **Dad's Creamy Cucumber Dressing**

1 cup plain nonfat yogurt
½ medium cucumber, finely chopped
1 teaspoon fresh-squeezed lemon juice
1 clove garlic, very finely minced
½ teaspoon salt
½ teaspoon white pepper

Blend ingredients together in a jar. This makes a delicious dressing not only for salads but also for sandwiches. I just love it with chicken and lettuce on French bread. *Makes about 2 cups.*

• • • • • • • • • • • • • • • **Mom's Low-Calorie Blue Cheese Dressing**

1 cup low-fat cottage cheese
1 tablespoon lemon juice
¼ teaspoon onion salt
⅓ cup skim milk
2 ounces blue cheese

Place the cottage cheese in a strainer and rinse off the cream so that cottage cheese is now virtually fat free. Combine the cottage cheese curds, lemon juice, onion salt, and milk in a blender or food processor and blend until smooth. Crumble the blue cheese and mix into the dressing. A 2-tablespoon serving contains less than 1 gram of fat! *Makes about 1¾ cups.*

• • • • • • • • • • • • • • **Yogurt Fruit Dressing**

1 cup plain nonfat yogurt
1 tablespoon light corn syrup
2 teaspoons honey
2 teaspoons fresh-squeezed lemon juice
1 teaspoon grated lemon peel
¼ teaspoon ground allspice

Blend all the ingredients in a jar and store in refrigerator for up to 3 weeks. Use liberally over fresh fruit salads. Look at those ingredients; they contain no fat whatsoever. *Makes about 1¼ cups.*

NOTE: There are a number of nonfat, no-oil dressings now on the market. Experiment with them to see which ones your family enjoys in addition to the recipes I've just listed.

You can also substitute ingredients for packaged dressing mixes. Use reduced-calorie mayonnaise instead of regular to save up to 7 grams of fat per tablespoon. Cut the oil in half and substitute half corn syrup instead. In some dressings, you may even be able to substitute corn syrup entirely.

Since salad dressings are the only problem with restaurant salad bars, we take little containers of our own dressings along with us when we go out. It's really no problem, and it's a lot more pleasant to see the kids using our own dressing rather than watching to be sure they don't use too much of the fat-laden dressings available on the restaurant's salad bar.

GRILLED CHEESE SANDWICHES AND SOUP

Let's say you're going out to dinner, and the sitter is due in just a few minutes but the kids have to be fed before you can leave. For this or other squeezed-time dilemmas, turn to the kids' favorite standard. You can even do it without much fat.

Spray one side of a slice of bread with butter-flavor Pam. Place sprayed-side down in a nonstick pan set over medium heat. Put 1½ slices of Borden Lite-Line cheese on the bread and cover with another slice of bread. Spray the top with Pam and toast until underside is browned. Flip the sandwich over and toast the other side. You're done.

Serve sandwiches with a bowl of chicken and vegetable soup —a brand you know has few grams of fat per serving. Soup and a sandwich add up to 5 or 6 grams of fat. That means that as your kids grow, you can give them two sandwiches and two bowls of soup and still feel good about the meal.

While the soup is simmering and the sandwiches are toasting, slice a few pieces of fruit to put on the plates. If you do, the kids will eat them; it's as simple as that. You've given them a fairly balanced meal, and you'll be on time for your dinner reservation.

TERIYAKI CHICKEN DINNER

This recipe is so easy and such a family-pleaser that it's sure to become a regular in your house just as it has in ours. The kids and adults enjoy it equally.

• • • • • • • • • • • • • • • • **Teriyaki Chicken**

1–2 pounds chicken parts, with bones, but skinned

½ cup low-sodium soy sauce or teriyaki sauce

2 tablespoons brown sugar

2 garlic cloves, minced

1 tablespoon dry sherry

1 tablespoon freshly grated ginger, or 1 teaspoon dried

Mix marinade ingredients in a 1-gallon storage bag. Add the chicken parts and marinate in refrigerator for at least 1 hour. Drain chicken and broil over charcoal or in kitchen broiler for about 30 minutes. *Serves 2–4.*

VARIATION: Here's an idea that kids love—for a meal, snack, or appetizer. Slice boneless, skinless chicken breasts into thin strips and thread onto bamboo or metal skewers. Broil 6 to 10 minutes.

Serve this chicken dish with rice and Oriental vegetables. Of course you can buy the vegetables precut and frozen in the supermarket. But if you want a truly tasty vegetable dish, try this next recipe. You and the children will like it much more.

• • • • • • • • • • • • • • • **Oriental Vegetables**

Marinade from Teriyaki Chicken recipe

1 tablespoon brown sugar

Green bell peppers, cut into strips

Carrots, cut into strips

Onion, sliced into rings (optional)

When you make the chicken marinade, just make about half again as much. Add the brown sugar to the extra marinade and set aside. Soak the strips of vegetables in another storage bag. (I deliberately left out specific quantities of vegetables because that depends on your family. For

(*continued*)

Oriental Vegetables, Continued

my family of four, I use 1 pound of carrots and 1 large green pepper. My kids hate onion, so I use it only when I'm making the recipe for myself and other adults.) Spray a nonstick pan with Pam. Drain the vegetables and sauté them for about 3 minutes. Then add marinade to the pan to a depth of ½ inch and simmer for 8 minutes, or until the vegetables are tender. There will be very little sauce left, leaving a thickened glaze on the vegetables.

NOTE: If your child absolutely, positively won't eat such food, don't force the issue. Just set aside a few carrot and green pepper strips and let the youngster eat them raw along with the chicken.

BACKWARDS BREAKFASTS

Even on weekends, there never seems to be enough time to prepare big, hearty breakfasts and to sit down and enjoy them as a family. Typically we settle for cereal in the morning. So it's nice to turn things around now and then and have what my kids call "backwards breakfast." Happily, too, the recipes I've worked out allow us to enjoy foods that we just wouldn't order in a restaurant because of the fat and cholesterol levels in such staples as eggs, bacon, and sausage.

• • • • • • • • • • • • • • • • **French Toast**

This is one of the easiest of breakfast meals to fix in a hurry. Heat the griddle so it's good and hot by the time you're ready to put on the toast (350°F on an electric griddle). Pour 1 carton of Egg Beaters (equivalent to 4 eggs) into a large bowl for every 4 pieces of toast. (I prefer using large slabs of sourdough bread, since it stands up to the eggs without getting soggy.) Dip bread slices into egg and coat well. Spray Pam onto the griddle and drop the egg-coated bread onto the hot surface. Cook each side about 3 minutes. Serve with real maple syrup, fruit syrups, or fruit compote. On the side, have some low-fat ham slices, Canadian bacon, or specially prepared turkey sausage.

We alternate between the following two recipes for pancakes and the Breakfast Pancakes on page 168. Each is delicious and filled with low-fat nutrition. Try them all.

• • • • • • • • • • • • • • • **Buttermilk Pancakes**

1 cup self-rising flour
1 cup whole wheat flour
1 cup oat bran
1 tablespoon baking powder
3 tablespoons sugar
6 egg whites, or 1½ cartons Egg Beaters
3 cups nonfat or low-fat buttermilk
3 tablespoons corn oil
3 tablespoons light corn syrup

Heat a griddle until very hot (350°F on an electric griddle) Blend the flours, oat bran, baking powder, and sugar. Add the moist ingredients and mix until smooth. Spray griddle with Pam, drop batter in large spoonfuls onto griddle, and cook until steam stops rising. Turn pancakes and cook on other side.

There's no need to put any butter or even margarine on these pancakes. Simply serve with syrup or fruit compotes. You and the children will never miss the fat. *Makes 36 small pancakes.*

• • • • • • • • • • • • • • **Rice-Bran Pancakes**

1 cup all-purpose flour
1 cup Vita-Fiber rice bran
2 teaspoons baking powder
1 tablespoon sugar
1 teaspoon salt
6 egg whites, or ¾ carton Egg Beaters
3 tablespoons corn oil
3 tablespoons light corn syrup

Heat a griddle until very hot (350°F on an electric griddle). Blend the flour, rice bran, baking powder, sugar, and salt. Add the moist ingredients and mix until smooth. Spray griddle with Pam and drop batter in large spoonfuls onto griddle. Cook pancakes until steam stops rising, then turn and cook on other side.

Here's another way to get some
(*continued*)

Rice-Bran Pancakes, Continued

of that wonderful water-soluble fiber into the diet, this time in the form of rice bran instead of oat bran. *Makes 24 small pancakes.*

• • • • • • • • • • • • • • • **Waffles**

1 cup oat bran
1 cup self-rising flour
1 teaspoon baking powder
4 egg whites, or ½ carton Egg Beaters
2 cups skim milk
1 tablespoon corn oil
2 tablespoons light corn syrup

Heat the waffle iron until very hot. In a large bowl, blend the oat bran, flour, and baking powder, then add the moist ingredients. Spray the waffle iron with Pam, pour in some of the batter, and bake until the steam stops rising. Continue making waffles until batter is used up. *Makes 9 medium waffles.*

NOTE: Waffles freeze beautifully. Make and freeze plenty of extras so that when your family needs a snack you can simply pop one or two into the toaster. Also, if you're looking for a really wonderful summertime treat, make a waffle sandwich filled with frozen nonfat yogurt. It's so good my mouth is watering even as I write this. You've just got to try it!

Bacon and sausage are loaded with fats, sodium, and nitrites. Even families not concerned about cholesterol levels are cutting back on those foods. As substitutes we use slices of low-fat ham and Canadian bacon. And you can make your own turkey sausage with one of the two recipes that follow. Also, look for Schilling Breakfast Sausage Seasoning mix in your supermarket. You can add it directly to ground turkey breast to make a very nice sausage.

•••••••••••••••• **Turkey Breast Sausage**

1 packet Butter Buds
¼ teaspoon *each* ground
    cumin, dried
    marjoram, black
    pepper, dried
    oregano, ground red
    pepper
½ teaspoon *each* dried
    basil, dried thyme,
    powdered sage
⅛ teaspoon *each* garlic
    powder, grated
    nutmeg, ground
    ginger
1 tablespoon oat bran or
    Vita-Fiber rice bran
1 pound ground turkey
    breast

If you and your family enjoy the typically seasoned breakfast sausage, this recipe is for you. If you prefer a milder seasoning, cut the spices by half. To prepare, mix the dry ingredients, then add the turkey. Refrigerate for at least 1 hour, then form into patties and fry in a nonstick pan sprayed with a bit of Pam. *Makes 8 patties.*

NOTE: You can freeze the sausages either before or after cooking.

•••••••••••••••• **Garlic Turkey Sausage**

1   pound ground
    turkey breast
¾ teaspoon ground
    coriander
½ teaspoon salt
½ teaspoon black
    pepper
1–3 garlic cloves, finely
    minced

Whoa!!! You might say, "My kid would never eat foods highly seasoned with garlic." I'll bet you're wrong. Kids actually love garlic, but they just don't know it. Try them on this sausage and I think you'll agree.

Mix the ingredients well and chill for at least 1 hour before forming into patties. Fry in a nonstick pan sprayed with Pam. *Makes 8 patties.*

This sausage is especially good for dinner. Serve with mashed potatoes and brown gravy, and applesauce. Accompany with a nice green salad, and you have an easily prepared meal in a jiffy—something really different.

When I was a child, my mother prepared pork sausages and gravy in the same way. I won't eat the pork sausages anymore, so I make this turkey recipe and use Durkee (my particular favorite) Pork Gravy, which is virtually devoid of fat. It's a savory treat especially on a cool autumn evening.

TURKEY BURGERS

Instead of the usual hamburger meat, use ground turkey breast to make your next batch of burgers for the family. Mix 1 pound of meat with ¼ cup oat bran to better form the burgers. Serve with all the usual trimmings: tomatoes, onions, lettuce. And since turkey is so low in fat, you can afford to melt a slice of Borden's Lite-Line cheese over each burger. Serve with boiled sweet corn and Broasted Potatoes (see page 248).

SALMON PATTIES AND OTHER CANNED FISH DELIGHTS

• • • • • • • • • • • • • • **Salmon Patties**

1 (15½-ounce) can
   salmon
½ carton Egg Beaters
⅔ cup oat bran
1 small onion, minced
1 tablespoon finely
   chopped fresh
   parsley
1 tablespoon fresh-
   squeezed lemon
   juice

One of our favorite quick meals is Salmon Patties, served with mashed potatoes and boiled peas.

Mix all ingredients and form 8 patties. Spray a nonstick pan with Pam and fry patties until crisp on both sides. My mother served salmon patties with mashed potatoes, corn, and some ketchup, and I still love them this way. *Serves 4 (maybe more if your kids are still very small).*

• • • • • • • • • • • • • • • • **Salmon Salad Sandwiches**

1 (15½-ounce) can
   salmon
½ cup low-fat cottage
   cheese
1 tablespoon finely
   minced onion (so
   fine they won't see
   it)
1 tablespoon finely
   minced celery
1 tablespoon lemon juice
1 teaspoon prepared
   horseradish
½ teaspoon salt
¼ teaspoon white pepper

*Most children enjoy tuna
sandwiches, so it's just a small step
to get them to like salmon salad
sandwiches as well. This filling
can be used for sandwiches, or
spread on crackers or toast points
for a snack. Serve with gherkins or
sweet pickles.*

Clean the salmon of skin and
mince any bones until they can't
be detected. Place the cottage
cheese in a strainer and rinse off
excess milk and cream under
running water. In a bowl, mash the
cottage cheese curds and blend
with the salmon. Combine with all
the other ingredients and blend
until smooth. *Enough for 6
sandwiches.*

   This is a great staple to keep in
the refrigerator for healthful snacks
at any time. You'll also find that it
makes a wonderful dip—very
suitable for serving at the most
festive party. And the best part is
getting another serving of fish into
your family's diet.

TUNA SANDWICHES

While we're talking about tuna and salmon, I just couldn't resist sharing my favorite recipe for tuna sandwiches. When my wife first saw me making this, she couldn't believe the weird combination of ingredients. Then she tried it and agreed it was fantastic. Try it on your kids.

• • • • • • • • • • • • • • • • **Tuna Spread**

1 (6½-ounce) can white albacore tuna, packed in water, drained
½ apple, finely minced
2 large pimento-stuffed olives, chopped
1 tablespoon finely minced onion
1 celery stalk, finely chopped
¼ teaspoon celery salt
1 tablespoon fresh-squeezed lemon juice
2 tablespoons Weight Watchers Reduced-calorie Mayonnaise

Blend all the ingredients and serve on toast, or whatever kind of bread you and your family prefer.
Enough for 3 sandwiches.

WAGON WHEEL PASTA AND MARINARA SAUCE

I don't think a child has been born who doesn't like pasta. This is a boon to all of us trying to cut down on fat. So take advantage of this natural taste preference by serving pasta often. Provide variety by choosing different shapes such as wagon wheels, shells, and hundreds of others, as well as different flavors—spinach, tomato, whole wheat, or regular. Serving pasta with marinara sauce and some vegetables starts children off on a lifelong habit of enjoying vegetarian meals once in a while rather than having meat every evening.

• • • • • • • • • • • • • • • • **Pasta**

Regardless of the shape you choose, the trick to making good pasta is using a large enough pot. Get the biggest one you have, half fill it with water, bring to a boil, and cook the pasta for 6 to 8 minutes or until tender.

• • • • • • • • • • • • • • • **Marinara Sauce**

2 tablespoons minced
  onion
2 garlic cloves, minced
3 fresh basil leaves (or 1
  teaspoon dried)
1 bay leaf
2 teaspoons olive oil
1 (16-ounce) can
  tomatoes

The easiest thing to do, of course, is to open a jar of commercial sauce; the kids like them, and they're convenient, but these sauces are also heavy in sodium. And adults generally have more refined taste buds, so that the meal wouldn't please everyone at the table. Here's my recipe for quick marinara sauce from scratch.

Sauté the onion, garlic, basil, and bay leaf in olive oil until onion is limp. Discard bay leaf. Drain and chop tomatoes, then add to pan and simmer for 10 minutes.
Serves 4.

MEAT LOAF, MEAT BALLS, ETC

This basic recipe can be used to make meat loaf, meat balls, or any other shape you might want. It's a good recipe to make extra portions of, so you can freeze them.

• • • • • • • • • • • • • • • **Meat Loaf**

1 pound very lean
    ground veal
1 pound ground turkey
    breast
1 packet Butter Buds
1 tablespoon
    Worcestershire sauce
1 tablespoon tomato
    ketchup
1 teaspoon dry mustard
1 small onion, minced
2 large garlic cloves,
    minced
½ cup oat bran,
    approximately

Preheat oven to 350°F. Mix the ground meats with all the other ingredients except the oat bran. Gradually add the oat bran until the mixture can be formed into a loaf; you may need a bit less than the ½ cup. Place in baking pan and bake for about 50 minutes. *Serves 8.*

NOTE: Figure ¼ pound of meat per person, or a bit less for younger children. Serve with potatoes, gravy, and vegetables.

CHILI WITH MACARONI

Here's another meal in a bowl. For 4 servings, follow the instructions on any brand of commercial chili mix, but instead of beef use ½ pound of ground turkey breast and ½ pound of lean veal. Drain off what little fat develops during browning. Cook the macaroni, drain well, and place in individual bowls. Pour chili mixture over and serve.

• • • • • • • • • • • • • • • **Chili Extra**

1 pound ground turkey
    breast
1 pound ground veal

I like to add beans to my chili. And, since the chili also freezes well, I make double amounts for

2 (1 ¾-ounce) packages
  chili mix (any brand)
1 (16-ounce) can
  tomatoes
3 (15½-ounce) cans chili
  beans
1 (7-ounce) box macaroni

another meal. Here's my version of chili.

Brown meats in a nonstick skillet and drain off fat. Add chili mix, tomatoes, and beans. Heat through. While chili simmers, make the macaroni. Bring a large pot of water to a boil, add macaroni, and cook until al dente. Serve chili over the macaroni. *Serves 8.*

TURKEY CUTLET DINNER

Turkey breast cutlets are the perfect substitute for veal in practically any recipe. Simply have your butcher cut a turkey breast into slices as he would cut veal. You can use any of your own favorite recipes, or try this one.

• • • • • • • • • • • • • • • **Turkey Cutlets**

1 pound turkey breast
  cutlets
½ carton Egg Beaters
½ cup oat bran
1 (1 ¼-ounce) package
  gravy mix

Dip the cutlets into the Egg Beaters and then dredge in the oat bran to coat thoroughly. Allow to set for 10 minutes; this helps keep the coating firm. Spray a nonstick pan with Pam and fry until crispy on the outside and still tender on the inside. Prepare gravy according to directions on package, and serve with cutlets. *Serves 4.*

NOTE: Depending on the tastes of your family, you can season the oat bran before coating the cutlets. Onion or garlic powder, powdered sage, dried thyme, and other herbs

(continued)

Turkey Cutlets, Continued

and spices can be sprinkled in for extra flavor.

For a variation, cut the turkey breast into strips. Coat with oat bran mixed with a bit of fried-chicken seasoning. Fry strips in a nonstick pan sprayed with Pam or bake in a 350°F oven for 20 minutes.

And since you're trying to avoid fatty foods such as fast-food chicken nuggets, have the butcher cut that turkey breast (or chicken breast) into cubes, so you can make your own healthy version of nuggets.

HEARTY VEGETABLE SOUP

This is truly a back-to-basics meal. The only work involved is in cutting the vegetables, and that's something the children can help with. The soup freezes beautifully, so you'll want to make enough for two meals. Serve with chunks of good sourdough or rye bread.

• • • • • • • • • • • • • • • • Vegetable Soup

1½ pounds chicken breast or lean beef
1 quart water
2 bay leaves
¼ teaspoon dried marjoram leaves
¼ teaspoon dried thyme leaves
2 garlic cloves
6 peppercorns, cracked
½ cup chopped celery

In a large, heavy pot, cover the meat or chicken with water and heat to boiling. Add the seasonings. Reduce heat and simmer for 30 minutes for chicken or 1 hour for beef. Remove the meat and cut into bite-size pieces. Return the meat to the cooking liquid and add the vegetables and barley. Simmer until the vegetables are tender. Season

½ cup chopped onions
1 (16-ounce) can
  tomatoes
½ cup garbanzo beans
  (chick-peas)
3 carrots, chopped
½ cup pearled barley
  Salt or salt substitute

lightly with salt or salt substitute to taste. *Serves 8.*

COLONEL KOWALSKI'S FRIED CHICKEN

First there was pan-fried chicken done in the southern manner. Next came the fat-laden fast-food variety, whereby a perfectly healthy chicken is rendered to an artery-clogging horror. Then came the packets and mixtures such as Shake 'n Bake and Oven Fry. Those aren't bad, but they contain some hydrogenated fats. So I came up with a method that's sure to please the most finicky palate, young and old alike.

Select the leaner pieces of chicken such as the breasts, drumsticks, and wings; avoid the thighs and backs. Skin the chicken so that the fat won't be absorbed into the meat while cooking. Dip the skinned chicken pieces into a bowl of Egg Beaters (½ carton of Egg Beaters is enough for 1 pound of chicken.) Preheat oven to 400°F.

Now here's the real secret: Measure out 2 cups of bread crumbs or oat bran, or a mixture of the two. Add 2 tablespoons Schilling Fried Chicken Seasoning mix; it comes in a little shaker bottle. Blend the seasoning with the crumbs or oat bran in a large plastic bag (1-gallon size). Add one or two chicken pieces at a time and shake in the bag until well coated. Place the chicken pieces on a baking sheet and spray with Pam. Bake for 30 to 40 minutes, depending on the size of the pieces and the amount.

You'll love the crispy, tender, delicious result. Serve with oven fried potatoes as described on page 248 and fresh corn on the cob.

• • • • • • • • • • • • • • • **Vegetable Pasta and Pepper Sauce**

2 teaspoons olive oil
1 large or 2 small garlic cloves, peeled and sliced
1 small green bell pepper, cut in strips
1 small red bell pepper, cut in strips
1 (6-ounce) can tomato paste
1 pound colored pasta
Grated parmesan cheese

Just when the kids think they've seen every kind of pasta, surprise them with a rainbow-colored treat. You can find rotelli, fusilli, and other shapes of pasta colored red and green which have been made with tomatoes and spinach. Add an equally colorful pepper sauce and you're in for compliments.

Bring a large pot of salted water to a boil to cook the pasta. Meantime, start to prepare the sauce. Place the oil in a large skillet and sauté the garlic and pepper strips until tender but not soft. Add the tomato paste and 3 cans of hot water. Simmer over a low heat for 10 minutes. By now the water will be boiling; add the pasta and cook for 8 minutes. Drain the pasta and cover with sauce. Sprinkle with grated parmesan cheese. Serve with a salad. *Serves 4.*

HOT TURKEY SANDWICHES

When my mother took me shoe-shopping as a child, we would eat at a restaurant near the shoe store that served a wonderful steaming plate of a hot turkey sandwich and mashed potatoes, all covered with rich brown gravy and a side dish of cranberry sauce. I'll never forget how good it tasted; but surely that's the kind of meal we must avoid now, right? Wrong. Here's how to enjoy it without guilt.

First, as we know, turkey breast is low in fat; choose the breast, not other parts with dark meat. Second, potatoes are devoid of fat; it's the stuff we mash into them that poses the problem. And the gravy? My favorite turkey gravy is made by Durkee. So I wrote to them to ask about the fat content of the packet I buy in the super-market. The answer is that such mixes (Durkee as well as other brands) are almost devoid of fat, so you can use as much as you want.

You can buy turkey breasts pre-cooked and ready to serve. Just slice, place over pieces of sourdough bread, and pour on the gravy. We prefer the sourdough bread, since it stands up to the gravy better than softer breads.

And here's my recipe for mashed potatoes.

• • • • • • • • • • • • • • • Guilt-free Mashed Potatoes

Per person:

1   medium potato, peeled and cut into chunks
1   tablespoon Butter Buds
1–2   tablespoons evaporated skim milk

Place the potato chunks into a pot of cold water and bring to a boil. Boil for about 20 minutes or until quite tender when probed with a fork. Drain off water and coarsely mash the potatoes. Sprinkle on the Butter Buds, add the evaporated milk, and whip until smooth.

The Butter Buds provide all the flavor of butter, and the evaporated milk gives the dish the smooth, velvety texture you'd expect from cream. (Plain skim milk doesn't do as good a job.)

NOTE: Did you know you can freeze mashed potatoes? By all means! Double the amount and store the remainder for another time when your schedule is more frantic. They come out best when microwaved right out of the freezer. In fact, you can even make little "TV dinners" for the kids by putting some turkey, potatoes, and gravy into a segmented plate and freezing it for later. It's a great time-saver and one the children won't complain about at all.

(continued)

Guilt-Free Mashed Potatoes, Continued

Serve the meal with some cranberry sauce. You can make it from scratch, but it's a lot of work, and kids generally don't like it nearly as well as the kind that comes straight from a can.

Every meal should have the option of a fresh vegetable. This menu is particularly good with carrots. Or perhaps you'd prefer a dinner salad. If pressed for time, and the kids are yelling about hunger pangs, peel a few carrots and cucumbers for them to eat raw before the rest of the meal is completed. It saves you the work of cooking the vegetables, you satisfy their hunger, and you get some solid nutrition into their growing bodies. Not a bad deal.

BARBECUED CHICKEN SANDWICHES

There's a fast-food chain in the west—Carl's Jr.—that sells a delicious broiled chicken sandwich which my family and I enjoy when we want a fast meal without the fat. So I decided to experiment with making such sandwiches at home. It's really easy, and I think you'll love the results.

For a family of four, use 1 pound of boneless chicken breasts. Skin the breasts and, with a very sharp knife, slice them to make two filets of each breast. Sprinkle with a small amount of Adolph's Meat Tenderizer about 10 minutes before you're ready to cook the chicken. I prefer to grill the chicken over the charcoal, but a broiler will do the job very nicely, too. Cooking takes just a few minutes —about 3 minutes per side. When you see the chicken turning white around the edges, turn it over to do the other side. Don't overcook.

Serve the chicken on hamburger rolls selected on the basis of their fat content—avoid rolls made with hydrogenated oils or coconut oil. Let your kids pile on the sliced tomatoes, onions, and lettuce. A baked potato topped with some Mock Sour Cream (see page 248) goes with this meal beautifully.

• • • • • • • • • • • • • • • **Barbecue Sauce**

1 cup tomato ketchup
2 tablespoons brown
    sugar

Combine ingredients in a bottle or jar to serve on the table and then put into the refrigerator or

1 teaspoon distilled
   white vinegar
1 tablespoon
   Worcestershire sauce

cupboard for easy storage until
next time.

FRUIT PLATTER WITH YOGURT

There are times when nobody in the family wants a big meal.
Maybe it's one of those muggy summer evenings, and the idea of
hot food of any kind is a real turn-off. This is the perfect time to
bring out some fruit platters.

For some reason, fruit tastes so much better when it's attractively prepared and served. And children's interest in food has a lot
to do with its appearance. Take a few extra moments to design the
fruit platter cleverly. I find that my kids go bonkers when I design a
flower, a bird, a palm tree, or Mickey Mouse—all out of pieces of
fruit.

For example, to make a palm tree use a banana sliced lengthwise for the trunk. The palm fronds can be green pepper strips.
Marashino cherries become the coconuts; a slice of orange serves
as the sun; and grated carrots are the summer-bleached grass. Start
thinking of fruits and vegetables as art supplies: raisins for eyes,
carrots for birds' beaks, circles of apples for faces, lengthwise
slices of pears for bodies—and on it goes.

Along with the fruit and vegetable platter, serve a chilled bowl
of fruit-flavored nonfat yogurt. There are more and more brands
coming onto the market each day. Yoplait makes a nonfat type they
call "150," which stands for the total number of calories. Alta Deña
has a wonderful custard texture. And kids love them.

BEATING LUNCH BAG BLUES

Even though you don't want your child to eat the typical school
lunch, you probably dread the idea of coming up every day with
bagged lunches the kids will eat. Dawn got tired of asking the kids
what they wanted for lunch, only to get the same reply, "I don't
know." The trick was to form a list that she could repeat every two

weeks, just as they do in the school-lunch program. Let your child help you build the schedule, so there are no unpleasant surprises. Here's the way our school-lunch list looks:

1. Tuna sandwiches with carrot sticks and apple slices
2. Cold pizza slices with a snack box of raisins
3. Low-fat ham sandwiches on toast with a small can of fruit
4. Cold barbecued chicken on bread spread with honey
5. Peanut butter and jelly sandwiches with a banana
6. Borden's Lite-Line cheese sandwiches with canned pears
7. Sliced turkey sandwiches with cranberry sauce
8. Cut vegetables with yogurt dip and bread
9. Meat loaf sandwiches on French bread with ketchup
10. Hot dog or bratwurst sandwiches (made with turkey)

Does your child have a locker or space where a lunch bag can be stored during the day? If so, you might want to buy a wide-mouth Thermos jug so you can provide some hot lunches as well. Things to consider would be:

1. Soup
2. Spaghetti
3. Other pastas
4. Leftovers from night before

Most parents might think cold pizza a terrible lunch, but kids feel it's great, even for breakfast. The same goes for other foods you might not think of eating cold. Ross and Jenny both love cold tacos, for example.

The important thing is not necessarily to follow my list, but rather to make your own list by planning with your children well in advance. As time goes on, add to that list other foods that become favorites.

You can also add variety to the lunches by mixing and matching foods. One day include some canned fruit, another day some tortilla chips, some snack boxes of dried fruit, a granola bar, some oat-bran cookies, vegetable sticks, and so on.

Ask what the other kids bring to school, and whether your child would like to have that once in a while. Make sure food isn't being tossed in the waste can or traded for something you'd rather they didn't have. The only way to do that is by providing brown-bag lunches that please.

SUPER SHAKES

Whether as a snack or as part of a meal, these super shakes provide lots of nutrition without the fat and cholesterol found in the fast-food restaurant versions. Use your own imagination and personal tastes to engineer even more varieties. In all cases, simply blend the ingredients and serve.

• • • • • • • • • • • • • • • **Banana Smoothee**

1 cup skim milk
1 egg white
1 ripe banana
2 tablespoons frozen
    apple-juice
    concentrate

• • • • • • • • • • • • • • • **Fruit Fluid Medley**

2 egg whites
1 ripe banana
1 peeled and cored pear
½ cup watermelon,
    cantaloupe, or
    honeydew melon
    chunks

• • • • • • • • • • • • • • • **Strawberry Sweety**

1 cup skim milk
1 egg white
½ cup strawberries
1 tablespoon honey

• • • • • • • • • • • • • • • **Very Berry Delight**

2 tablespoons frozen
 cranberry or
 raspberry-juice
 concentrate
¼ cup *each* blueberries,
 raspberries, seedless
 grapes
1 tablespoon light corn
 syrup
½ cup water

CHOCOLATE SYRUP (AND WHAT TO DO WITH IT)

Of all the foods in the candy category that Ross and I love and miss when trying to avoid fat, chocolate heads the list. Unfortunately the better the chocolate, the higher the fat content. So I came up with an idea that has gone a long way toward satisfying that chocolate craving. I start by making some fat-free chocolate syrup.

Commercial chocolate syrup is made with cocoa and oil, often hydrogenated oil. Chocolate candy goes a step further by adding butterfat. So I experimented with making my own syrup, and found it surprisingly easy. Just blend ½ cup of cocoa with ⅔ cup light corn syrup. For a lighter, sweeter syrup, increase the corn syrup to 1 cup. Now you have chocolate syrup which you can use in many ways.

• • • • • • • • • • • • • • • **Dessert Fondue**

For a fantastic treat that kids and adults love equally, set out a bowl of chocolate syrup with a platter of cut fruit and berries. Give everyone a fork and let each spear a strawberry, a chunk of apple, a piece of pear, or whatever, then dip it into the chocolate for a delicious dessert.

• • • • • • • • • • • • • • Frozen Bananas

You can make your own frozen bananas simply by dipping peeled bananas into the chocolate syrup, sprinkling them with a bit of chopped peanuts, and freezing them on a sheet of wax paper. I've never had much luck putting the sticks into the bananas, so my kids eat them without the holders.

• • • • • • • • • • • • • • • Chocolate Sundae

How about a delicious chocolate sundae? I've mentioned before that frozen nonfat yogurt is taking the country by storm. Instead of buying the high-fat (and expensive) toppings in the store, bring the yogurt home and pour on the nonfat chocolate syrup. You can even top your sundae off with a maraschino cherry.

• • • • • • • • • • • • • • Chocolate Milkshake

Chocolate syrup can turn plain skim milk into a real treat. Or go all the way and make a chocolate milkshake by blending a cup of skim milk, 2 tablespoons of chocolate syrup, 1 egg white, 1 tablespoon malted milk powder, and 1 tablespoon oat bran. (The oat bran is optional, but this is another opportunity to get the bran into the kids. It gives the shake a bit of texture.)

• • • • • • • • • • • • • • Chocolate Phosphate

Are you old enough to remember chocolate phosphates made in old-fashioned ice cream parlors or drug stores? My father was a pharmacist and had a store with a soda fountain where I learned to love those drinks. Now I can share that pleasure with my kids. Here's my "soda jerk" recipe: Pour 1 tablespoon chocolate syrup into a glass, add 1 or 2 teaspoons skim milk and 1 tablespoon club soda; mix well, then fill the glass with the rest of the club soda. Easterners call this a chocolate egg cream. Wonderful!

I'll bet you'll come up with lots of other ways to use this chocolate syrup. Why not make a batch today and keep it on hand? It can be stored for weeks in a bottle or jar in the refrigerator.

19

The Diet-Heart Newsletter

Information about diet and heart disease increases on a daily basis. Laboratories perform new research. Studies shed additional light on issues. New products enter the market, offering tasty ways to control cholesterol without deprivation. To keep you up to date on what's happening in the field, I've developed *The Diet-Heart Newsletter*.

This quarterly publication summarizes current articles in the medical literature, shares insights from medical meetings, answers questions that come up from readers, and continues the flow of ideas about foods to enjoy.

For a sample of *The Diet-Heart Newsletter* and subscription information send a stamped, self-addressed business-size (large) envelope to:

> The Diet-Heart Newsletter
> P.O. Box 2039
> Venice, CA 90294

20
Food and Diet Tables

FOOD COMPOSITION TABLE

I've put together the following information to give you an idea of the calorie, fat, cholesterol, and sodium content of foods you probably consume frequently. The idea is not to memorize Table 17 but to develop an appreciation as to general trends. For example, from the table you'll learn that beef products certainly have more fat per serving than poultry. But you'll also see that some beef selections may be better than certain poultry choices. As time goes on, you'll know the foods to eat frequently and those to have just once in a while or not at all. See Table 18, Making a Low-Fat Diet Part of Your Life.

This table has been compiled from a number of sources, including manufacturers themselves, the U.S. Department of Agriculture, and various textbooks. It would, of course, be impossible to list all foods. If you would like to have a more complete listing, I recommend *Food Values of Portions Commonly Used,* by Jean Pennington and Helen Church. It's available in large-format paperback from Harper & Row in most major bookstores.

In addition to reading the table, you'll want to read the labels on foods in your supermarket. Soon you'll know almost exactly how much fat and cholesterol your family is really eating. And you'll all be healthier for it.

Table 17. CALORIE, FAT, CHOLESTEROL, AND SODIUM CONTENT OF FOODS

Food	Serving Size	Calories	Fat (grams)	Cholesterol (mgs)	Sodium (mgs)
Candy, Nuts, Snacks					
CANDY:					
Carnation Breakfast Bar	1 bar	210	11.0	1	140–220
M & Ms (plain)	1.59 oz.	220	10.0	—	—
Milk chocolate bar or 6–7 Kisses	1 oz.	150	9.2	5	7
Milk chocolate bar with almonds	1 oz.	155	9.3	4	22
Peanut Butter Cups	2 pieces	223	12.5	—	136
3 Musketeers bar	2.28 oz.	280	8.0	—	—
Twix bar	1.73 oz.	120	6.0	—	—
NUTS AND SEEDS:					
Almonds	12–15	90	8.1	—	—
Cashews	6–8	84	6.9	—	2
Chestnuts	3	29	0.2	—	—
Coconut (fresh)	2 tbsp.	53	3.6	—	29
Coconut (fresh)	½ cup	174	16.3	—	373
Macadamias	6	109	11.7	—	—
Peanuts (roasted, salted)	1 oz.	158	13.1	—	129
Pecans	12 halves	105	11.0	—	—
Pinenuts (piñons, Pignolis)	2 tbsp.	95	9.2	—	—
Walnuts (English)	8–15 halves	98	9.7	—	—
Sunflower seeds	1 oz.	157	13.2	—	8
SNACKS*					
Virginia peanuts (salted, oil roasted)	1¼ oz.	228	19.5	—	229
Sunflower seeds (salted, oil roasted)	1 oz.	190	17.1	—	125
Smoke-flavored almonds	1¾ oz.	318	27.6	—	337
Caramel corn	1½ oz.	184	4.7	—	155
Potato chips	1 oz.	150	9.1	—	196
Corn chips	1½ oz.	237	15.1	—	353
Tortilla chips	1 oz.	137	6.2	—	204
Cheese puffs	1¾ oz.	254	13.1	—	573
Popcorn	3½ oz.	456	21.8	—	1940

* Data provided by Laura Scudder for its products; figures are representative of other brands as well.

Food	Serving Size	Calories	Fat (grams)	Cholesterol (mgs)	Sodium (mgs)
Pretzel sticks (Rold Gold)	1 oz.	109	0.8	—	39

Cheese

Food	Serving Size	Calories	Fat (grams)	Cholesterol (mgs)	Sodium (mgs)
American	1 oz.	105	8.4	27	318
Blue	1 oz.	103	8.5	21	390
Brick	1 oz.	103	8.5	25	157
Brie	1 oz.	94	7.8	28	176
Camembert	1 oz.	84	6.9	20	236
Cheddar	1 oz.	112	9.1	30	197
Colby	1 oz.	110	9.0	27	169
Cottage (1% fat)	½ cup	82	1.6	5	460
Cottage (2% fat)	½ cup	100	2.2	9	460
Cottage (4% fat)	½ cup	120	4.7	12	460
Cream cheese	2 tbsp.	99	9.9	34	84
Edam	1 oz.	87	5.7	25	270
Feta	1 oz.	74	6.0	25	312
Gouda	1 oz.	100	7.7	3.2	229
Gruyère	1 oz.	115	8.9	31	94
Monterey Jack	1 oz.	105	8.5	30	150
Mozzarella	1 oz.	79	6.1	22	104
Mozzarella (part skim)	1 oz.	78	4.8	15	148
Muenster	1 oz.	104	8.5	27	178
Neufchâtel	1 oz.	73	6.6	21	112
Parmesan (grated)	1 tbsp.	23	1.5	4	93
Parmesan (hard)	1 oz.	111	7.3	19	454
Provolone	1 oz.	98	7.3	19	245
Ricotta (13% fat)	½ cup	216	16.1	63	104
Ricotta (8% fat)	½ cup	171	9.8	40	155
Romano	1 oz.	110	7.6	29	340
Roquefort	1 oz.	105	8.7	26	513
Swiss (pasteurized processed)	1 oz.	95	7.1	26	388
Cheezola	1 oz.	89	6.4	1	448
Countdown	1 oz.	39	0.3	1	434
Lite-Line	1 oz.	50	2.0	10	410
Light n' Lively	1 oz.	70	4.0	15	350+
Cheeze Whiz spread	1 oz.	80	6.0	15	490
Lo-Chol	1 oz.	105	9.0	4	130

(continued)

Table 17. (*continued*)

Food	Serving Size	Calories	Fat (grams)	Cholesterol (mgs)	Sodium (mgs)
Cheddamelt	1 oz.	80	6.0	5	310
Pizza-Mate	1 oz.	90	7.0	5	—
Combination Foods					
Beefaroni	7 oz.	229	7.9	50	1044
Beef pot pie	1 pie	443	25.4	41	1008
Beef stew	1 cup	186	7.3	33	966
Chicken & noodles	6 oz.	151	4.9	20	816
Dennison's Chili con Carne	16-oz. can	320	17.0	30	10
Egg roll	3½ oz.	210+	6.7+	12+	530+
Morton Salisbury Steak Dinner	1 oz.	373	15.6	47	1213
Franco-American Macaroni and Cheese	1 cup	180	8.0	26	900
ARMOUR CLASSIC LITE DINNERS:					
Beef Pepper Steak	1	270	9.0	55	900
Chicken Burgundy	1	230	4.0	75	920
Chicken Oriental	1	240	4.0	75	730
Fillet of Cod Divan	1	280	7.0	80	990
Chicken Breast Marsala	1	270	7.0	—	—
Seafood, Natural Herbs	1	240	5.0	25	1440
Sliced Beef with Broccoli	1	280	7.0	70	2140
Turf n Surf	1	260	8.0	105	690
Turkey Parmesan	1	260	7.0	75	960
Veal Pepper Steak	1	280	8.0	90	480
LEAN CUISINE (STOUFFER'S):					
Cheese Cannelloni	1	270	10.0	45	950
Chicken & Vegetables with Vermicelli	1	260	7.0	40	1250
Chicken Cacciatore with Vermicelli	1	280	10.0	40	1040
Chicken Chow Mein	1	250	5.0	25	1160
Fillet of Fish Florentine	1	240	9.0	100	800
Glazed Chicken	1	270	8.0	55	840
Linguini/Clam	1	260	7.0	40	860
Meatball Stew	1	250	9.0	65	1165
Oriental Beef	1	260	8.0	35	1270
Oriental Scallops	1	220	3.0	20	1200

Food	Serving Size	Calories	Fat (grams)	Cholesterol (mgs)	Sodium (mgs)
Spaghetti	1	280	7.0	20	1400
Stuffed Cabbage	1	210	9.0	40	830
Zucchini Lasagna	1	260	7.0	20	1050
KRAFT:					
Macaroni & Cheese	¾ cup	290	13.0	5	530
Spiral Mac. & Cheese	¾ cup	330	17.0	10	560
Egg Noodles & Cheese	¾ cup	340	17.0	50	630
Egg Noodles & Chicken	¾ cup	240	9.0	35	880
Spaghetti Dinner	1 cup	310	8.0	5	730
Spaghetti Dinner Meat Sauce	1 cup	370	14.0	15	720
Velveeta Shells & Cheese	¾ cup	260	10.0	25	720

Condiments

Food	Serving Size	Calories	Fat (grams)	Cholesterol (mgs)	Sodium (mgs)
Mayonnaise	1 tbsp.	100	11.0	5	80
Tartar sauce	1 tbsp.	95	10.0	10	141
White sauce	2 tbsp.	54	4.1	4	125
Diet mayo.	1 tbsp.	45	5.0	5	90
Imitation mayo.	1 tbsp.	60	4.0	10	100
Miracle Whip	1 tbsp.	70	7.0	5	85
Kraft sandwich spread	1 tbsp.	50	5.0	5	75

Dairy Foods

Food	Serving Size	Calories	Fat (grams)	Cholesterol (mgs)	Sodium (mgs)
Whole milk	1 cup	150	8.1	34	120
Low-fat milk	1 cup	122	4.7	20	122
Skim milk	1 cup	89	0.4	5	128
Nonfat dry	1 cup	81	0.2	4	124
Canned evaporated skim	1 oz.	23	trace	1	35
Buttermilk (nonfat)	1 cup	88	0.2	10	318
Goat milk	1 cup	163	9.8	27	83
Yogurt (nonfat)	1 cup	127	0.4	4	174
Yogurt (low-fat)	1 cup	143	3.4	14	159
Yogurt (whole-milk)	1 cup	141	7.7	30	107
Half & half	1 tbsp.	20	1.7	6	6
Light cream	1 tbsp.	29	2.9	10	6
Medium cream	1 tbsp.	37	3.8	13	6
Light whipped cream	1 tbsp.	44	4.6	17	5
Heavy whipped cream	1 tbsp.	52	5.6	20	6
Sour cream	1 tbsp.	26	2.5	5	6

(*continued*)

Table 17. (*continued*)

Food	Serving Size	Calories	Fat (grams)	Cholesterol (mgs)	Sodium (mgs)
Aerosol whipped-cream topping	¼ cup	25	2.0	10	10

Desserts

Food	Serving Size	Calories	Fat (grams)	Cholesterol (mgs)	Sodium (mgs)
Cinnamon roll	1 ave.	174	5.0	39	214
Brownie	1 ave.	146	9.4	25	75
Angel-food cake	2 oz.	161	0.1	0	170
Carrot cake	3½ oz.	356	20.4	30	246
Devil's-food cake	3 oz.	323	15.0	37	357
Gingerbread	2 oz.	175	4.3	0.6	190
Marble cake	3 oz.	288	7.6	40	225
Choco.-chip cookies	1 ave.	52	2.3	6	44
Ladyfingers	1 large	50	1.1	50	10
McDonald's cookies	1 box	292	10.5	9	328
Oatmeal cookies	1 ave.	63	2.2	7	23
Peanut-butter cookies	1 ave.	57	2.3	7	21
Hostess Devil's Food Cupcakes	1	185	6.0	5	282
Hostess Ding Dongs	1	187	10.5	10	121
Hostess Ho Hos	1	118	6.0	14	63
Hostess Suzy Qs	1	256	10.9	10	301
Hostess Twinkies	1	152	6.2	20	203
Custard mixes	½ cup	143	4.6	19–24	125+
Doughnuts	1 ave.	125+	6–12	8–100+	75+
Ice Cream:					
16% fat	1 cup	349	23.8	84	108
10% fat	1 cup	257	14.1	53	116
sandwich	1	238	8.5	34	100+
Eskimo Pie	1	270	19.1	35	100+
Ice milk	1 cup	222	4.6	13	163
Frozen yogurt	1 cup	244	3.0	10	121
Tofu dessert	1 cup	130	10.8	0	95
Sherbet	1 cup	268	4.0	7	92
PIES:					
Hostess Apple	3½ oz.	331	18.1	35	320
Hostess Cherry	3½ oz.	352	17.1	10	180
Sara Lee Bavarian Cream	3½ oz.	352	25.1	23	80
Morton Coconut Custard	3¼ oz.	290	15.0	60	150
Lemon Meringue	3½ oz.	227	7.5	93	282

Food	Serving Size	Calories	Fat (grams)	Cholesterol (mgs)	Sodium (mgs)
Morton Peach	3½ oz.	260	12.0	10	230
Morton Pumpkin	3½ oz.	210	8.0	40	270
PUDDINGS:					
Canned tapioca	3½ oz.	129	3.1	53	185
Vanilla (whole-milk)	½ cup	175	4.1	16	251
Vanilla (skim-milk)	½ cup	147	0.3	3	258

Dips

Food	Serving Size	Calories	Fat (grams)	Cholesterol (mgs)	Sodium (mgs)
Kraft Premium (various types)	1 oz.	50	4.0	10–20	150+
Guacamole	2 tbsp.	50	4.0	0	210
Buttermilk	2 tbsp.	70	6.0	0	240
French onion	2 tbsp.	60	4.0	0	260
Green onion	2 tbsp.	60	4.0	0	170
Bacon-horseradish	2 tbsp.	60	5.0	0	200
Clam	2 tbsp.	60	5.0	0	250
Garlic	2 tbsp.	60	4.0	0	160

Eggs & Substitutes

Food	Serving Size	Calories	Fat (grams)	Cholesterol (mgs)	Sodium (mgs)
Whole egg	1 med.	78	5.5	250	59
Egg yolk	1 med.	59	5.2	250	12
Egg white	1 med.	16	trace	0	47
Eggnog	1 cup	352	19.0	149	138
Egg Beaters	¼ cup	25	0	0	80
Eggstra	¼ cup	30	0.8	23	56
Eggtime	¼ cup	40	1.0	0	120
Lucern	¼ cup	50	2.0	trace	—
Second Nature	¼ cup	35	1.6	0	79
Scramblers	¼ cup	60	3.0	0	150

Fast Foods*   One Order

Food	Serving Size	Calories	Fat (grams)	Cholesterol (mgs)	Sodium (mgs)
ARBY'S:					
Roast Beef Sand.		350	15	45	880
Jr. Roast Beef		220	9	35	530
Super Roast Beef		620	28	85	1420

* Not all data for sodium and cholesterol are available. Sodium levels are expected to be comparable for similar foods from various restaurants. Cholesterol content is also expected to be similar from food to food, regardless of restaurant. Moreover, cholesterol levels reflect the original, raw animal food ingredients. An ounce of cheese contains about 7 grams of fat and 18 milligrams of cholesterol. Cholesterol levels of beef, pork, and chicken are listed under "meats" in this table. Levels will not vary, whether prepared at home or in restaurants. Pay particular attention to *fat content* of fast-food items.

(*continued*)

Table 17. (*continued*)

Food	Serving Size	Calories	Fat (grams)	Cholesterol (mgs)	Sodium (mgs)
Beef 'n' Cheddar		484	21	55	1745
French Dip		386	12	—	1111
Roast Beef Deluxe		486	23	—	1288
Sub (no dress.)		484	16	—	1354
Ham 'n' Cheese		484	21	60	1745
Chicken Breast Sand.		584	28	—	1323
Potato Cakes (2)		190	9	—	476
French Fries		216	12	—	39
ARTHUR TREACHER'S (FISH, CHIPS, COLE SLAW):					
3-piece dinner		1100	65	—	—
2-piece dinner		905	51	—	—
BURGER CHEF:					
Hamburger		250	12	27	—
Cheeseburger		304	17	39	—
Dbl. Hamburger		325	15	54	—
Dbl. Cheeseburger		434	26	78	—
Big Chef		535	30	81	—
Super Chef		600	37	105	—
Skipper's Treat		604	37	—	—
Rancher Platter		640	38	106	—
Mariner Platter		680	24	35	—
French Fries		187	9	—	—
Milkshake (Chocolate)		310	9	36	—
BURGER KING:					
Hamburger		290	13	—	525
Cheeseburger		350	17	—	730
Dbl. Cheeseburger		530	31	—	990
Whopper		630	36	—	990
Whopper/Cheese		740	45	—	1435
Dbl. Whopper		850	52	—	1080
Dbl. Whopper/Cheese		950	60	—	1535
Whopper Jr.		370	20	—	560
Whopper Jr./Cheese		420	25	—	785
Onion Rings		270	16	—	450
French Fries		210	11	—	230
Chocolate Shake		340	10	—	280
Vanilla Shake		340	11	—	320

Food	Serving Size	Calories	Fat (grams)	Cholesterol (mgs)	Sodium (mgs)
CARL'S JR.:					
Famous Star Burger		530	32	—	705
Super Star		780	50	—	785
Western Bacon Burger		670	40	—	1330
Oldtime Star		450	20	—	625
Happy Star		330	13	—	670
Char. Chicken Sand.		450	14	—	1380
Char. Steak Sand.		630	33	—	700
Calif. Roast Beef Sand.		300	7	—	505
Filet of Fish		570	27	—	790
Crispirito		670	40	—	1050
Original Hot Dog		320	16	—	880
Chili Dog		330	17	—	640
Chili Cheese Dog		380	21	—	740
French Fries		250	15	—	460
Onion Rings		330	17	—	75
Vanilla Shake		490	8	—	350
JACK IN THE BOX:					
Hamburger		263	11	26	566
Cheeseburger		310	15	32	877
Jumbo Jack Hamburger		551	29	80	1134
Jumbo Jack/Cheese		628	35	110	1666
Regular Taco		189	11	22	460
Super Taco		285	17	37	968
Moby Jack		455	26	56	837
Chicken Supreme		700	45	—	—
Ham & Cheese Supreme		500	22	—	—
Bacon Cheeseburger Supreme		790	54	—	—
Beef & Cheese Supreme		595	33	—	—
Club Supreme		426	22	—	—
French Fries		270	15	—	128
Onion Rings		351	23	24	318
Vanilla Shake		342	9	36	263
Chocolate Shake		365	9	35	294
KENTUCKY FRIED CHICKEN:					
Original Recipe					
Wing		136	9	55	302
Drumstick		117	6	63	207

(continued)

Table 17. (*continued*)

Food	Serving Size	Calories	Fat (grams)	Cholesterol (mgs)	Sodium (mgs)
Side Breast		199	12	63	558
Thigh		257	17	109	566
Extra Crispy					
Wing		201	13	59	312
Drumstick		155	9	59	263
Side Breast		286	18	65	564
Thigh		343	23	109	549
Breast Fillet Sand.		436	22	—	1092
Mashed Potatoes		64	1	—	268
Gravy		23	2	—	57
Roll		61	1	—	118
Corn		169	3	—	11
Cole Slaw		121	7	—	225
French Fries		184	7	—	174
LONG JOHN SILVER (FISH, CHIPS, COLE SLAW):					
3-piece dinner		1190	63	—	—
2-piece dinner		955	50	—	—
McDONALD'S:					
Hamburger		255	10	25	520
Cheeseburger		307	14	37	767
Quarter Pounder		424	22	67	735
Quarter Pounder/Cheese		524	31	96	1236
Big Mac		563	33	86	1010
Filet-O-Fish		432	25	47	781
French Fries		220	12	9	109
Vanilla Shake		352	8	30	201
Chocolate Shake		383	9	30	300
Chicken McNuggets (6)		314	19	76	525
PIZZA HUT:					
Standard Cheese (½ 13″ med., Thin 'n' Crispy)		680	22	—	1800
Supreme (½ 13″ med., Thin 'n' Crispy)		800	34	—	2400
TACO BELL:					
Bean Burrito		343	12	—	272
Beef Burrito		466	21	—	327
Beefy Tostada		331	18	—	138

Food	Serving Size	Calories	Fat (grams)	Cholesterol (mgs)	Sodium (mgs)
Bellbeefer		221	7	—	231
Bellbeefer/cheese		278	12	—	330
Burrito Supreme		457	22	—	367
Combination Burrito		404	16	—	300
Enchirito		454	21	—	1175
Taco		192	11	—	79
Tostada		259	11	—	101
Taco Supreme		237	15	—	—
Bell Bellgrande		410	26	—	—
Taco Light		390	26	—	—
WENDY'S:					
Single Hamburger		472	26	70	774
Double Hamburger		669	40	125	980
Triple Hamburger		853	51	205	1217
Single Cheese		577	34	90	1085
Double Cheese		797	48	155	1414
Triple Cheese		1036	68	225	1848
Chili		228	8	25	1065
Chicken Sandwich		468	19	—	963
Chicken/Cheese		496	25	—	1195
Taco Salad		460	24	—	1297
French Fries		327	16	5	112
Frosty		391	16	45	247

Fats & Oils

Food	Serving Size	Calories	Fat (grams)	Cholesterol (mgs)	Sodium (mgs)
Bacon fat	1 tbsp.	126	14.0	11	150+
Beef suet	1 tbsp.	216	23.3	21	18
Chicken fat	1 tbsp.	126	14.0	9	0
Lard	1 tbsp.	126	14.0	13	0
Vegetable oil	1 tbsp.	120	13.5	0	0
Butter	1 tbsp.	108	12.2	36	124
Margarine	1 tbsp.	108	12.0	0	Variable
Butter Buds	1 oz.	12	0	0	—

Fish & Shellfish

Food	Serving Size	Calories	Fat (grams)	Cholesterol (mgs)	Sodium (mgs)
Caviar (sturgeon)	1 tsp.	26	1.5	25	220
Clams (canned)	½ cup	52	0.7	80	36
Clams (raw)	3½ oz.	82	1.9	50	36

(continued)

Table 17. (*continued*)

Food	Serving Size	Calories	Fat (grams)	Cholesterol (mgs)	Sodium (mgs)
Cod (raw)	3½ oz.	78	0.3	50	70
Crab (king)	3½ oz.	93	1.9	60	Variable
Fish sticks (frozen)	3½ oz.	176	8.9	70	180
Flatfish	3½ oz.	79	0.8	61	78
Haddock	3½ oz.	141	6.6	60	71
Halibut	3½ oz.	214	8.8	60	168
Herring	3½ oz.	176	11.3	85	74
Lobster	3½ oz.	91	1.9	100	210
Mackerel	3½ oz.	191	12.2	95	148
Oysters	3½ oz.	66	1.8	50	73
Salmon	3½ oz.	182	7.4	47	50
Salmon (canned chinook)	3½ oz.	210	14.0	60	300+
Sardines (canned in oil)	3½ oz.	311	24.4	120	510
Scallops	3½ oz.	81	0.2	35	255
Shrimp	3½ oz.	91	0.8	100	140
Trout (brook)	3½ oz.	101	2.1	55	50
Trout (rainbow)	3½ oz.	195	11.4	55	50
Tuna (raw)	3½ oz.	133	3.0	60	37
Tuna (canned in oil)	3½ oz.	197	8.2	63	800+
Tuna (canned in water)	3½ oz.	127	0.8	63	41

Grain Products

BREADS:

Food	Serving Size	Calories	Fat (grams)	Cholesterol (mgs)	Sodium (mgs)
Cracked-wheat	1 slice	66	0.6	0	132
English muffin	1 slice	133	1.0	0	203
French	1 slice	75	0.5	0	140
Pita (pocket)	1 slice	145	1.0	0	86
Pumpernickel	1 slice	79	0.4	0	182
Raisin	1 slice	66	0.7	0	91
Rye	1 slice	61	0.3	0	139
White	1 slice	68	0.8	0	127
Whole-wheat	1 slice	61	0.8	0	132

CRACKERS:

Food	Serving Size	Calories	Fat (grams)	Cholesterol (mgs)	Sodium (mgs)
Matzo	1	118	0.3	0	10
Melba toast	3	60	2.0	0.6	2
Saltines	4	48	1.3	1.0	123
Egg noodles	1 cup	200	2.4	50	3
Pancake mix	1 ave.	367	5.0	33	1192
Stuffing mix	½ cup	198	8.0	45	515

Meats

Food	Serving Size	Calories	Fat (grams)	Cholesterol (mgs)	Sodium (mgs)
BEEF:					
Cooked, well-trimmed					
Composite	3 oz.	192	9.4	73	57
Eye round steak	3 oz.	158	6.0	59	52
Top round steak	3 oz.	166	5.9	72	52
Tip roast	3 oz.	167	7.0	69	55
Bottom round	3 oz.	201	9.3	81	44
Sirloin steak	3 oz.	185	8.3	75	56
Top sirloin	3 oz.	182	8.7	65	57
Rib steak	3 oz.	200	10.9	68	58
Rib roast	3 oz.	217	12.9	68	62
Blade pot roast	3 oz.	241	14.3	90	60
Arm pot roast	3 oz.	205	9.3	85	56
Brisket	3 oz.	230	14.3	77	66
Tenderloin	3 oz.	183	8.9	72	54
Ground beef (27% fat)	3 oz.	251	16.9	86	71
Ground beef (18% fat)	3 oz.	233	14.4	86	69
LAMB:					
Cooked, trimmed					
Composite	3 oz.	176	8.1	78	71
Lamb shank	3 oz.	156	6.0	81	54
Lamb loin chop	3 oz.	188	8.9	82	71
Lamb blade chop	3 oz.	195	10.9	82	80
Lamb rib roast	3 oz.	211	12.9	78	67
PORK:					
Cooked, trimmed					
Composite	3 oz.	198	11.1	79	50
Leg roast	3 oz.	187	9.4	80	55
Top loin chop	3 oz.	219	12.7	80	57
Top loin roast	3 oz.	208	11.7	67	39
Shoulder blade	3 oz.	250	15.0	99	64
Spareribs	3 oz.	338	25.8	103	79
Center loin chop	3 oz.	196	8.9	83	66
Tenderloin	3 oz.	141	4.1	79	57
Sirloin roast	3 oz.	221	11.1	94	50
Center rib chop	3 oz.	219	12.7	80	57
Center rib roast	3 oz.	208	11.7	67	39

(*continued*)

Table 17. (*continued*)

Food	Serving Size	Calories	Fat (grams)	Cholesterol (mgs)	Sodium (mgs)
Bacon	1 slice	40	3.0	5	120
Ham (3% fat)	3 oz.	120	6.0	45	240
CHICKEN:					
Light, no skin	3 oz.	153	4.2	66	54
Dark, no skin	3 oz.	156	5.4	78	72
Dark & white, with skin	3 oz.	210	12.6	75	66
Chicken gizzard	1 cup	215	4.8	283	83
Chicken liver	1 cup	200	5.0	800	68
TURKEY:					
Light, no skin	3 oz.	153	4.2	66	54
Dark, no skin	3 oz.	156	5.4	78	72
Light & dark, with skin	3 oz.	210	12.6	75	66
Bologna, franks	1 oz.	71	5.4	37	336
Ham	1 oz.	40	1.5	28	280
Pastrami	1 oz.	34	1.6	29	525
Salami	1 oz.	50	3.5	26	454
VEAL:					
Lean only (leg, loin, cutlet)	3 oz.	120	2.7	84	48
Lean & fat (most cuts)	3 oz.	183	9.0	84	39
Lean & fat (rib, breast)	3 oz.	267	23.1	87	42
DUCK:					
Flesh only	3 oz.	141	6.9	62	63
Flesh & skin	3 oz.	276	24.3	60	63
GOOSE:					
Flesh only	3 oz.	135	6.0	63	72
ORGAN MEATS:					
Beef kidney	3½ oz.	252	12.0	375	253
Beef liver	3½ oz.	140	4.7	300	73
Chicken liver	3½ oz.	165	4.4	746	61
Beef tongue	3½ oz.	244	16.7	140	61
Beef heart	3½ oz.	179	5.7	274	104
Brains	3½ oz.	106	7.3	2100	106
Sweetbreads	3½ oz.	90	6.6	132	99
LUNCHEON MEATS: (Oscar Mayer)					
Bologna	1 oz.	88	8.1	15+	292
Canadian bacon	1 oz.	45	2.0	13	384

Food	Serving Size	Calories	Fat (grams)	Cholesterol (mgs)	Sodium (mgs)
Chopped ham	1 oz.	64	4.8	14	387
Ham & cheese loaf	1 oz.	70	5.6		372
Headcheese	1 oz.	55	4.1	28	
Honey loaf	1 oz.	39	1.7	8	377
Liverwurst	1 oz.	139	9.1	35	81
Olive loaf	1 oz.	64	4.5	10	416
Salami (dry)	1 oz.	112	9.8	22	540
Spam (Hormel)	1 oz.	87	7.4	15	336
Hot dog	1.6 oz.	142	13.5	23	464
Ham	3½ oz.	120	5.0	50	1527
Salad Dressings					
Blue cheese	1 tbsp.	71	7.3	4–10	153
Green goddess	1 tbsp.	68	7.0	1	150
Russian	1 tbsp.	74	7.6	7–10	130
Thousand Island	1 tbsp.	70	7.0	9	98
French	1 tbsp.	66	6.2	0	219
Italian	1 tbsp.	83	9.0	0	314

Table 18. MAKING A LOW-FAT DIET PART OF YOUR LIFE

Food Group & Minimum Recommended Amount	First-Choice Foods	Second-Choice Foods	Make-It-Scarce Foods
Milk Products			
1 serving = 1 cup milk 1 cup yogurt 1½ oz. cheese 2 cups cottage cheese* 1¾ cups ice cream* (Supplies calcium, riboflavin, protein)	skim or 1% milk (fortified w/vitamins A & D)—fluid, evaporated, nonfat dry, or buttermilk nonfat or low-fat yogurt—preferably with little or no added sugar (e.g., plain, vanilla, lemon) low-fat cheeses—no more than 2 grams fat/oz. (e.g., Borden Lite-Line or Weight Watchers cheese slices) low-fat cottage cheese—1 to 2% fat nonfat frozen yogurt	2% milk low-fat yogurt cheeses in the 3–5 grams fat/oz. range (e.g., part-skim mozzarella) regular cottage cheese part-skim ricotta cheese ice milk	whole milk—regular, evaporated, condensed; half and half whole-milk yogurt regular cheeses (e.g., American, cheddar, Swiss) whole-milk ricotta cheese ice cream
Protein Foods			
1 serving = 2 oz. cooked fish, poultry, or meat 2 eggs 1 cup cooked, dried beans or peas 4 tablespoons peanut butter* (2 oz. cheese can also be counted as a protein serving) (Supplies protein, B vitamins, iron, zinc)	most fresh, frozen, and canned (in water) fish—3 to 7 times/week. (Eat a mix of high, medium, & low-fat fish) skinless chicken and turkey lean, fat-trimmed beef, veal, pork, and lamb egg whites or cholesterol-free egg substitutes dried beans and peas—cooked without fat and used in place of some meat tofu (soybean curd) low-fat cold cuts—turkey breast, lean boiled ham (no more than 2 grams fat/oz.) wild game (skinless and fat trimmed)	shrimp, lobster, squid, crawfish (all are low in total fat, but higher in cholesterol than other fish) eel tuna or sardines, canned in oil (drained) containing no more than 15% fat (by weight) peanut butter	fish roe, caviar chicken and turkey with skin highly marbled, fatty meats—beef, veal, pork, and lamb regular ground beef organ meats (e.g., liver, heart, kidneys) egg yolks—no more than 3/week hot dogs sausage, bacon high-fat cold cuts (e.g., bologna, pastrami, salami) duck (domestic)
Fruits & Vegetables			
1 serving = ½ cup juice ½ cup cooked vegetables or fruit 1 cup raw vegetables or fruit 1 medium fresh fruit	all plain, fresh, and frozen fruits and vegetables are First-Choice foods. (Canned vegetables are good low-fat choices too, but tend to be much higher in sodium; try to use fruits without added sugar)	fruits and vegetables with small amounts of First-Choice fats	fruits and vegetables with added butter, sour cream, cream, sauces, and cheese

	First-Choice Foods	Second-Choice Foods	Make-It-Scarce Foods
(Supplies vitamins A and C, potassium, fiber)	note that avocados and olives are considered fats (see fats, below) for vitamin A—have a dark green or orange vegetable at least 3–4 times/week for vitamin C—have at least 1 good daily source (citrus fruits, strawberries, cantaloupe, tomatoes, green peppers, broccoli, cabbage, dark greens)		
Grain Products (whole-grain or enriched)			
1 serving = 1 slice bread 4–6 crackers[b] 1 cup flake-type cereal[b] ½ cup cooked cereal ½ cup cooked pasta, rice, or bulgur (Supplies B vitamins, iron, fiber)	plain bread—whole wheat, rye, oatmeal, bran, white low-fat rolls—hamburger & hotdog rolls, English muffins, Syrian bread, bagels low-fat crackers—saltines, melba, matzoh, oyster, flatbread, graham, enriched pretzels, rice cakes hot and cold cereals (preferably with little sugar) pasta, rice, bulgur—without added fat low-fat cookies—ginger snaps, animal crackers, vanilla wafers, fig bars angel food cake	egg breads, noodles, and bagels quick breads made with First-Choice fats and milk products (e.g., muffins, biscuits, pancakes, waffles) First-Choice grain products with small amounts of First-Choice fats	butter rolls, cheese breads croissants, doughnuts pies, cakes, cookies, and other baked goods made with Make-It-Scarce fats higher-fat crackers (e.g., made with cheese, butter, palm or coconut oil) potato and corn chips granola-type cereals made with coconut or coconut oil First-Choice grain products served with Make-It-Scarce fats, sauces, and regular cheese
Calorie-Booster Foods			
fats, sugars, alcoholic beverages—there is no recommended amount; try to eat as little as possible (The American Heart Association recommends no more than 5–8 servings of polyunsaturated fats per day. 1 serving = 1 teaspoon vegetable oil or margarine; 2 teaspoons diet margarine, regular mayonnaise, or salad dressing) (Supplies calories, fat)	*Best selections:* reduced-calorie margarine, mayonnaise, and salad dressings vegetable oils—corn, cottonseed, olive, safflower, sesame, soybean, sunflower regular margarine—with a *liquid* First-Choice oil listed as the first ingredient regular mayonnaise and salad dressings made with First-Choice oils avocados, olives nuts and seeds nondairy creamers made with First-Choice oils	peanut oil partially hydrogenated First-Choice oils reduced-fat sour cream and cream cheese	butter, lard, bacon fat, shortening cream, sour cream, cream cheese nondairy creamers and dessert toppings made with coconut or palm oils palm, palm kernel, and coconut oils chocolate coconut

[a] These choices provide more calories than others in the same group. For example, you have to eat about 400 calories of low-fat cottage cheese to get the same amount of calcium contained in a 100-calorie cup of low-fat milk.

[b] These products vary widely in calorie content—read labels to select a portion size that provides between 70 and 100 calories.

Notes

Chapter 3. The Kids' Cholesterol Connection

1. Holman, R. L. "Atherosclerosis—A Pediatric Nutrition Problem?" *American Journal of Clinical Nutrition,* 1961: volume 9, pages 565–69.

2. Kannel, W. B. "Pediatric Aspects of Lipid-induced Atherosclerosis." *Journal of the American College of Nutrition,* 1984: volume 3, pages 139–46.

3. "The Lipid Research Clinics Coronary Primary Prevention Trial Results." *Journal of the American Medical Association,* 1984: volume 251, number 3, pages 365–74.

4. Consensus Conference. "Lowering blood cholesterol to prevent heart disease." *Journal of the American Medical Association,* 1985: volume 253, number 14, pages 2080–86.

5. Strong, W. B., et al. "Primary Prevention of Atherosclerosis." *Southern Medical Journal,* 1975: volume 68, pages 319–27.

6. Glueck, C. J. "Therapy of Familial and Acquired Hyperlipoproteinemia in Children and Adolescents." *Preventive Medicine,* 1983: volume 12, pages 835–47.

7. Gilliam, T. B., et al. "Prevalence of Coronary Heart Disease Risk Factors in Active Children, 7 to 12 Years of Age." *Medicine and Science in Sports,* 1977: volume 9, pages 21–25.

8. Turner, R. W. D. "Perspectives in Coronary Prevention." *Postgraduate Medical Journal,* 1978: volume 54, pages 141–48.

9. Wilmore, J. H. and J. J. McNamara. "Prevalence of Coronary Heart Disease Risk Factors in Boys, 8 to 12 Years of Age." *Journal of Pediatrics,* 1974: volume 84, pages 527–33.

10. Lauer, R. M., et al. "Coronary Heart Disease Risk Factors in School Children: The Muscatine Study." *Journal of Pediatrics,* 1975: volume 86, pages 697–706.

11. Data from Rifkind, B. M. and P. Segal. "Lipid Research Clinics Reference Values for Hyperlipidemia and Hypolipidemia." *Journal of the American Medical Association,* 1983: volume 250, number 14, pages 1869–72.

12. Voors, A. W., et al. "Resting Heart Rate and Pressure-rate Product of Children in a Total Biracial Community." *American Journal of Epidemiology,* 1982: volume 116, pages 276–86.

13. Owen, G. M., et al. "A Study of Nutritional Status of Preschool Children in the United States, 1968–70." *Journal of Pediatrics,* 1974: volume 55, pages 597–606.

14. Freedman, D. S., et al. "Tracking of Serum Lipids and Lipoproteins in Children over an 8-Year Period: The Bogalusa Study." *Preventive Medicine,* 1985: volume 14, pages 203–16.

15. Laskarzewski, P., et al. "Lipid and Lipoprotein Tracking in 108 Children over a Four-year Period." *Journal of Pediatrics,* 1979: volume 64, pages 584–91.

16. Donahue, R. P. et al. "Lipids and Lipoproteins in a Young Adult Population: The Beaver County Lipid Study." *American Journal of Epidemiology,* 1985: volume 122, number 3, pages 458–67.

17. Enos, W. F. and R. H. Holmes. "Coronary Disease among United States Soldiers Killed in Action in Korea." *Journal of the American Medical Association,* 1953: volume 182, pages 1090–93.

18. McNamara, J. J., et al. "Coronary Artery Disease in Combat Casualties in Vietnam." *Journal of the American Medical Association,* 1971: volume 216, pages 1185–87.

19. Newman, W. P., et al. "Relation of Serum Lipoprotein Levels and Systolic Blood Pressure to Early Atherosclerosis: The Bogalusa Study." *New England Journal of Medicine,* 1986: volume 314, number 3, pages 138–44.

20. Moll, P. P., et al. "Total Cholesterol and Lipoproteins in School Children: Prediction of Coronary Heart Disease in Adult Relatives." *Circulation,* 1983: volume 67, number 1, pages 127–34.

21. Laskarzewski, P. M., et al. "Parent-Child Coronary Heart Disease Risk Factor Associations." *American Journal of Epidemiology,* 1981: volume 114, number 6, pages 827–35.

22. Laskarzewski, P. M., et al. "Parent-Child Nutrient Intake Interrelationships in School Children Ages 6 to 19: The Princeton School District Study." *American Journal of Clinical Nutrition,* 1980: volume 33, pages 2350–55.

23. Knuiman, J. T., et al. "Determinants of Total and High Density Lipoprotein Cholesterol in Boys from Finland, the Netherlands, Italy, the Philippines and Ghana with Special Reference to Diet." *Human Nutrition: Clinical Nutrition,* 1983: volume 37, pages 237–54.

24. Neufeld, H. N. and U. Goldbourt. "Coronary Heart Disease: Genetic Aspects." *Circulation,* 1983: volume 67, number 5, pages 943–54.

25. American Heart Association. "Nutrition Education in the Young: A Statement for Health Professionals." *Circulation,* 1980: volume 62, pages 918–23.

26. Glueck, C. J. "Pediatric Primary Prevention of Atherosclerosis" (editorial). *New England Journal of Medicine,* 1986: volume 314, number 3, pages 175–77.

Index

Fat(s), blood levels of, effects of
elevated, 19
Fat(s), dietary, 169–76. *See also* Monounsaturated fats; Polyunsaturated fats;
Saturated fats
in baked goods, 154–55
calorie, fat, cholesterol, and sodium
content of, 285
grams of, 49–50
hydrogenated, 173–74, 188
in cereals, 204–5
in nondairy products, 229–30
need for, 129–30
as percentage of caloric intake, 17, 41,
48–50, 126
shopping and, 187–89
in various foods (table), 275–89
Fiber, 136–37
insoluble, 137, 149–50
soluble, 137. *See also* Oat bran
Fish. *See also specific kinds of fish*
calorie, fat, cholesterol, and sodium
content of, 286
EPA in, 171–73
shopping for, 196–97
Fish-oil capsules, 197
Fitness. *See* Physical fitness
"Fitness for Youth" program, 89
Fluoridated water, 136
Folic acid (folacin), 133, 141
Fondue, dessert, 272
Food composition table, 275–89
Food Values of Portions Commonly Used
(Pennington and Church), 275
French toast, 254
Fried foods, 228–30
Friedman, Meyer, 97, 100
Friends, children's, 56
eating at homes of, 59
Frozen foods, 206
calorie, fat, cholesterol, and sodium
content of, 278–79
Fruit(s)
first-choice, second-choice, and make-
it-scarce foods (table), 290–91
fluid medley, 271
platter with yogurt, 269
for preschool children, 142
salad dressing, yogurt, 251
shopping for, 199–201
as snacks, 60, 61
Fudge brownies, 166

Gardening, 62–63
Garlic turkey sausages, 257
Genetic factors
coronary heart disease and, 32
in familial homozygous hypercholesterolemia, 37–38
obesity and, 80
Type A behavior and, 104
Glueck, Charles, 25, 41–42, 112–13

Go For Health program, 223–24
Gotto, Antonio, Jr., 35
Grannis, Larry, 222
Granola bars, 155, 164
Green-goddess dressing, tofu, 250
Grundy, Scott, 174, 175

Halloween, 58–59
Ham, 189
with raisin sauce, 246
Hamburgers, 193
McDonald's, 64–68
Heart disease, 19. *See also* Coronary
heart disease
statistics on, 20–21
unconditional love and, 105
Heart Smart program, 224
Herbs, 230
growing your own, 62–63
Hiccups, cure for, 108–9
High-density lipoproteins (HDL),
17–18, 31, 32, 34
monosaturated fats and, 174
oat bran and, 152
smoking and, 113
Hirsch, Jules, 74
HMG Co-A reductase, 16
Hospitals, fast-food restaurants in, 66–67
Hostility, Type A personality and, 101
Hot dogs, 195, 231–32
Hugging, 108
Hydrogenated fats or oils, 173–74, 188
in cereals, 204–5
in nondairy products, 229–30
Hypercholesterolemia, 18, 37–38
Hyperlipidemia, 18
Hyperlipoproteinemia, 18–19
Hypertension (high blood pressure),
115–17
Type A personality and, 98

Inactivity. *See* Sedentary lifestyle
Institute for Social Research (University
of Michigan), 89–90
Iodine, 134, 141
Iron, 134, 141
Iron supplement, 71, 134
for teenagers, 145
Ischemic heart disease. *See* Coronary
heart disease

Jack in the Box, calorie, fat, cholesterol,
and sodium content of foods
served by, 283
Japan, 116
Johnson, Timothy, 35
Juices, fruit, 201

Kannel, William, 22, 25, 27, 33
Kentucky Fried Chicken, calorie, fat,
cholesterol, and sodium content
of foods served by, 283–84